Praise for Roger Lowenstein's
When Genius Failed: The Rise and Fall of Long-Term Capital Management

"Lowenstein, one of the best financial [...] convincing argument that the strategy [...] doomed to eventual failure."

"With such a complex and demanding story, you need a safe pair of journalistic hands. Mr. Lowenstein possesses these. What he possesses also is a quiet but beautifully controlled grasp of manners and social milieu.... Mr. Lowenstein is enthralling." —*The New York Observer*

"[A] very engrossing, smoothly written book."
—*Booklist* (one of *Booklist*'s Top 10 Business Books of 2000)

"Ninety-five percent of all the books written about investing are worthless.... But over the years there have been some great ones, and, in fact, I have a shelf of maybe thirty-five titles. The criteria for inclusion are that the book has to give an important insight in how to invest, or help with the emotional aspects of managing money, or deepen your understanding of the nature of the beast. Maybe once a year at most I add a new title, and now with passion I am adding Roger Lowenstein's *When Genius Failed*. . . .[It] should be read by every serious investor, manager of investors, and trader. . . . *When Genius Failed* is a remarkable and frightening book that will broaden and deepen your understanding of risk."
—BARTON M. BIGGS, chairman, Morgan Stanley Asset Management

"A very good account of LTCM: clear, entertaining, informative and judicious. The narrative has drama; the fate of the financial world was briefly at stake. It has complexity; there are serious issues of mathematics, statistics, and social science behind this story. Most of all, there is here a haunting portrait of our financial culture, where very ordinary people control extraordinary amounts of money." —*The Washington Monthly*

"A crackling good read." —TheStreet.com

"Strongly reported and clearly written. . . . Lowenstein adds fresh detail, personality, and even drama to the tale. . . . He does a particularly good job at explaining the essence of LTCM's arbitrage trades that were at first so profitable and later disastrous." —*Barron's*

"A kind of '90s sequel to *Liar's Poker*. . . . [Lowenstein] excels at explaining financial matters in a concise way that illuminates without oversimplifying. It's rare enough for someone to be able to explain business so smoothly and cogently, but Lowenstein also has a deftness with descriptions."
—Salon.com

"Compelling. . . . The story of Long-Term is in some ways the ideal parable. . . . What's more, the fund was long cloaked in secrecy, making the story of its rise . . . and its ultimate destruction that much more fascinating."
—*The Washington Post*

"Imagine a drama that revolves around a cast of brainy, quirky characters, is set against a backdrop of phenomenal wealth, and has a plot that threatens to bring the entire financial system to its knees. Then go out and read *When Genius Failed*." —*The International Economy*

ALSO BY ROGER LOWENSTEIN

Buffett: The Making of an American Capitalist

JOHN NAMBOIS

ROGER LOWENSTEIN, author of the bestselling *Buffett: The Making of an American Capitalist,* reported for *The Wall Street Journal* for more than a decade and wrote the *Journal*'s stock market column "Heard on the Street" from 1989 to 1991 and the "Intrinsic Value" column from 1995 to 1997. He now writes a column in *Smart Money* magazine, and has written for *The New York Times* and *The New Republic,* among other publications. He has three children and lives in Westfield, New Jersey.

ROGER LOWENSTEIN

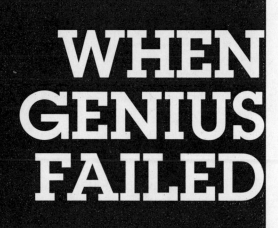

WHEN GENIUS FAILED

The Rise and Fall of Long-Term Capital Management

 RANDOM HOUSE TRADE PAPERBACKS
NEW YORK

Library of Congress Cataloging-in-Publication Data

Lowenstein, Roger.
When genius failed : the rise and fall of Long-Term Capital Management / Roger Lowenstein.
p.   cm.
Includes index.
ISBN 0-375-75825-9
1. Hedge funds—United States.   I. Long-Term Capital Management (Firm)
II. Title.
HG4930 .L69 2000
332.6—dc21   00-028091

Random House website address: www.atrandom.com

Printed in the United States of America

19 18 17 16 15 14 13 12 11 10

Book design by Carole Lowenstein

To
Maury Lasky
and
Jane Ruth Mairs

Past may be prologue, but which past?

—HENRY HU

Author's Note and Acknowledgments

This history of Long-Term Capital Management is unauthorized. At the project's outset, I was granted several formal interviews with two of the firm's partners, Eric Rosenfeld and David Mullins, but such formal cooperation quickly ceased. Subsequent attempts to resume the interviews, and to gain formal access to John W. Meriwether, the founder, and others of the partners, proved fruitless. Nonetheless, over the course of my research, I repeatedly conveyed (via e-mail and telephone) seemingly endless lists of questions to Rosenfeld, and he generously consented to answer many of my queries. In addition, various Long-Term employees at all levels of the firm privately aided me in my research, helping me to understand both the inner workings of the firm and the nuances of many of the individual partners; I am deeply grateful to them.

My other primary sources were interviews conducted at the major Wall Street investment banks, including the six banks that played a crucial role in the genesis and ultimate rescue of Long-Term. Without the cooperation of many people at Bear Stearns, Goldman Sachs, J. P. Morgan, Merrill Lynch, Salomon Smith Barney, and Union Bank of Switzerland, this book could not have been written.

I also had generous tutors in economics. There were others, but Peter Bernstein, Eugene Fama, John Gilster, Bruce Jacobs, Christopher May, and Mark Rubinstein helped me to understand the world of options, hedging, bell curves, and fat tails where Long-Term plied its trade.

In addition, the confidential memorandum on the fund's debacle prepared by Long-Term's partners in January 1999 provided facts and figures on the fund's capital, asset totals, leverage, and monthly returns throughout the life of the fund, as well as information on the results of investors. It was an invaluable resource and, indeed, the source of many of the figures in this book. Finally, I am grateful to the Federal Reserve Bank of New York for its free-spirited cooperation.

Whenever possible, sources are indicated by an endnote. However, in many cases, I had to rely on sources that declined to be identified. Writing recent history is always a touchy business, and the Long-Term story—essentially, one of failure and disappointment—was particularly delicate. Long-Term's partners are by nature private people who would have been uncomfortable with such a project during the best of times; that they were unenthusiastic about a history of such a titanic failure is only human. Therefore, I must ask the reader's indulgence for the much material that is unattributed.

■

I am deeply grateful to Viken Berberian, a research aide who proved to be not only an intrepid gatherer of facts but a resourceful and insightful assistant. Neil Barsky, Jeffrey Tannenbaum, and Louis Lowenstein—two dear friends and a nonpareil dad—tirelessly read this manuscript in crude form and provided me with invaluable and much-needed suggestions; their inspired handiwork graces every page. Melanie Jackson, my agent, and Ann Godoff, my editor, as unerring a team as Montana-to-Rice, skillfully shepherded this project from conception to finish. Their repeated shows of confidence lightened many otherwise solitary hours. And my three children, Matt, Zack, and Alli, were a continuing inspiration. Many others helped the author, both professionally and personally, during the course of writing this book, and my gratitude to them knows no bounds.

Contents

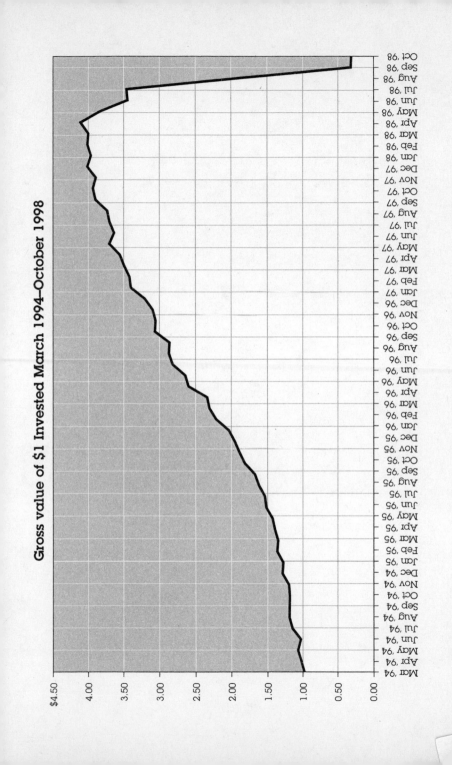

Gross value of $1 Invested March 1994–October 1998

Introduction

The Federal Reserve Bank of New York is perched in a gray sand-stone slab in the heart of Wall Street. Though a city landmark building constructed in 1924, the bank is a muted, almost unseen presence among its lively, entrepreneurial neighbors. The area is dotted with discount stores and luncheonettes—and, almost everywhere, brokerage firms and banks. The Fed's immediate neighbors include a shoe repair stand and a teriyaki house, and also Chase Manhattan Bank; J. P. Morgan is a few blocks away. A bit farther to the west, Merrill Lynch, the people's brokerage, gazes at the Hudson River, across which lie the rest of America and most of Merrill's customers. The bank skyscrapers project an open, accommodative air, but the Fed building, a Florentine Renaissance showpiece, is distinctly forbidding. Its arched windows are encased in metal grille, and its main entrance, on Liberty Street, is guarded by a row of black cast-iron sentries.

The New York Fed is only a spoke, though the most important spoke, in the U.S. Federal Reserve System, America's central bank. Because of the New York Fed's proximity to Wall Street, it acts as the eyes and ears into markets for the bank's governing board, in Washington, which is run by the oracular Alan Greenspan. William J. McDonough, the beefy president of the New York Fed, talks to bankers and traders often. McDonough wants to be kept abreast of the gossip that traders share with one another. He especially wants to hear about anything that might upset markets or, in the extreme, the financial system. But McDonough tries to stay in the background. The Fed has always been a controversial regulator—a servant of the people that is elbow to elbow with Wall Street, a cloistered agency amid the democratic chaos of markets. For McDonough to intervene, even in a small way, would take a crisis, perhaps a war. And in the first days of the autumn of 1998, McDonough did intervene—and not in a small way.

The source of the trouble seemed so small, so laughably remote, as to be insignificant. But isn't it always that way? A load of tea is dumped into a harbor, an archduke is shot, and suddenly a tinderbox is lit, a crisis erupts, and the world is different. In this case, the shot was Long-Term Capital Management, a private investment partnership with its headquarters in Greenwich, Connecticut, a posh suburb some forty miles from Wall Street. LTCM managed money for only one hundred investors; it employed not quite two hundred people, and surely not one American in a hundred had ever heard of it. Indeed, five years earlier, LTCM had not even existed.

But on the Wednesday afternoon of September 23, 1998, Long-Term did not seem small. On account of a crisis at LTCM, McDonough had summoned—"invited," in the Fed's restrained idiom—the heads of every major Wall Street bank. For the first time, the chiefs of Bankers Trust, Bear Stearns, Chase Manhattan, Goldman Sachs, J. P. Morgan, Lehman Brothers, Merrill Lynch, Morgan Stanley Dean Witter, and Salomon Smith Barney gathered under the oil portraits in the Fed's tenth-floor boardroom—not to bail out a Latin American nation but to consider a rescue of one of their own. The chairman of the New York Stock Exchange joined them, as did representatives from major European banks. Unaccustomed to hosting such a large gathering, the Fed did not have enough leather-backed chairs to go around, so the chief executives had to squeeze into folding metal seats.

Although McDonough was a public official, the meeting was secret. As far as the public knew, America was in the salad days of one of history's great bull markets, although recently, as in many previous

INTRODUCTION • xix

autumns, it had seen some backsliding. Since mid-August, when Russia had defaulted on its ruble debt, the global bond markets in particular had been highly unsettled. But that wasn't why McDonough had called the bankers.

Long-Term, a bond-trading firm, was on the brink of failing. The fund was run by John W. Meriwether, formerly a well-known trader at Salomon Brothers. Meriwether, a congenial though cautious midwesterner, had been popular among the bankers. It was because of him, mainly, that the bankers had agreed to give financing to Long-Term—and had agreed on highly generous terms. But Meriwether was only the public face of Long-Term. The heart of the fund was a group of brainy, Ph.D.-certified arbitrageurs. Many of them had been professors. Two had won the Nobel Prize. All of them were very smart. And they knew they were very smart.

For four years, Long-Term had been the envy of Wall Street. The fund had racked up returns of more than 40 percent a year, with no losing stretches, no volatility, seemingly no risk at all. Its intellectual supermen had apparently been able to reduce an uncertain world to rigorous, cold-blooded odds—on form, they were the very best that modern finance had to offer.

This one obscure arbitrage fund had amassed an amazing $100 billion in assets, virtually all of it borrowed—borrowed, that is, from the bankers at McDonough's table. As monstrous as this indebtedness was, it was by no means the worst of Long-Term's problems. The fund had entered into thousands of derivative contracts, which had endlessly intertwined it with every bank on Wall Street. These contracts, essentially side bets on market prices, covered an astronomical sum—more than $1 trillion worth of exposure.

If Long-Term defaulted, all of the banks in the room would be left holding one side of a contract for which the other side no longer existed. In other words, they would be exposed to tremendous—and untenable—risks. Undoubtedly, there would be a frenzy as every bank rushed to escape its now one-sided obligations and tried to sell its collateral from Long-Term.

Panics are as old as markets, but derivatives were relatively new. Regulators had worried about the potential risks of these inventive new securities, which linked the country's financial institutions in a complex chain of reciprocal obligations. Officials had wondered what would happen if one big link in the chain should fail. McDonough feared that the markets would stop working; that trading would cease; that the system itself would come crashing down.

James Cayne, the cigar-chomping chief executive of Bear Stearns, had been vowing that he would stop clearing Long-Term's trades—which would put it out of business—if the fund's available cash fell below $500 million. At the start of the year, that would have seemed remote, for Long-Term's capital had been $4.7 *billion*. But during the past five weeks, or since Russia's default, Long-Term had suffered numbing losses—day after day after day. Its capital was down to the minimum. Cayne didn't think it would survive another day.

The fund had already asked Warren Buffett for money. It had gone to George Soros. It had gone to Merrill Lynch. One by one, it had asked every bank it could think of. Now it had no place left to go. That was why, like a godfather summoning rival and potentially warring families, McDonough had invited the bankers. If each one moved to unload bonds individually, the result could be a worldwide panic. If they acted in concert, perhaps a catastrophe could be avoided. Although McDonough didn't say so, he wanted the banks to invest $4 billion and rescue the fund. He wanted them to do it right then—tomorrow would be too late.

But the bankers felt that Long-Term had already caused them more than enough trouble. Long-Term's secretive, close-knit mathematicians had treated everyone else on Wall Street with utter disdain. Merrill Lynch, the firm that had brought Long-Term into being, had long tried to establish a profitable, mutually rewarding relationship with the fund. So had many other banks. But Long-Term had spurned them. The professors had been willing to trade on their terms and only on theirs—not to meet the banks halfway. The bankers did not like it that the once haughty Long-Term was pleading for their help.

And the bankers themselves were hurting from the turmoil that Long-Term had helped to unleash. Goldman Sachs's CEO, Jon Corzine, was facing a revolt by his partners, who were horrified by Goldman's recent trading losses and who, unlike Corzine, did not want to use their diminishing capital to help a competitor. Sanford I. Weill, chairman of Travelers/Salomon Smith Barney, had suffered big losses, too. Weill was worried that the losses would jeopardize his company's pending merger with Citicorp, which Weill saw as the crowning gem to his lustrous career. He had recently shuttered his own arbitrage unit—which, years earlier, had been the launching pad for Meriwether's career—and was not keen to bail out another one.

As McDonough looked around the table, every one of his guests was in greater or lesser trouble, many of them directly on account of Long-Term. The value of the bankers' stocks had fallen precipitously. The bankers were afraid, as was McDonough, that the global storm that had begun, so innocently, with devaluations in Asia, and had spread to Russia, Brazil, and now to Long-Term Capital, would envelop all of Wall Street.

Richard Fuld, chairman of Lehman Brothers, was fighting off rumors that *his* company was on the verge of failing due to its supposed overexposure to Long-Term. David Solo, who represented the giant Swiss bank Union Bank of Switzerland, thought his bank was already in far too deeply; it had foolishly invested in Long-Term and had suffered titanic losses. Thomas Labrecque's Chase Manhattan had sponsored a loan to the hedge fund of $500 million; before Labrecque thought about investing more, he wanted that loan repaid.

David Komansky, the portly Merrill chairman, was worried most of all. In a matter of two months, Merrill's stock had fallen by half—$19 billion of its market value had simply melted away. Merrill had suffered shocking bond-trading losses, too. Now its own credit rating was at risk.

Komansky, who personally had invested almost $1 million in the fund, was terrified of the chaos that would result if Long-Term collapsed. But he knew how much antipathy there was in the room toward Long-Term. He thought the odds of getting the bankers to agree were long at best.

Komansky recognized that Cayne, the maverick Bear Stearns chief executive, would be a pivotal player. Bear, which cleared Long-Term's trades, knew the guts of the hedge fund better than any other firm. As the other bankers nervously shifted in their seats, Herbert Allison, Komansky's number two, asked Cayne where he stood.

Cayne stated his position clearly: Bear Stearns would not invest a nickel in Long-Term Capital.

For a moment the bankers, the cream of Wall Street, were silent. And then the room exploded.

THE RISE OF LONG-TERM CAPITAL MANAGEMENT

MERIWETHER

IF THERE WAS one article of faith that John Meriwether discovered at Salomon Brothers, it was to ride your losses until they turned into gains. It is possible to pinpoint the moment of Meriwether's revelation. In 1979, a securities dealer named J. F. Eckstein & Co. was on the brink of failing. A panicked Eckstein went to Salomon and met with a group that included several of Salomon's partners and also Meriwether, then a cherub-faced trader of thirty-one. "I got a great trade, but I can't stay in it," Eckstein pleaded with them. "How about buying me out?"

The situation was this: Eckstein traded in Treasury bill futures—which, as the name suggests, are contracts that provide for the delivery of U.S. Treasury bills, at a fixed price in the future. They often traded at a slight discount to the price of the actual, underlying bills. In a classic bit of arbitrage, Eckstein would buy the futures, sell the bills, and then wait for the two prices to converge. Since most people would pay about the same to own a bill in the proximate future as they would to own it now, it was reasonable to think that the prices *would* converge. And there was a bit of magic in the trade, which was the secret of Eckstein's business, of Long-Term Capital's future business, and indeed of every arbitrageur who has ever plied the trade.

Eckstein didn't know whether the two securities' prices would go up or down, *and Eckstein didn't care.* All that mattered to him was how the two prices would change relative to each other.

By buying the bill futures and shorting (that is, betting on a decline in the prices of) the actual bills, Eckstein really had *two* bets going, each in opposite directions.* Depending on whether prices moved up or down, he would expect to make money on one trade and lose it on the other. But as long as the cheaper asset—the futures—rose by a little more (or fell by a little less) than did the bills, Eckstein's profit on his winning trade would be greater than his loss on the other side. This is the basic idea of arbitrage.

Eckstein had made this bet many times, typically with success. As he made more money, he gradually raised his stake. For some reason, in June 1979, the normal pattern was reversed: futures got *more* expensive than bills. Confident that the customary relationship would reassert itself, Eckstein put on a *very* big trade. But instead of converging, the gap widened even further. Eckstein was hit with massive margin calls and became desperate to sell.

Meriwether, as it had happened, had recently set up a bond-arbitrage group within Salomon. He instantly saw that Eckstein's trade made sense, because sooner or later, the prices *should* converge. But in the meantime, Salomon would be risking tens of millions of its capital, which totaled only about $200 million. The partners were nervous but agreed to take over Eckstein's position. For the next couple of weeks, the spread continued to widen, and Salomon suffered a serious loss. The firm's capital account used to be scribbled in a little book, left outside the office of a partner named Allan Fine, and each afternoon the partners would nervously tiptoe over to Fine's to see how much they had lost. Meriwether coolly insisted that they would come out ahead. "We better," John Gutfreund, the managing partner, told him, "or you'll be fired."

The prices did converge, and Salomon made a bundle. Hardly anyone traded financial futures then, but Meriwether understood them. He was promoted to partner the very next year. More important, his little section, the inauspiciously titled Domestic Fixed Income Arbi-

---

* In practical terms, those who go short sell a security they have borrowed. They must return the security later—by which time, they believe, the price will have declined. The principle of buying cheap and selling dear still holds. Short sellers merely reverse the order: sell dear, *then* buy cheap.

trage Group, now had carte blanche to do spread trades with Salomon's capital. Meriwether, in fact, had found his life's work.

Born in 1947, Meriwether had grown up in the Rosemoor section of Roseland on the South Side of Chicago, a Democratic, Irish Catholic stronghold of Mayor Richard Daley. He was one of three children but part of a larger extended family, including four cousins across an alleyway. In reality, the entire neighborhood was family. Meriwether knew virtually everyone in the area, a self-contained world that revolved around the basketball lot, soda shop, and parish. It was bordered to the east by the tracks of the Illinois Central Railroad and to the north by a red board fence, beyond which lay a no-man's-land of train yards and factories. If it wasn't a poor neighborhood, it certainly wasn't rich. Meriwether's father was an accountant; his mother worked for the Board of Education. Both parents were strict. The Meriwethers lived in a smallish, cinnamon-brick house with a trim lawn and tidy garden, much as most of their neighbors did. Everyone sent their children to parochial schools (the few who didn't were ostracized as "publics"). Meriwether, attired in a pale blue shirt and dark blue tie, attended St. John de la Salle Elementary and later Mendel Catholic High School, taught by Augustinian priests. Discipline was harsh. The boys were rapped with a ruler or, in the extreme, made to kneel on their knuckles for an entire class. Educated in such a Joycean regime, Meriwether grew up accustomed to a pervasive sense of order. As one of Meriwether's friends, a barber's son, recalled, "We were afraid to goof around at [elementary] school because the nuns would punish you for life and you'd be sent to Hell." As for their mortal destination, it was said, only half in jest, that the young men of Rosemoor had three choices: go to college, become a cop, or go to jail. Meriwether had no doubt about his own choice, nor did any of his peers.

A popular, bright student, he was seemingly headed for success. He qualified for the National Honor Society, scoring especially high marks in mathematics—an indispensable subject for a bond trader. Perhaps the orderliness of mathematics appealed to him. He was ever guided by a sense of restraint, as if to step out of bounds would invite the ruler's slap. Although Meriwether had a bit of a mouth on him, as one chum recalled, he never got into serious trouble.[1] Private with his feelings, he kept any reckless impulse strictly under wraps and cloaked his drive behind a comely reserve. He was clever but not a prodigy, well liked but not a standout. He was, indeed, average enough in a neighborhood and time in which it would have been hell to have been anything *but* average.

Meriwether also liked to gamble, but only when the odds were sufficiently in his favor to give him an edge. Gambling, indeed, was a field in which his cautious approach to risk-taking could be applied to his advantage. He learned to bet on horses and also to play blackjack, the latter courtesy of a card-playing grandma. Parlaying an innate sense of the odds, he would bet on the Chicago Cubs, but not until he got the weather report so he knew how the winds would be blowing at Wrigley Field.[2] His first foray into investments was at age twelve or so, but it would be wrong to suggest that it occurred to any of his peers, or even to Meriwether himself, that this modestly built, chestnut-haired boy was a Horatio Alger hero destined for glory on Wall Street. "John and his older brother made money in high school buying stocks," his mother recalled decades later. "His father advised him." And that was that.

Meriwether made his escape from Rosemoor by means of a singular passion: not investing but golf. From an early age, he had haunted the courses at public parks, an unusual pastime for a Rosemoor boy. He was a standout member of the Mendel school team and twice won the Chicago Suburban Catholic League golf tournament. He also caddied at the Flossmoor Country Club, which involved a significant train or bus ride south of the city. The superintendents at Flossmoor took a shine to the earnest, likable young man and let him caddy for the richest players—a lucrative privilege. One of the members tabbed him for a Chick Evans scholarship, named for an early-twentieth-century golfer who had had the happy idea of endowing a college scholarship for caddies. Meriwether picked Northwestern University, in Evanston, Illinois, on the chilly waters of Lake Michigan, twenty-five miles and a world away from Rosemoor. His life story up to then had highlighted two rather conflicting verities. The first was the sense of well-being to be derived from fitting into a group such as a neighborhood or church: from religiously adhering to its values and rites. Order and custom were virtues in themselves. But second, Meriwether had learned, it paid to develop an edge—a low handicap at a game that nobody else on the block even played.

After Northwestern, he taught high school math for a year, then went to the University of Chicago for a business degree, where a grain farmer's son named Jon Corzine (later Meriwether's rival on Wall Street) was one of his classmates. Meriwether worked his way through business school as an analyst at CNA Financial Corporation, and graduated in 1973. The next year, Meriwether, now a sturdily built twenty-seven-year-old with beguiling eyes and round, dimpled cheeks, was hired by Salomon. It was still a small firm, but it was in the center of great changes that were convulsing bond markets everywhere.

Until the mid-1960s, bond trading had been a dull sport. An investor bought bonds, often from the trust department of his local bank, for steady income, and as long as the bonds didn't default, he was generally happy with his purchase, if indeed he gave it any further thought. Few investors actively traded bonds, and the notion of *managing* a bond portfolio to achieve a higher return than the next guy or, say, to beat a benchmark index, was totally foreign. That was a good thing, because no such index existed. The reigning bond guru was Salomon's own Sidney Homer, a Harvard-educated classicist, distant relative of the painter Winslow Homer, and son of a Metropolitan Opera soprano. Homer, author of the massive tome *A History of Interest Rates: 2000 BC to the Present,* was a gentleman scholar—a breed on Wall Street that was shortly to disappear.

Homer's markets, at least in contrast to those of today, were characterized by fixed relationships: fixed currencies, regulated interest rates, and a fixed gold price ($35 an ounce). But the epidemic of inflation that infected the West in the late 1960s destroyed this cozy world forever. As inflation rose, so did interest rates, and those gilt-edged bonds, bought when a 4 percent rate seemed attractive, lost half their value or more. In 1971, the United States freed the gold price; then the Arabs embargoed oil. If bondholders still harbored any illusion of stability, the bankruptcy of the Penn Central Railroad, which was widely owned by blue-chip accounts, wrecked the illusion forever. Bond investors, most of them knee-deep in losses, were no longer comfortable standing pat. Gradually, governments around the globe were forced to drop their restrictions on interest rates and on currencies. The world of fixed relationships was dead.

Soybeans suddenly seemed quaint; *money* was the hot commodity now. Futures exchanges devised new contracts in financial goods such as Treasury bills and bonds and Japanese yen, and everywhere there were new instruments, new options, new bonds to trade, just when professional portfolio managers were waking up and wanting to trade them. By the end of the 1970s, firms such as Salomon were slicing and dicing bonds in ways that Homer had never dreamed of: blending mortgages together, for instance, and distilling them into bite-sized, easily chewable securities.

The other big change was the computer. As late as the end of the 1960s, whenever traders wanted to price a bond, they would look it up in a thick blue book. In 1969, Salomon hired a mathematician, Martin Leibowitz, who got Salomon's first computer. Leibowitz became the most popular mathematician in history, or so it seemed when the bond market was hot and Salomon's traders, who no longer had time to page through the blue book, crowded around him to get bond prices that they now needed on the double. By the early 1970s, traders had their own crude handheld calculators, which subtly quickened the rhythm of the bond markets.

Meriwether, who joined Salomon on the financing desk, known as the Repo Department, got there just as the bond world was turning topsy-turvy. Once predictable and relatively low risk, the bond world was pulsating with change and opportunity, especially for younger, sharp-eyed analysts. Meriwether, who didn't know a soul when he arrived in New York, rented a room at a Manhattan athletic club and soon discovered that bonds were made for him. Bonds have a particular appeal to mathematical types because so much of what determines their value is readily quantifiable. Essentially, two factors dictate a bond's price. One can be gleaned from the coupon on the bond itself. If you can lend money at 10 percent today, you would pay a premium for a bond that yielded 12 percent. How much of a premium? That would depend on the maturity of the bond, the timing of the payments, your outlook (if you have one) for interest rates in the future, plus all manner of wrinkles devised by clever issuers, such as whether the bond is callable, convertible into equity, and so forth.

The other factor is the risk of default. In most cases, that is not strictly quantifiable, nor is it very great. Still, it exists. General Electric is a good risk, but not as good as Uncle Sam. Hewlett-Packard is somewhat riskier than GE; Amazon.com, riskier still. Therefore, bond investors demand a higher interest rate when they lend to Amazon as compared with GE, or to Bolivia as compared with France. Deciding how much higher is the heart of bond trading, but the point is that bonds trade on a mathematical *spread*. The riskier the bond, the wider the spread—that is, the greater the difference between the yield on it and the yield on (virtually risk free) Treasurys. Generally, though not always, the spread also increases with time—that is, investors demand a slightly higher yield on a two-year note than on a thirty-day bill because the uncertainty is greater.

These rules are the catechism of bond trading; they ordain a vast matrix of yields and spreads on debt securities throughout the world. They are as intricate and immutable as the rules of a great religion, and it is no wonder that Meriwether, who kept rosary beads and prayer cards in his briefcase, found them satisfying. Eager to learn, he peppered his bosses with questions like a divinity student. Sensing his promise, the suits at Salomon put him to trading government agency bonds. Soon after, New York City nearly defaulted, and the spreads on various agency bonds soared. Meriwether reckoned that the market had goofed—surely, not every government entity was about to go bust—and he bought all the bonds he could. Spreads did contract, and Meriwether's trades made millions.[3]

The Arbitrage Group, which he formed in 1977, marked a subtle but important shift in Salomon's evolution. It was also the model that Long-Term Capital was to replicate, brick for brick, in the 1990s—a laboratory in which Meriwether would become accustomed to, and comfortable with, taking big risks. Although Salomon had always traded bonds, its primary focus had been the relatively safer business of buying and selling bonds for customers. But the Arbitrage Group, led by Meriwether, became a principal, risking Salomon's own capital. Because the field was new, Meriwether had few competitors, and the pickings were rich. As in the Eckstein trade, he often bet that a spread—say, between a futures contract and the underlying bond, or between two bonds—would converge. He could also bet on spreads to widen, but convergence was his dominant theme. The people on the other side of his trades might be insurers, banks, or speculators; Meriwether wouldn't know, and usually he wouldn't care. Occasionally, these other investors might get scared and withdraw their capital, causing spreads to widen further and causing Meriwether to lose money, at least temporarily. But if he had the capital to stay the course, he'd be rewarded in the long run, or so his experience seemed to prove. Eventually, spreads always came in; that was the lesson he had learned from the Eckstein affair, and it was a lesson he would count on, years later, at Long-Term Capital. But there was a different lesson, equally valuable, that Meriwether might have drawn from the Eckstein business, had his success not come so fast: while a losing trade may well turn around *eventually* (assuming, of course, that it was properly conceived to begin with), the turn could arrive too late to do the trader any good—meaning, of course, that he might go broke in the interim.

■

By the early 1980s, Meriwether was one of Salomon's bright young stars. His shyness and implacable poker face played perfectly to his skill as a trader. William McIntosh, the Salomon partner who had interviewed him, said, "John has a steel-trap mind. You have no clue to what he's thinking." Meriwether's former colleague, the writer Michael Lewis, echoed this assessment of Meriwether in *Liar's Poker*:

> He wore the same blank half-tense expression when he won as he did when he lost. He had, I think, a profound ability to control the two emotions that commonly destroy traders—fear and greed—and it made him as noble as a man who pursues his self-interest so fiercely can be.[4]

It was a pity that the book emphasized a supposed incident in which Meriwether allegedly dared Gutfreund to play a single hand of poker for $10 million, not merely because the story seems apocryphal, but because it canonized Meriwether for a recklessness that wasn't his.[5] Meriwether was the priest of the *calculated* gamble. He was cautious to a fault; he gave away nothing of himself. His background, his family, his entire past were as much of a blank to colleagues as if, one said, he had "drawn a line in the sand." He was so intensely private that even when the Long-Term Capital affair was front-page news, a *New York Times* writer, after trying to determine if Meriwether had any siblings, settled for citing the inaccurate opinion of friends who thought him an only child.[6] Such reticence was a perfect attribute for a trader, but it was not enough. What Meriwether lacked, he must have sensed, was an *edge*—some special forte like the one he had developed on the links in high school, something that would distinguish Salomon from every other bond trader.

His solution was deceptively simple: Why not hire traders who were *smarter*? Traders who would treat markets as an intellectual discipline, as opposed to the folkloric, unscientific Neanderthals who traded from their bellies? Academia was teeming with nerdy mathematicians who had been publishing unintelligible dissertations on markets for years. Wall Street had started to hire them, but only for research, where they'd be out of harm's way. On Wall Street, the eggheads were stigmatized as "quants," unfit for the man's game of trading. Craig Coats, Jr., head of government-bond trading at Salomon, was a type typical of trading floors: tall, likable, handsome, bound to get along with clients. Sure, he had been a goof-off in college, but he had played forward on the basketball team, and he had trading in his heart. It was just this element of passion that Meriwether wanted to eliminate; he preferred the cool discipline of scholars, with their rigorous and highly quantitative approach to markets.

Most Wall Street executives were mystified by the academic world, but Meriwether, a math teacher with an M.B.A. from Chicago, was comfortable with it. *That would be his edge.* In 1983, Meriwether called Eric Rosenfeld, a sweet-natured MIT-trained Harvard Business School assistant professor, to see if Rosenfeld could recommend any of his students. The son of a modestly successful Concord, Massachusetts, money manager, Rosenfeld was a computer freak who had already been using quantitative methods to make investments. At Harvard, he was struggling.[7] Laconic and dry, Rosenfeld was compellingly bright, but he was less than commanding in a classroom. At a distance, he looked like a thin, bespectacled mouse. The students were tough on him; "they beat the shit out of him," according to a future colleague. Rosenfeld, who was grading exams when Meriwether called and was making, as he recalled, roughly $30,000 a year, instantly offered to audition for Salomon himself. Ten days later, he was hired.[8]

Meriwether didn't stop there. After Rosenfeld, he hired Victor J. Haghani, an Iranian American with a master's degree in finance from the London School of Economics; Gregory Hawkins, an Arkansan who had helped run Bill Clinton's campaign for state attorney general and had then gotten a Ph.D. in financial economics from MIT; and William Krasker, an intense, mathematically minded economist with a Ph.D. from—once again—MIT and a colleague of Rosenfeld at Harvard. Probably the nerdiest, and surely the smartest, was Lawrence Hilibrand, who had *two* degrees from MIT. Hilibrand was hired by Salomon's research department, the traditional home of quants, but Meriwether quickly moved him into the Arbitrage Group, which, of course, was the heart of the future Long-Term Capital.

The eggheads immediately took to Wall Street. They downloaded into their computers all of the past bond prices they could get their hands on. They distilled the bonds' historical relationships, and they modeled how these prices should behave in the future. And then, when a market price somewhere, somehow got out of line, the computer models told them.

The models didn't *order* them to trade; they provided a contextual argument for the human computers to consider. They simplified a complicated world. Maybe the yield on two-year Treasury notes was a bit closer than it ordinarily was to the yield on ten-year bonds; or maybe the spread between the two was unusually narrow, compared with a similar spread for some other country's paper. The models condensed the markets into a pointed inquiry. As one of the group said, "Given the state of things around the world—the shape of yield curves, volatilities, interest rates—are the financial markets making statements that are inconsistent with each other?" This is how they talked, and this is how they thought. Every price was a "statement"; if two statements were in conflict, there might be an opportunity for arbitrage.

The whole experiment would surely have failed, except for two happy circumstances. First, the professors *were* smart. They stuck to their knitting, and opportunities were plentiful, especially in newer markets such as derivatives. The professors spoke of opportunities as *inefficiencies;* in a perfectly efficient market, in which all prices were correct, no one would have anything to trade. Since the markets they traded in were still evolving, though, prices were often incorrect and there were opportunities aplenty. Moreover, the professors brought to the job an abiding credo, learned from academia, that over time, *all* markets tend to get more efficient.

In particular, they believed, spreads between riskier and less risky bonds would tend to narrow. This followed logically because spreads reflect, in part, the *uncertainty* that is attached to chancier assets. Over time, if markets did become more efficient, such riskier bonds would be less volatile and therefore more certain-seeming, and so the premium demanded by investors would tend to shrink. In the early 1980s, for instance, the spreads on swaps—a type of derivative trade, of which more later—were 2 percentage points. "They looked at this and said, 'It can't be right; there can't be that much risk,'" a junior member of Arbitrage recalled. "They said, 'There is going to be a secular trend toward a more efficient market.'"

And swap spreads did tighten—to 1 percentage point and eventually to a quarter point. All of Wall Street did this trade, including the Salomon government desk, run by the increasingly wary Coats. The difference was that Meriwether's Arbitrage Group did it in *very* big dollars. If a trade went against them, the arbitrageurs, especially the ever-confident Hilibrand, merely redoubled the bet. Backed by their models, they felt more *certain* than others did—almost invincible. Given enough time, given enough capital, the young geniuses from academe felt they could do no wrong, and Meriwether, who regularly journeyed to academic conferences to recruit such talent, began to believe that the geniuses were right.

That was the second happy circumstance: the professors had a protector who shielded them from company politics and got them the capital to trade. But for Meriwether, the experiment *couldn't* have worked; the professors were simply too out of place. Hilibrand, an engineer's son from Cherry Hill, New Jersey, was like an academic version of Al Gore; socially awkward, he answered the simplest-seeming questions with wooden and technical—albeit mathematically precise—replies. Once, a trader not in the Arbitrage Group tried to talk Hilibrand out of buying and selling a certain pair of securities. Hilibrand replied, as if conducting a tutorial, "But they are priced so *egregiously*." His colleague, accustomed to the profane banter of the trading floor, shot back, "I was thinking the same thing— 'egregiously'!" Surrounded by unruly traders, the arbitrageurs were quiet intellectuals. Krasker, the cautious professor who built many of the group's models, had all the charisma of a tabletop. Rosenfeld had a wry sense of humor, but in a firm in which many of the partners hadn't gone to college, much less graduate school at MIT, he was shy and taciturn.

Meriwether had the particular genius to bring this group to Wall Street—a move that Salomon's competitors would later imitate. "He took a bunch of guys who in the corporate world were considered freaks," noted Jay Higgins, then an investment banker at Salomon. "Those guys would be playing with their slide rules at Bell Labs if it wasn't for John, and they knew it."[9]

The professors were brilliant at reducing a trade to pluses and minuses; they could strip a ham sandwich to its component risks; but they could barely carry on a normal conversation. Meriwether created a safe, self-contained place for them to develop their skills; he adoringly made Arbitrage into a world apart. Because of Meriwether, the traders fraternized with one another, and they didn't feel the need to fraternize with anyone else.

Meriwether would say, "We're playing golf on Sunday," and he didn't have to add, "I'd like you to be there." The traders who hadn't played golf before, such as Hilibrand and Rosenfeld, quickly learned. Meriwether also developed a passion for horses and acquired some thoroughbreds; naturally, he took his traders to the track, too. He even shepherded the gang and their spouses to Antigua every year. He didn't want them just during trading hours, he wanted all of them, all the time. He nurtured his traders, all the while building a protective fence around the group as sturdy as the red board fence in Rosemoor.

Typical of Meriwether, he made gambling an intimate part of the group's shared life. The arbitrageurs devised elaborate betting pools over golf weekends; they bet on horses; they took day trips to Atlantic City together. They bet on elections. They bet on anything that aroused their passion for odds. When they talked sports, it wasn't about the game; it was about the *point spread*.

Meriwether loved for his traders to play liar's poker, a game that involves making poker hands from the serial numbers on dollar bills. He liked to test his traders; he thought the game honed their instincts, and he would get churlish and threaten to quit when they played poorly. It started as fun, but then it got serious; the traders would play for hours, occasionally for stakes in the tens of thousands of dollars. Rosenfeld kept an envelope stuffed with hundreds of single bills in his desk. Then, when it seemed that certain bills were cropping up too often, they did away with bills and got a computer to generate random lists of numbers. The Arbitrage boys seemed addicted to gambling: "You could never go out to dinner with J.M.'s guys without playing liar's poker to see who would pick up the check," Gerald Rosenfeld, Salomon's chief financial officer, recalled. Meriwether was a good player, and so was Eric Rosenfeld (no relation), who had an inscrutable poker face. The straight-arrow Hilibrand was a bit too literal. He was incapable of lying and for a long time never bluffed; mustachioed and eerily intelligent, he had a detachment that was almost extrahuman. Once, when asked whether it was awkward to have a wife who worked in mortgages (which Hilibrand traded), he answered flatly, "Well, I never talk to my wife about business."

The Arbitrage Group, about twelve in all, became incredibly close. They sat in a double row of desks in the middle of Salomon's raucous trading floor, which was the model for the investment bank in Tom Wolfe's *The Bonfire of the Vanities*. Randy Hiller, a mortgage trader in Arbitrage, found its cliquish aspect overbearing and left. Another defector was treated like a traitor; Meriwether vengefully ordered the crew not to even golf with him. But very few traders left, and those who remained all but worshiped Meriwether. They spoke of him in hushed tones, as of a Moses who had brought their tribe to Palestine. Meriwether didn't exactly return the praise, but he gave them something more worthwhile. His interest and curiosity stimulated the professors; it challenged them and made them better. And he rewarded them with heartfelt loyalty. He never screamed, but it wouldn't have mattered if he had. To the traders, the two initials "J.M."—for that was his unfailing sobriquet—were as powerful as any two letters could be.

Though he had a private office upstairs, Meriwether usually sat on the trading floor, at a tiny desk squeezed in with the others. He would chain-smoke while doing Eurodollar trades, and supervise the professors by asking probing questions. Somehow, he sheathed great ambition in an affecting modesty. He liked to say that he never hired anyone who wasn't smarter than he was. He didn't talk about himself, but no one noticed because he was genuinely interested in what the others were doing. He didn't build the models, but he grasped what the models were saying. And he trusted the models because *his* guys had built them. One time, a trader named Andy who was losing money on a mortgage trade asked for permission to double up, and J.M. gave it rather offhandedly. "Don't you want to know more about this trade?" Andy asked. Meriwether's trusting reply deeply affected the trader. J.M. said, "My trade was when I hired you."

Meriwether had married Mimi Murray, a serious equestrian from California, in 1981, and the two of them lived in a modest two-bedroom apartment on York Avenue on the Upper East Side. They wanted children, according to a colleague, but remained childless.

Aside from Mimi, J.M.'s family was Salomon. He didn't leave his desk even for lunch; in fact, his noontime was as routinized as the professors' models. Salomon did a china-service lunch, and for a long time, every day, a waiter would waft over to Meriwether bearing a bologna sandwich on white bread, two apples, and a Tab hidden under a silver dome. J.M. would eat one of the apples and randomly offer the other to one of the troops as a sort of token. The rest of the gang might order Chinese food, and if any sauce leaked onto his desk, J.M., his precious territory violated, would scowl and say, "Look, I guess I'm going to have to give up my desk and go back to my office and work there."

A misfit among Wall Street's Waspish bankers, J.M. identified more with the parochial school boys he had grown up with than with the rich executives whose number he had joined. Unlike other financiers in the roaring eighties, who were fast becoming trendy habitués of the social pages, Meriwether disdained attention (he purged his picture from Salomon's annual report) and refused to dine on any food that smacked of French. When in Tokyo, he went to McDonald's. Ever an outsider, he molded his group into a tribe of outsiders as cohesive, loyal, and protective as the world he had left in Rosemoor. His cohorts were known by schoolboy nicknames such as Vic, the Sheik, E.R., and Hawk.

Although J.M. knew his markets, his reputation as a trader was overwrought. His real skill was in shaping people, which he did in singularly understated style. He was awkward when speaking to a group; his words came out in uneven bunches, leaving others to piece together their meaning.[10] But his confidence in his troops was written on his face, and it worked on their spirits like a tonic. Combined with the traders' uncommon self-confidence, Meriwether's faith in them was a potent but potentially combustible mix. It inflated their already supreme self-assurance. Moreover, J.M.'s willingness to bankroll Hilibrand and the others with Salomon's capital dangerously conditioned the troops to think that they would always have access to more.

As Arbitrage made more money, the group's turf inevitably expanded. Meriwether, eclipsing rivals such as Coats, gained command over all bond trading, including government bonds, mortgages, high-yield corporate bonds, European bonds, and Japanese warrants. It seemed logical, for the group to apply its models in new and greener pastures. But others in Salomon began to seethe. J.M. would send one of his boys—Hilibrand or Victor Haghani—to Salomon's London office or its Tokyo office, and the emissary would declare, "This trade is very good, but you should be ten times bigger in it." Not two times, but *ten* times! As if they *couldn't* fail. Hilibrand and Haghani were in their twenties, and they might be talking to guys twice their age. Then they started to say, "Don't do this trade; we're better at this than anyone else, so we'll do all of this trade on the arbitrage desk."

Hilibrand was particularly annoying. He was formal and polite, but he struck old hands as condescending, infuriating them with his mathematical certitude. One time, he tried to persuade some commodity traders that they should bet on oil prices following a pattern similar to that of bond prices. The traders listened dubiously while Hilibrand bobbed his head back and forth. Suddenly he raised a hand and sonorously declaimed, "Consider the following hypothesis." It was as if he were delivering an edict from on high, to be etched in stone.

Traders had an anxious life; they'd spend the day shouting into a phone, hollering across the room, and nervously eyeballing a computer screen. The Arbitrage Group, right in the middle of this controlled pandemonium, seemed to be a mysterious, privileged subculture. Half the time, the boys were discussing trades in obscure, esoteric language, as if in a seminar; the other half, they were laughing and playing liar's poker. In their cheap suits and with their leisurely mien, they could seemingly cherry-pick the best trades while everyone else worked at a frenetic pace.

The group was extremely private; it seemed to have adopted J.M.'s innate secretiveness as a protective coloring. Though any trader is well advised to be discreet, the professors' refusal to share any information with their Salomon colleagues fueled the resentment felt by Coats and others. Though Arbitrage soaked up all of the valuable tidbits that passed through a premier bond-trading floor, it set up its own private research arm and strictly forbade others in Salomon to learn about its trades. One time, the rival Prudential-Bache hired away a Salomon mortgage trader, which was considered a coup. "What was the first thing he wanted?" a then-Pru-Bache manager laughingly remembered. "Analytics? Better computer system or software? No. He wanted locks on the filing cabinet. It reflected their mentality!" Driven by fanatical loyalty to Meriwether, the Arbitrage Group nurtured an us-against-them clannishness that would leave the future Long-Term dangerously remote from the rest of Wall Street. Hilibrand became so obsessed with his privacy that he even refused to let Salomon Brothers take his picture.[11]

■ ·

As other areas of Salomon floundered, Arbitrage increasingly threw its weight around. Hilibrand pressed the firm to eliminate investment banking, which, he argued with some justification, took home too much in bonuses and was failing to carry its weight. Then he declared that Arbitrage shouldn't have to pay for its share of the company cafeteria, because the group didn't eat there. True to his right-wing, libertarian principles, Hilibrand complained about being saddled with "monopoly vendors," as if every trader and every clerk should negotiate his own deal for lunch. The deeper truth was that Hilibrand and his mates in Arbitrage had little respect for their mostly older Salomon colleagues who worked in other areas of the firm. "It was like they were a capsule inside a spaceship," Higgins said of J.M.'s underlings. "They didn't breathe the air that everybody else did."

Hilibrand and Rosenfeld continually pressed J.M. for more money. They viewed Salomon's compensation arrangement, which liberally spread the wealth to all departments, as socialistic. Since Arbitrage was making most of the money, they felt, they and they alone should reap the rewards.

In 1987, the raider Ronald Perelman made a hostile bid for Salomon. Gutfreund feared, with ample justification, that if Perelman won, Salomon's reputation as a trusted banker would go down the tubes (indeed, Salomon's corporate clients could likely find themselves on Perelman's hit list). Gutfreund fended Perelman off by selling control of the firm to a distinctly friendly investor, the billionaire Warren Buffett. Hilibrand, who weighed everything in mathematical terms, was incensed over what he reckoned was a poor deal for Salomon. The twenty-seven-year-old wunderkind, though unswervingly honest himself, couldn't see that an intangible such as Salomon's ethical image was also worth a price. He actually flew out to Omaha to try to persuade Buffett, now a member of Salomon's board, to sell back his investment, but Buffett, of course, refused.

J.M. tried to temper his impatient young Turks and imbue them with loyalty to the greater firm. When the traders' protests got louder, J.M. invited Hilibrand and Rosenfeld to a dinner with William McIntosh, an older partner, to hear about Salomon's history. A liberal Democrat in the Irish Catholic tradition, J.M. had a stronger sense of the firm's common welfare and a grace that softened the hard edge of his cutthroat profession. He shrugged off his lieutenants' occasional cries that Arbitrage should separate from Salomon. He would tell them, "I've got loyalty to people here. And anyway, you're being greedy. Look at the people in Harlem." He pressed Salomon to clean house, but not without showing concern for other departments. Thoughtfully, when the need arose, he would tell the chief financial officer, "We have a big trade on; we could lose a lot—I just want you to know." In the crash of 1987, Arbitrage did drop $120 million in one day.[12] Others at Salomon weren't sure quite what the group was doing or what its leverage was, but they instinctively trusted Meriwether. Even his rivals in the firm liked him. And then it all came crashing down.

■

Pressed by his young traders, who simply wouldn't give up, in 1989 Meriwether persuaded Gutfreund to adopt a formula under which his arbitrageurs would get paid a fixed, 15 percent share of the group's profits. The deal was cut in secret, after Hilibrand had threatened to bolt.[13] Typically, J.M. left himself out of the arrangement, telling Gutfreund to pay him whatever he thought was fair. Then Arbitrage had a banner year, and Hilibrand, who got the biggest share, took home a phenomenal $23 million. Although Hilibrand modestly continued to ride the train to work and drive a Lexus, news of his pay brought to the surface long-simmering resentments, particularly as no other Salomon department was paid under such a formula. As Charlie Munger, Buffett's partner and a Salomon director, put it, "The more hyperthyroid at Salomon went stark, raving mad."

In particular, a thirty-four-year-old trader named Paul Mozer was enraged. Mozer had been part of Arbitrage, but a couple of years earlier he had been forced to leave that lucrative area to run the government desk. Mozer had a wiry frame, close-set eyes, and an intense manner. In 1991, a year after the storm over Hilibrand's pay, Mozer went to Meriwether and made a startling confession: he had submitted a false bid to the U.S. Treasury to gain an unauthorized share of a government-bond auction.

Stunned, Meriwether asked, "Is there anything else?" Mozer said there wasn't.

Meriwether took the matter to Gutfreund. The pair, along with two other top executives, agreed that the matter was serious, but they somehow did nothing about it. Although upset with Mozer, Meriwether stayed loyal to him. It is hard to imagine the clannish, faithful J.M. doing otherwise. He defended Mozer as a hard worker who had slipped but once and left him in charge of the government desk. This was a mistake—not an ethical mistake but an error in judgment brought on by J.M.'s singular code of allegiance. In fact, Mozer was a volatile trader who—motivated more by pique than by a realistic hope for profit—had repeatedly and recklessly broken the rules, jeopardizing the reputation of Meriwether, his supervisor, and the entire firm. It must be said that Mozer's crime had been so foolish as to be easily slipped by his superiors. Quite naturally, Meriwether, now head of Salomon's bond business, hadn't thought to inquire if one of his traders had been lying to the U.S. Treasury. But J.M.'s lenience after the fact is hard to fathom. A few months later, in August, Salomon discovered that Mozer's confession to Meriwether had itself been a lie, for he had committed numerous other infractions, too. Though now Salomon did report the matter, the Treasury and Fed were furious. The scandal set off an uproar seemingly out of proportion to the modest wrongdoing that had inspired it.[14] No matter; one simply did not—could not—deceive the U.S. Treasury. Gutfreund, a lion of Wall Street, was forced to quit.

Buffett flew in from Omaha and became the new, though interim, CEO. He immediately asked the frazzled Salomon executives, "Is there any way we can save J.M.?" Meriwether, of course, was the firm's top moneymaker and known as impeccably ethical. His traders heatedly defended him, pointing out that J.M. had immediately reported the matter to *his* superior. But pressure mounted on all involved in the scandal. McIntosh, the partner who had first brought Meriwether into Salomon, trekked up to J.M.'s forty-second-floor office and told him that he should quit for the good of the firm. And almost before the Arbitrage Group could fathom it, their chief had resigned. It was so unexpected, Meriwether felt it was surreal; moreover, he suffered for being front-page news. "I'm a fairly shy, introspective person," he later noted to *Business Week*.[15] The full truth was more bitter: J.M. was being pushed aside—even implicitly blamed—despite, in his opinion, having done no wrong. This painful dollop of limelight made him even more secretive, to Long-Term Capital's later regret. Meanwhile, within the Arbitrage Group, resurrecting J.M. became a crusade. Hilibrand and Rosenfeld kept J.M.'s office intact, with his golf club, desk, and computer, as if he were merely on an extended holiday. Deryck Maughan, the new CEO, astutely surmised that as long as this shrine to J.M. remained, J.M. was alive as his potential rival. Sure enough, a year later, when Meriwether resolved his legal issues stemming from the Mozer affair, Hilibrand and Rosenfeld, now the heads of Arbitrage and the government desk, respectively, lobbied for J.M.'s return as co-CEO.*

Maughan, a bureaucrat, was too smart to go for this and tried to refashion Salomon into a global, full-service bank, with Arbitrage as a mere department. Hilibrand, who was dead opposed to this course, increasingly asserted himself in J.M.'s absence. He wanted Salomon to fire its investment bankers and retrench around Arbitrage. Meanwhile, he made a near-catastrophic bet in mortgages and fell behind by $400 million. Most traders in that situation would have called it a day, but Hilibrand was just warming up; he coolly proposed that Salomon double its commitment! Because Hilibrand believed in his trade so devoutly, he could take pain as no other trader could. He said that the market was like a Slinky out of shape—eventually it would spring back. It was said that only once had he ever suffered a permanent loss, a testament to the fact that he was not a gambler. But his supreme conviction in his own rightness cried out for some restraining influence, lest it develop a reckless edge.

Doubling up was too much, but management let Hilibrand keep the trade he had. Eventually, it *was* profitable, but it reminded Salomon's managers that while Hilibrand was critiquing various departments as being so much extra baggage, Arbitrage felt free to call on Salomon's capital whenever it was down. The executives could never agree on just how much capital Arbitrage was tying up or how much risk its trades entailed, matters on which the dogmatic Hili-

---

* The Securities and Exchange Commission filed a civil complaint charging that Meriwether had failed to properly supervise Mozer. Without admitting or denying guilt, Meriwether settled the case, agreeing to a three-month suspension from the securities industry and a $50,000 fine.

brand lectured them for hours. In short, how much—if, sometime, the Slinky did not bounce back—could Arbitrage potentially lose? Neither Buffett nor Munger ever felt quite comfortable with the mathematical tenor of Hilibrand's replies.[16] Buffett agreed to take J.M. back—but not, as Hilibrand wanted, to trust him with the entire firm.

Of course, there was no way Meriwether would settle for such a qualified homecoming. The Mozer scandal had ended any hope that J.M. would take his place at the top of Salomon, but it had sown the seeds of a greater drama. Now forty-five, with hair that dipped in a wavy, boyish arc toward impenetrable eyes, J.M. broke off talks with Salomon. He laid plans for a new and independent arbitrage fund, perhaps a hedge fund, and he proceeded to raid the Arbitrage Group that he had, so lovingly, assembled.

2

HEDGE FUND

I love a hedge, sir.
—HENRY FIELDING, 1736

Prophesy as much as you like, but always hedge.
—OLIVER WENDELL HOLMES, 1861

BY THE EARLY 1990s, as Meriwether began to resuscitate his career, investing had entered a golden age. More Americans owned investments than ever before, and stock prices were rising to astonishing heights. Time and again, the market indexes soared past once unthinkable barriers. Time and again, new records were set and old standards eclipsed. Investors were giddy, but they were far from complacent. It was a golden age, but also a nervous one. Americans filled their empty moments by gazing anxiously at luminescent monitors that registered the market's latest move. Stock screens were everywhere—in gyms, at airports, in singles bars. Pundits repeatedly prophesied a correction or a crash; though always wrong, they were hard to ignore. Investors were greedy but wary, too. People who had gotten rich beyond their wildest dreams wanted a place to reinvest, but one that would not unduly suffer if—or when—the stock market finally crashed.

And there were plenty of rich people about. Thanks in large part to the stock market boom, no fewer than 6 million people around the world counted themselves as dollar millionaires, with a total of $17 trillion in assets.[1] For these lucky 6 million, at least, investing in hedge funds had a special allure.

As far as securities law is concerned, there is no such thing as a *hedge fund*. In practice, the term refers to a limited partnership, at least a small number of which have operated since the 1920s. Benjamin Graham, known as the father of value investing, ran what was perhaps the first. Unlike mutual funds, their more common cousins, these partnerships operate in Wall Street's shadows; they are private and largely unregulated investment pools for the rich. They need not register with the Securities and Exchange Commission, though some must make limited filings to another Washington agency, the Commodity Futures Trading Commission. For the most part, they keep the contents of their portfolios hidden. They can borrow as much as they choose (or as much as their bankers will lend them—which often amounts to the same thing). And, unlike mutual funds, they can concentrate their portfolios with no thought to diversification. In fact, hedge funds are free to sample any or all of the more exotic species of investment flora, such as options, derivatives, short sales, extremely high leverage, and so forth.

In return for such freedom, hedge funds must limit access to a select few investors; indeed, they operate like private clubs. By law, funds can sign up no more than ninety-nine investors, people, or institutions each worth at least $1 million, or up to five hundred investors, assuming that each has a portfolio of at least $5 million. The implicit logic is that *if* a fund is open to only a small group of millionaires and institutions, agencies such as the SEC need not trouble to monitor it. Presumably, millionaires know what they are doing; if not, their losses are nobody's business but their own.

Until recently, hedge fund managers were complete unknowns. But in the 1980s and '90s, a few large operators gained notoriety, most notably the émigré currency speculator George Soros. In 1992, Soros's Quantum Fund became celebrated for "breaking" the Bank of England and forcing it to devalue the pound (which he had relentlessly sold short), a coup that netted him a $1 billion profit. A few years later, Soros was blamed—perhaps unjustifiably—for forcing sharp devaluations in Southeast Asian currencies. Thanks to Soros and a few other high-profile managers, such as Julian Robertson and Michael Steinhardt, hedge fund operators acquired an image of daring buccaneers capable of roiling markets. Steinhardt bragged that he and his fellows were one of the few remaining bastions of frontier capitalism.[2] The popular image was of swashbuckling risk takers who captured outsized profits or suffered horrendous losses; the 1998 *Webster's College Dictionary* defined hedge funds as those that use "high-risk speculative methods."

Despite their bravura image, however, most hedge funds are rather tame; indeed, that is their true appeal. The term "hedge fund" is a colloquialism derived from the expression "to hedge one's bets," meaning to limit the possibility of loss on a speculation by betting on the other side. This usage evolved from the notion of the common garden hedge as a boundary or limit and was used by Shakespeare ("England hedg'd in with the maine"[3]). No one had thought to apply the term to an investment fund until Alfred Winslow Jones, the true predecessor of Meriwether, organized a partnership in 1949.[4] Though such partnerships had long been in existence, Jones, an Australian-born *Fortune* writer, was the first to run a balanced, or *hedged*, portfolio. Fearing that his stocks would fall during general market slumps, Jones decided to neutralize the market factor by hedging—that is, by going both long and short. Like most investors, he bought stocks he deemed to be cheap, but he also sold short seemingly overpriced stocks. At least in theory, Jones's portfolio was "market neutral." Any event—war, impeachment, a change in the weather—that moved the market either up or down would simply elevate one half of Jones's portfolio and depress the other half. His net return would depend only on his ability to single out the *relative* best and worst.

This is a conservative approach, likely to make less but also to lose less, which appealed to the nervous investor of the 1990s. Eschewing the daring of Soros, most modern hedge funds boasted of their steadiness as much as of their profits. Over time, they expected to make handsome returns but *not* to track the broader market blip for blip. Ideally, they would make as much as or more than generalized stock funds yet hold their own when the averages suffered.

At a time when Americans compared investment returns as obsessively as they once had soaring home prices, these hedge funds—though dimly understood—attained a mysterious cachet, for they had seemingly found a route to riches while circumventing the usual risks. People at barbecues talked of nothing but their mutual funds, but a mutual fund was so—common! For people of means, for people who summered in the Hamptons and decorated their homes with Warhols, for patrons of the arts and charity dinners, investing in a hedge fund denoted a certain status, an inclusion among Wall

Street's smartest and savviest. When the world was talking invest-ments, what could be more thrilling than to demurely drop, at court-side, the name of a young, sophisticated hedge fund manager who, discreetly, shrewdly, and auspiciously, was handling one's resources? Hedge funds became a symbol of the richest *and* the best. Paradox-ically, the princely fees that hedge fund managers charged enhanced their allure, for who could get away with such gaudy fees except the exceptionally talented? Not only did hedge fund managers pocket a fat share of their investors' profits, they greedily claimed a percent-age of the assets.

For such reasons, the number of hedge funds in the United States exploded. In 1968, when the SEC went looking, it could find only 215 of them.[5] By the 1990s there were perhaps 3,000 (no one knows the exact number), spread among many investing styles and asset types. Most were small; all told, they held perhaps $300 billion in capital, compared with $3.2 trillion in equity mutual funds.[6] How-ever, investors were hungry for more. They were seeking an alterna-tive to plain vanilla that was both bold *and* safe: not the riskiest investing style but the most certain; not the loudest, merely the smartest. This was exactly the sort of hedge fund Meriwether had in mind.

Emulating Alfred Jones, Meriwether envisioned that Long-Term Capital Management would concentrate on "relative value" trades in bond markets. Thus, Long-Term would buy some bonds and sell some others. It would bet on spreads between *pairs* of bonds to either widen or contract. If interest rates in Italy were significantly higher than in Germany, meaning that Italy's bonds were cheaper than Ger-many's, a trader who invested in Italy and shorted Germany would profit if, and as, this differential narrowed. This is a relatively low-risk strategy. Since bonds usually rise and fall in sync, spreads don't move as much as the bonds themselves. As with Jones's fund, Long-Term would in theory be unaffected if markets rose or fell, or even if they crashed.

But there was one significant difference: Meriwether planned from the very start that Long-Term would leverage its capital twenty to thirty times or even more. This was a necessary part of Long-Term's strategy, because the gaps between the bonds it intended to buy and those it intended to sell were, most often, minuscule. To make a de-cent profit on such tiny spreads, Long-Term would have to multiply its bet many, many times by borrowing. The allure of this strategy is apparent to anyone who has visited a playground. Just as a seesaw enables a child to raise a much greater weight than he could on his own, financial leverage multiplies your "strength"—that is, your earning power—because it enables you to earn a return on the capital you have borrowed as well as on your own money. Of course, your power to lose is also multiplied. If for some reason Long-Term's strategy ever failed, its losses would be vastly greater and accrue more quickly; indeed, they might be life-threatening—an eventuality that surely seemed remote.

■

Early in 1993, Meriwether paid a call on Daniel Tully, chairman of Merrill Lynch. Still anxious about the unfair tarnish on his name from the Mozer affair, J.M. immediately asked, "Am I damaged goods?" Tully said he wasn't. Tully put Meriwether in touch with the Merrill Lynch people who raised capital for hedge funds, and shortly thereafter, Merrill agreed to take on the assignment of raising capital for Long-Term.

J.M.'s design was staggeringly ambitious. He wanted nothing less than to replicate the Arbitrage Group, with its global reach and ability to take huge positions, but without the backing of Salomon's billions in capital, credit lines, information network, and seven thousand employees. Having done so much for Salomon, he was bitter about having been forced into exile under a cloud and eager to be vindicated, perhaps by creating something better.

And Meriwether wanted to raise a colossal sum, $2.5 billion. (The typical fund starts with perhaps 1 percent as much.) Indeed, everything about Long-Term was ambitious. Its fees would be considerably higher than average. J.M. and his partners would rake in 25 percent of the profits, *in addition to* a yearly 2 percent charge on assets. (Most funds took only 20 percent of profits and 1 percent on assets.) Such fees, J.M. felt, were needed to sustain a global operation—but this only pointed to the far-reaching nature of his aspirations.

Moreover, the fund insisted that investors commit for at least three years, an almost unheard-of lockup in the hedge fund world. The lockup made sense; if fickle markets turned against it, Long-Term would have a cushion of truly "long-term" capital; it would be the bank that could tell depositors, "Come back tomorrow." Still, it was asking investors to show enormous trust—particularly since J.M. did not have a formal track record to show them. While it was known anecdotally that Arbitrage had accounted for most of Salomon's recent earnings, the group's profits hadn't been disclosed. Even investors who had an inkling of *what* Arbitrage had earned had no understanding of *how* it had earned it. The nuts and bolts—the models, the spreads, the exotic derivatives—were too obscure. Moreover, people had serious qualms about investing with Meriwether so soon after he had been sanctioned by the SEC in the Mozer affair.

As Merrill began to chart a strategy for raising money, J.M.'s old team began to peel off from Salomon. Eric Rosenfeld left early in 1993. Victor Haghani, the Iranian Sephardi, was next; he got an ovation on Salomon's trading floor when he broke the news. In July, Greg Hawkins quit. Although J.M. still lacked Hilibrand, who was ambivalent in the face of Salomon's desperate pleas that he stay, Meriwether was now hatching plans with a nucleus of his top traders. He still felt a strong loyalty to his former colleagues, and he touchingly offered the job of nonexecutive chairman to Gutfreund, Salomon's fallen chief—on the condition that Gutfreund give up an acrimonious fight that he was waging with Salomon for back pay. Though overlooked, Gutfreund had played a pivotal role in the Arbitrage Group's success: he had been the brake on the traders' occasional tendencies to overreach. But it was not to be. At Long-Term, J.M. would have to restrain his own disciples.

In any case, J.M. wanted more cachet than Gutfreund or even his talented but unheralded young arbitrageurs could deliver. He needed an edge—something to justify his bold plans with investors. He had to recast his group, to showcase them as not just a bunch of bond traders but as a grander experiment in finance. This time, it would not do to recruit an unknown assistant professor—not if he wanted to raise $2.5 billion. This time, Meriwether went to the very top of academia. Harvard's Robert C. Merton was the leading scholar in finance, considered a genius by many in his field. He had trained several generations of Wall Street traders, including Eric Rosenfeld. In the 1980s, Rosenfeld had persuaded Merton to become a consultant to Salomon, so Merton was already friendly with the Arbitrage Group. More important, Merton's was a name that would instantly open doors, not only in America but also in Europe and Asia.

Merton was the son of a prominent Columbia University social scientist, Robert K. Merton, who had studied the behavior of scientists. Shortly after his son was born, Merton *père* coined the idea of the "self-fulfilling prophecy," a phenomenon, he suggested, that was illustrated by depositors who made a run on a bank out of fear of a default—for his son, a prophetic illustration.[7] The younger Merton, who grew up in Hastings-on-Hudson, outside New York City, showed a knack for devising systematic approaches to whatever he tackled. A devotee of baseball and cars, he studiously memorized first the batting averages of players and then the engine specs of virtually every American automobile.[8] Later, when he played poker, he would stare at a lightbulb to contract his pupils and throw off opponents. As if to emulate the scientists his father studied, he was already the person of whom a later writer would say that he "looked for order all around him."[9]

While he was an undergrad at Cal Tech, another interest, investing, blossomed. Merton often went to a local brokerage at 6:30 A.M., when the New York markets opened, to spend a few hours trading and watching the market. Providentially, he transferred to MIT to study economics. In the late 1960s, economists were just beginning to transform finance into a mathematical discipline. Merton, working under the wing of the famed Paul Samuelson, did nothing less than invent a new field. Up until then, economists had constructed models to describe how markets look—or in theory should look—at any point in time. Merton made a Newtonian leap, modeling prices in a series of infinitesimally tiny moments. He called this "continuous time finance." Years later, Stan Jonas, a derivatives specialist with the French-owned Société Générale, would observe, "Most everything else in finance has been a footnote on what Merton did in the 1970s." His mimeographed blue lecture notes became a keepsake.

In the early 1970s, Merton tackled a problem that had been partially solved by two other economists, Fischer Black and Myron S. Scholes: deriving a formula for the "correct" price of a stock option. Grasping the intimate relation between an option and the underlying stock, Merton completed the puzzle with an elegantly mathematical flourish. Then he graciously waited to publish until after his peers did; thus, the formula would ever be known as the Black-Scholes model. Few people would have cared, given that no active market for options existed. But coincidentally, a month before the formula appeared, the Chicago Board Options Exchange had begun to list stock options for trading. Soon, Texas Instruments was advertising in *The Wall Street Journal,* "Now you can find the Black-Scholes value using our . . . calculator."[10] This was the true beginning of the derivatives revolution. Never before had professors made such an impact on Wall Street.

In the 1980s, Meriwether and many other traders became accustomed to trading these newfangled instruments just as they did stocks and bonds. As opposed to actual securities, derivatives were simply contracts that derived (hence the name) their value from stocks, bonds, or other assets. For instance, the value of a stock option, the right to purchase a stock at a specific price and within a certain time period, varied with the price of the underlying shares.

Merton jumped at the opportunity to join Long-Term Capital because it seemed a chance to showcase his theories in the real world. Derivatives, he had recently been arguing, had blurred the lines between investment firms, banks, and other financial institutions. In the seamless world of derivatives, a world that Merton had helped to invent, anyone could assume the risk of loaning money, or of providing equity, simply by structuring an appropriate contract. It was function that mattered, not form. This had already been proved in the world of mortgages, once supplied exclusively by local banks and now largely funded by countless disparate investors who bought tiny pieces of securitized mortgage pools.

Indeed, Merton saw Long-Term Capital not as a "hedge fund," a term that he and the other partners sneered at, but as a state-of-the-art *financial intermediary* that provided capital to markets just as banks did. The bank on the corner borrowed from depositors and lent to local residents and businesses. It matched its assets—that is, its loans—with liabilities, attempting to earn a tiny spread by charging borrowers a slightly higher interest rate than it paid to depositors. Similarly, Long-Term Capital would "borrow" by selling one group of bonds and lend by purchasing another—presumably bonds that were slightly less in demand and that therefore yielded slightly higher interest rates. Thus, the fund would earn a spread, just like a bank. Though this description is highly simplified, Long-Term, by investing in the riskier (meaning higher-yielding) bonds, would be in the business of "providing liquidity" to markets. And what did a bank do but provide liquidity? Thanks to Merton, the nascent hedge fund began to think of itself in grander terms.

Unfortunately, Merton was of little use in selling the fund. He was too serious-minded, and he was busy with classes at Harvard. But in the summer of 1993, J.M. recruited a second academic star: Myron Scholes. Though regarded as less of a heavyweight by other academics, Scholes was better known on Wall Street, thanks to the Black-Scholes formula. Scholes had also worked at Salomon, so he, too, was close to the Meriwether group. And with *two* of the most brilliant minds in finance, each said to be on the shortlist of Nobel candidates, Long-Term had the equivalent of Michael Jordan and Muhammad Ali on the same team. "This was mystique taken to a very high extreme," said a money manager who ultimately invested in the fund.

In the fall of 1993, Merrill Lynch launched a madcap drive to recruit investors. Big-ticket clients were ferried by limousine to Merrill's headquarters, at the lower tip of Manhattan, where they were shown a presentation on the fund, sworn to secrecy, and then returned to their limos. Then Merrill and various groups of partners took their show on the road, making stops in New York, Boston, Philadelphia, Tallahassee, Atlanta, Chicago, St. Louis, Cincinnati, Madison, Kansas City, Dallas, Denver, Los Angeles, Amsterdam, London, Madrid, Paris, Brussels, Zurich, Rome, São Paulo, Buenos Aires, Tokyo, Hong Kong, Abu Dhabi, and Saudi Arabia. Long-Term set a minimum of $10 million per investor.

The road show started badly. J.M. was statesmanlike but reserved, as if afraid that anything he said would betray the group's secrets. "People all wanted to see J.M., but J.M. never talked," Merrill's Dale Meyer griped. The understated Rosenfeld was too low-key; he struck one investor as nearly comatose. Greg Hawkins, a former pupil of Merton, was the worst—full of Greek letters denoting algebraic symbols. The partners didn't know how to tell a story; they *sounded* like math professors. Even the fund's name lacked pizzazz; only the earnest Merton liked it. Investors had any number of reasons to shy away. Many were put off by J.M.'s unwillingness to discuss his investment strategies. Some were frightened by the prospective leverage, which J.M. was careful to disclose. Institutions such as the Rockefeller Foundation and Loews Corporation balked at paying such high fees. Long-Term's entire premise seemed untested, especially to the consultants who advise institutions and who decide where a lot of money gets invested.

Meriwether, who was continually angling to raise Long-Term's pedigree, went to Omaha for a steak dinner with Buffett, knowing that if Buffett invested, others would, too. The jovial billionaire was his usual self—friendly, encouraging, and perfectly unwilling to write a check.

Rebuffed by the country's richest investor, J.M. approached Jon Corzine, who had long envied Meriwether's unit at Salomon and who was trying to build a rival business at Goldman Sachs. Corzine dangled the prospect of Goldman's becoming a big investor or, perhaps, of its taking Meriwether's new fund in-house. Ultimately, it did neither. Union Bank of Switzerland took a long look, but it passed, too. Not winning these big banks hurt. Despite his bravura, J.M. was worried about being cut out of the loop at Salomon. He badly wanted an institutional anchor.

Turning necessity to advantage, J.M. next pursued a handful of foreign banks to be Long-Term's quasi partners, to give the fund an international gloss. Each partner—J.M. dubbed them "strategic investors"—would invest $100 million and share inside dope about its local market. In theory, at least, Long-Term would reciprocate. The plan was pure Meriwether, flattering potential investors by calling them "strategic." Merton loved the idea; it seemed to validate his theory that the old institutional relationships could be overcome. It opened up a second track, with J.M. independently courting foreign banks while Merrill worked on recruiting its clients.

Merrill moved the fund-raising forward by devising an ingenious system of "feeders" that enabled Long-Term to solicit funds from investors in every imaginable tax and legal domain. One feeder was for ordinary U.S. investors; another for tax-free pensions; another for Japanese who wanted their profits hedged in yen; still another for European institutions, which could invest only in shares that were listed on an exchange (this feeder got a dummy listing on the Irish Stock Exchange).

The feeders didn't keep the money; they were paper conduits that channeled the money to a central fund, known as Long-Term Capital Portfolio (LTCP), a Cayman Islands partnership. For all practical purposes, Long-Term Capital Portfolio *was* the fund: it was the entity that would buy and sell bonds and hold the assets. The vehicle that *ran* the fund was Long-Term Capital Management (LTCM), a Delaware partnership owned by J.M., his partners, and some of their

spouses. Though such a complicated organization might have dis-
suaded others, it was welcome to the partners, who viewed their ability to structure complex trades as one of their advantages over other
traders. Physically, of course, the partners were nowhere near either
the Caymans or Delaware but in offices in Greenwich, Connecticut,
and London.

The partners got a break just as they started the marketing. They
were at the office of their lawyer, Thomas Bell, a partner at Simpson
Thacher & Bartlett, when Rosenfeld excitedly jumped up and said,
"Look at this! Do you see what Salomon did?" He threw down a
piece of paper—Salomon's earnings statement. The bank had finally
decided to break out the earnings from Arbitrage, so Long-Term
could now point to its partners' prior record. Reading between the
lines, it was clear that J.M.'s group had been responsible for most of
Salomon's previous profits—more than $500 million a year during
his last five years at the firm. However, even this was not enough to
persuade investors. And despite Merrill's pleading, the partners remained far too tight-lipped about their strategies. Long-Term even refused to give examples of trades, so potential investors had little idea
of what the partners were proposing. Bond arbitrage wasn't widely
understood, after all.

Edson Mitchell, the chain-smoking Merrill executive who oversaw
the fund-raising, was desperate for J.M. to open up; it was as if J.M.
had forgotten that *he* was the one asking for money. Even in private
sessions with Mitchell, J.M. wouldn't reveal the names of the banks
he was calling; he treated every detail like a state secret. With such a
guarded client, Mitchell couldn't even sell the fund to his own bosses.
Although Mitchell suggested that Merrill become a strategic partner,
David Komansky, who oversaw capital markets for Merrill, warily
refused. He agreed to invest Merrill's fee, about $15 million, but
balked at putting in more.

At one point during the road show, a group including Scholes,
Hawkins, and some Merrill people took a grueling trip to Indi-
anapolis to visit Conseco, a big insurance company. They arrived exhausted. Scholes started to talk about how Long-Term could make
bundles even in relatively efficient markets. Suddenly, Andrew Chow,
a cheeky thirty-year-old derivatives trader, blurted out, "There aren't
that many opportunities; there is no way you can make that kind of
money in Treasury markets." Chow, whose academic credentials con-

sisted of merely a master's in finance, seemed not at all awed by the famed Black-Scholes inventor. Furious, Scholes angled forward in his leather-backed chair and said, "You're the reason—because of fools like you we can."[11] The Conseco people got huffy, and the meeting ended badly. Merrill demanded that Scholes apologize. Hawkins thought it was hilarious; he was holding his stomach laughing.

But in truth, Scholes was the fund's best salesman. Investors at least had heard of Scholes; a couple had even taken his class. And Scholes was a natural raconteur, temperamental but extroverted. He used a vivid metaphor to pitch the fund. Long-Term, he explained, would be earning a tiny spread on each of thousands of trades, as if it were vacuuming up nickels that others couldn't see. He would pluck a nickel seemingly from the sky as he spoke; a little showmanship never hurt. Even when it came to the fund's often arcane details, Scholes could glibly waltz through the math, leaving most of his prospects feeling like humble students. "They used Myron to blow you away," said Maxwell Bublitz, head of Conseco's investment arm.

The son of an Ontario dentist, Scholes was an unlikely scholar. Relentlessly entrepreneurial, he and his brother had gotten involved in a string of business ventures, such as publishing, and selling satin sheets.[12] After college, in 1962, the restless Scholes got a summer job as a computer programmer at the University of Chicago, despite knowing next to nothing about computers. The business school faculty had just awakened to the computer's power, and was promoting data-based research, in particular studies based on stock market prices. Scholes's computer work was so invaluable that the professors urged him to stick around and take up the study of markets himself.[13]

As it happened, Scholes had landed in a cauldron of neoconservative ferment. Scholars such as Eugene F. Fama and Merton H. Miller were developing what would become the central idea in modern finance: the Efficient Market Hypothesis. The premise of the hypothesis is that stock prices are always "right"; therefore, no one can divine the market's future direction, which, in turn, must be "random." For prices to be right, of course, the people who set them must be both rational and well informed. In effect, the hypothesis assumes that every trading floor and brokerage office around the world—or at least enough of them to determine prices—is staffed by a race of calm, collected Larry Hilibrands, who never pay more, never pay less than any security is "worth." According to Victor Niederhoffer, who studied with Scholes at Chicago and would later blow up a hedge fund of his own, Scholes was part of a "Random Walk Cosa Nostra," one of the disciples who methodically rejected any suggestion that markets could err. Swarthy and voluble, Scholes once lectured a real estate agent who urged him to buy in Hyde Park, near the university, and who claimed that housing prices in the area were supposed to rise by 12 percent a year. If that were true, Scholes shot back, people would buy all the houses now. Despite his credo, Scholes was never fully convinced that *he* couldn't beat the market. In the late 1960s, he put his salary into stocks and borrowed to pay his living expenses. When the market plummeted, he had to beg his banker for an extension to avoid being forced to sell at a heavy loss. Eventually, his stocks recovered—not the last time a Long-Term partner would learn the value of a friendly banker.[14]

While Merton was the consummate theoretician, Scholes was acclaimed for finding ingenious ways of *testing* theories. He was as argumentative as Merton was reserved, feverishly promoting one brainstorm after the next, most of which were unlikely to see the light of day but which often showed a creative spark. With his practical bent, he made a real contribution to Salomon, where he set up a derivative-trading subsidiary. And Scholes was a foremost expert on tax codes, both in the United States and overseas. He regarded taxes as a vast intellectual game: "No one actually *pays* taxes," he once snapped disdainfully.[15] Scholes could not believe there were people who would *not* go to extremes to avoid paying taxes, perhaps because they did not fit the Chicago School model of human beings as economic robots. At Long-Term, Scholes was the spearhead of a clever plan that let the partners defer their cut of the profits for up to ten years in order to put off paying taxes. He harangued the attorneys with details, but the partners tended to forgive his hot flashes. They were charmed by Scholes's energy and joie de vivre. He was perpetually reinventing himself, taking up new sports such as skiing and—on account of Meriwether—golf, which he played with passion.

With Scholes on board, the marketing campaign gradually picked up steam. The fund dangled a tantalizing plum before investors, who were told that annual returns on the order of 30 percent (after the

partners took their fees) would not be out of reach. Moreover, though
the partners stated clearly that risk was involved, they stressed that
they planned to diversify. With their portfolio spread around the
globe, they felt that their eggs would be safely scattered. Thus, no one
single market could pull the fund down.

The partners doggedly pursued the choicest investors, often invit-
ing prospects back to their pristine headquarters on Steamboat Road,
at the water's edge in Greenwich. Some investors met with partners
as many as seven or eight times. In their casual khakis and golf shirts,
the partners looked supremely confident. The fact was, they had
made a ton of money at Salomon, and investors warmed to the idea
that they could do it again. In the face of such intellectual brilliance,
investors—having little understanding of how Meriwether's gang actually operated—gradually forgot that they were taking a leap of
faith. "This was a constellation of people who knew how to make
money," Raymond Baer, a Swiss banker (and eventual investor),
noted. By the end of 1993, commitments for money were starting to
roll in, even though the fund had not yet opened and was well behind
schedule. The partners' morale got a big boost when Hilibrand finally
defected from Salomon and joined them. Merton and Scholes might
have added marketing luster, but Hilibrand was the guy who would
make the cash register sing.

J.M. also offered partnerships to two of his longtime golfing
cronies, Richard F. Leahy, an executive at Salomon, and James J.
McEntee, a close friend who had founded a bond-dealing firm. Neither fit the mold of Long-Term's nerdy traders. Leahy, an affable,
easygoing salesman, would be expected to deal with Wall Street
bankers—not the headstrong traders' strong suit. McEntee's role,
though, was a puzzle. After selling his business, he had lived in high
style, commuting via helicopter to a home in the Hamptons and jetting to an island in the Grenadines, which had earned him the sobriquet "the Sheik." In contrast to the egghead arbitrageurs, the
Bronx-born McEntee was a traditionalist who traded from his gut.
But Meriwether liked having such friends around; bantering with
these pals, he was relaxed and even gregarious. Not coincidentally,
Leahy and McEntee were fellow Irish Americans, a group with whom
J.M. always felt at home. Each was also a partner in the asset that
was closest to J.M.'s heart—a remote, exquisitely manicured golf
course, on the coast of southwestern Ireland, known as Waterville.

Early in 1994, J.M. bagged the most astonishing name of all: David W. Mullins, vice chairman of the U.S. Federal Reserve and second in the Fed's hierarchy to Alan Greenspan, the Fed chairman. Mullins, too, was a former student of Merton's at MIT who had gone on to teach at Harvard, where he and Rosenfeld had been friends. As a central banker, he gave Long-Term incomparable access to international banks. Moreover, Mullins had been the Fed's point man on the Mozer case. The implication was that Meriwether now had a clean bill of health from Washington.

Mullins, like Meriwether a onetime teenage investor, was the son of a University of Arkansas president and an enormously popular lecturer at Harvard. Ironically, he had launched his career in government as an expert on financial crises; he was expected to be Long-Term's disaster guru if markets came unstuck again. After the 1987 stock market crash, Mullins had helped write a blue-ribbon White House report, laying substantial blame on the new derivatives markets, where the snowball selling had gathered momentum. Then he had joined the Treasury, where he had helped draft the law to bail out the country's bankrupt savings and loans. As a regulator, he was acutely aware that markets—far from being perfect pricing machines—periodically and dangerously overshoot. "Our financial system is fast-paced, enormously creative. It's designed to have near misses with some frequency," he remarked a year before jumping ship for Long-Term. With more omniscience regarding his future fund than he could have dreamed, Mullins argued that part of the Fed's mission should be saving private institutions that were threatened by "liquidity problems."[16]

Wry and soft-spoken, the intellectual Mullins dressed like a banker and was thought to be a potential successor to Greenspan. Nicholas Brady, his former boss at Treasury, wondered when Mullins joined Long-Term what he was doing with "those guys." Investors, though, were soothed by the addition of the congenial Mullins, whose perspective on markets may have been much like their own. Indeed, by snaring a central banker, Long-Term gained unparalleled access for a private fund to the pots of money in quasi-governmental accounts around the world. Soon, Long-Term won commitments from the Hong Kong Land & Development Authority, the Government of Singapore Investment Corporation, the Bank of Taiwan, the Bank of Bangkok, and the Kuwaiti state-run pension fund. In a rare coup,

Long-Term even enticed the foreign exchange office of Italy's central bank to invest $100 million. Such entities simply do *not* invest in hedge funds. But Pierantonio Ciampicali, who oversaw investments for the Italian agency, thought of Long-Term not as a "hedge fund" but as an elite investing organization "with a solid reputation."[17]

Private investors were similarly awed by a fund boasting the best minds in finance and a resident central banker, who plausibly would be a step ahead in the obsessive Wall Street game of trying to outguess Greenspan. The list was impressive. In Japan, Long-Term signed up Sumitomo Bank for $100 million. In Europe, it corralled the giant German Dresdner Bank, the Liechtenstein Global Trust, and Bank Julius Baer, a private Swiss bank that pitched the fund to its million-aire clientele, for sums ranging from $30 million to $100 million. Re-public New York Corporation, a secretive organization run by international banker Edmond Safra, was mesmerized by Long-Term's credentials and seduced by the possibility of winning business from the fund.[18] It invested $65 million. Long-Term also snared Banco Garantia, Brazil's biggest investment bank.

In the United States, Long-Term got money from a diverse group of hotshot celebrities and institutions. Michael Ovitz, the Hollywood agent, invested; so did Phil Knight, chief executive of Nike, the sneaker giant, as well as partners at the elite consulting firm McKin-sey & Company and New York oil executive Robert Belfer. James Cayne, the chief executive of Bear Stearns, figured that Long-Term would make so much money that its fees wouldn't matter. Like others, Cayne was comforted by the willingness of J.M. and his partners to invest $146 million of their own. (Rosenfeld and others put their kids' money in, too.) Academe, where the professors' brilliance was well known, was an easy sell: St. John's University and Yeshiva University put in $10 million each; the University of Pittsburgh climbed aboard for half that. In Shaker Heights, Paragon Advisors put its wealthy clients into Long-Term. Terence Sullivan, president of Paragon, had read Merton and Scholes while getting a business degree; he felt the operation was low risk.[19]

In the corporate world, PaineWebber, thinking it would tap Long-Term for investing ideas, invested $100 million; Donald Marron, its chairman, added $10 million personally. Others included the Black & Decker Corporation pension fund, Continental Insurance of New York (later acquired by Loews), and Presidential Life Corporation.

Long-Term opened for business at the end of February 1994. Meriwether, Rosenfeld, Hawkins, and Leahy celebrated by purchasing a shipment of fine Burgundies ample enough to last for years. In addition to its eleven partners, the fund had about thirty traders and clerks and $10 million worth of SPARC workstations, the powerful Sun Microsystems machines favored by traders and engineers. Long-Term's fund-raising blitz had netted $1.25 billion—well short of J.M.'s goal but still the largest start-up ever.[20]

3

ON THE RUN

They [Long-Term] are in effect the best finance faculty in the world.
—INSTITUTIONAL INVESTOR

THE GODS SMILED on Long-Term. Having raised capital during the best of times, it put its money to work just as clouds began to gather over Wall Street. Investors long for steady waters, but paradoxically, the opportunities are richest when markets turn turbulent. When prices are flat, trading is a dull sport. When prices begin to gyrate, it is as if little eddies and currents begin to bubble in a formerly placid river. This security is dragged with the current, that one is washed upstream. Two bonds that once journeyed happily in tow are now wrenched apart, and once predictable spreads are jolted out of sync. Suddenly, investors feel cast adrift. Those who are weak or insecure may panic or at any rate sell. If enough do so, a dangerous undertow may distort the entire market. For the few who have hung on to their capital and their wits, this is when opportunity beckons.

In 1994, as Meriwether was wrapping up the fund-raising, Greenspan started to worry that the U.S. economy might be overheating. Mullins, who was cleaning out his desk at the Fed and preparing to jump to Long-Term, urged the Fed chief to tighten credit.[1] In February, just when interest rates were at their lowest—and, indeed, when investors were feeling their plummiest—

Greenspan stunned Wall Street by raising short-term interest rates. It was the first such hike in five years. But if the oracular Fed chief had in mind calming markets, the move backfired. Bond prices tumbled (bond prices, of course, move in the opposite direction of interest rates). And given the modest nature of Greenspan's quarter-point increase, bonds were falling more than they "should" have. Somebody was desperate to sell.

By May, barely two months after Long-Term's debut, the thirty-year Treasury bond had plunged 16 percent from its recent peak—a huge move in the relatively tame world of fixed-income securities—rising in yield from 6.2 percent to 7.6 percent. Bonds in Europe were crashing, too. Diverse investors, including hedge funds—many of which were up to their necks in debt—were fleeing from bonds. Michael Steinhardt, one such leveraged operator, watched in horror. Steinhardt, who had bet on European bonds, was losing $7 million with every *hundredth* of a percentage point move in interest rates. The swashbuckling Steinhardt lost $800 million of his investors' money in a mere four days. George Soros, who was jolted by a ricochet effect on international currencies, dropped $650 million for his clients in two days.[2]

For Meriwether, this tumult was the best of news. One morning during the heat of the selling, J.M. walked over to one of his traders. Glancing at the trader's screen, J.M. marveled, "It's wave after wave of guys throwing in the towel." As J.M. knew, panicky investors wouldn't be picky as they ran for the exits. In their eagerness to sell, they were pushing spreads wider, creating just the gaps that Meriwether was hoping to exploit. "The unusually high volatility in the bond markets . . . has generally been associated with a widening of spreads," he chirped in a—for him—unusually revealing letter to investors. "This widening has created further opportunities to add to LTCP's convergence and relative-value trading positions."[3] After two flat months, Long-Term rose 7 percent in May, beginning a stretch of heady profits. It would hardly have occurred to Meriwether that Long-Term would ever switch places with some of those panicked, overleveraged hedge funds. But the bond debacle of 1994, which unfolded during Long-Term's very first months, merited Long-Term's close attention.

Commentators began to see a new connectedness in international bond markets. *The Wall Street Journal* observed that "implosions in seemingly unrelated markets were reverberating in the U.S. Treasury bond market."[4] Such disparate developments as a slide in European bonds, news of trading losses at Bankers Trust, the collapse of Askin Capital Management, a hedge fund that had specialized in mortgage trades, and the assassination of Mexico's leading presidential contender all accentuated the slide in U.S. Treasurys that had begun with Greenspan's modest adjustment.

Suddenly markets were more closely *linked*—a development with pivotal significance for Long-Term. It meant that a trend in one market could spread to the next. An isolated slump could become a generalized rout. With derivatives, which could be custom-tailored to any market of one's fancy, it was a snap for a speculator in New York to take a flier on Japan or for one in Amsterdam to gamble on Brazil—raising the prospect that trouble on one front would leach into the next. For traders tethered to electronic screens, the distinction between markets—say, between mortgages in America and government loans in France—almost ceased to exist. They were all points on a continuum of risk, stitched together by derivatives. With traders scrambling to pay back debts, Neal Soss, an economist at Credit Suisse First Boston, explained to the *Journal,* "You don't sell what you should. You sell what you can." By leveraging one security, investors had potentially given up control of all of their others. This verity is well worth remembering: the securities might be unrelated, but the same investors owned them, implicitly linking them in times of stress. And when armies of financial soldiers were involved in the same securities, borders shrank. The very concept of safety through diversification—the basis of Long-Term's own security—would merit rethinking.

Steinhardt blamed his losses on a sudden evaporation of "liquidity," a term that would be on Long-Term's lips in years to come.[5] But "liquidity" is a straw man. Whenever markets plunge, investors are stunned to find that there are not enough buyers to go around. As Keynes observed, there cannot be "liquidity" for the community as a whole.[6] The mistake is in thinking that markets have a duty to stay liquid or that buyers will always be present to accommodate sellers. The real culprit in 1994 was leverage. If you aren't in debt, you can't go broke and can't be made to sell, in which case "liquidity" is irrelevant. But a leveraged firm may be *forced* to sell, lest fast-accumulating losses put it out of business. Leverage always gives rise to this same brutal dynamic, and its dangers cannot be stressed too often.

Long-Term was doubly fortunate: spreads widened before it invested much of its capital, and once opportunities did arise, Long-Term was one of a very few firms in a position to exploit the general distress. And its trades were good trades. They weren't risk-free; they weren't *so* good that the fund could leverage indiscriminately. But by and large, they were intelligent and opportunistic. Long-Term started to make money on them almost immediately.

One of its first trades involved the same thirty-year Treasury bond. Treasurys (of all durations) are, of course, issued by the U.S. government to finance the federal budget. Some $170 billion of them trade each day, and they are considered the least risky investments in the world. But a funny thing happens to thirty-year Treasurys six months or so after they are issued: investors stuff them into safes and drawers for long-term keeping. With fewer left in circulation, the bonds become harder to trade. Meanwhile, the Treasury issues a new thirty-year bond, which now has its day in the sun. On Wall Street, the older bond, which has about $29^{1}/_{2}$ years left to mature, is known as *off the run;* the shiny new model is *on the run.* Being less liquid, the off-the-run bond is considered less desirable. It begins to trade at a slight discount (that is, you can purchase it for a little less, or at what amounts to a slightly higher interest yield). As arbitrageurs would say, a spread opens.

In 1994, Long-Term noticed that this spread was unusually wide. The February 1993 issue was trading at a yield of 7.36 percent. The bond issued six months later, in August, was yielding only 7.24 percent, or 12 *basis points,* less. Every Tuesday, Long-Term's partners held a risk-management meeting, and at one of the early meetings, several proposed that they bet on this 12-point gap to narrow. It wasn't enough to say, "One bond is cheaper, one bond is dearer." The professors needed to know *why* a spread existed, which might shed light on the paramount issue of whether it was likely to persist or even to widen. In this case, the spread seemed almost silly. After all, the U.S. government is no less likely to pay off a bond that matures in $29^{1}/_{2}$ years than it is one that expires in thirty. But some institutions were so timid, so bureaucratic, that they refused to own anything but the most liquid paper. Long-Term believed that many opportunities arose from market distortions created by the sometimes arbitrary demands of institutions.[7] The latter were willing to pay a premium for on-the-run paper, and Long-Term's partners, who had often done this trade at Salomon, happily collected it. They called it a "snap trade," because the two bonds usually snapped together after only a few months. In effect, Long-Term would be collecting a fee for its willingness to own a less liquid bond.

"A lot of our trades were liquidity-providing," Rosenfeld noted. "We were buying the stuff that everyone wanted to sell." It apparently did not occur to Rosenfeld that since Long-Term tended to buy the less liquid security in every market, its assets were not entirely independent of one another, the way one dice roll is independent of the next. Indeed, its assets would be susceptible to falling in unison if a time came when, literally, "everyone" wanted to sell.

■

Twelve basis points is a tiny spread; ordinarily, it wouldn't be worth the trouble. The price difference was only $15.80 for each pair of $1,000 bonds. Even if the spread narrowed two thirds of the way, say in a few months' time, Long-Term would earn only $10, or 1 percent, on those $1,000 bonds. But what if, using leverage, that tiny spread could be multiplied? What if, indeed! With such a strategy in mind, Long-Term bought $1 *billion* of the cheaper, off-the-run bonds. It also sold $1 billion of the more expensive, on-the-run Treasurys. This was a staggering sum. Right off the bat, the partners were risking all of Long-Term's capital! To be sure, they weren't likely to lose very much of it. Since they were buying one bond and selling another, they were betting only that the bonds would converge, and, as noted, bond spreads vary much less than bonds themselves do. The price of your home could crash, but if it does, the price of your neighbor's house will likely crash as well. Of course, there was *some* risk that the spread could widen, at least for a brief period. If two bonds traded at a 12-point spread, who could say that the spread wouldn't go to 14 points—or, in a time of extreme stress, to 20 points?

Long-Term, with trademark precision, calculated that owning one bond and shorting another was one twenty-fifth as risky as owning either bond outright.[8] Thus, it reckoned that it could prudently leverage this long/short arbitrage twenty-five times. This multiplied its potential for profit but—as we have seen—also its potential for loss. In any case, borrow it did. It paid for the cheaper, off-the-run bonds with money that it borrowed from a Wall Street bank, or from several banks. And the other bonds, the ones it sold short, it obtained through a loan, as well.

Actually, the transaction was more involved, though it was among the simplest in Long-Term's repertoire. No sooner did Long-Term buy the off-the-run bonds than it loaned them to some other Wall Street firm, which then wired cash to Long-Term as collateral. Then Long-Term turned around and used this cash as collateral on the bonds that *it* borrowed. On Wall Street, such short-term, collateralized loans are known as "repo financing."

The beauty of the trade was that Long-Term's cash transactions were in perfect balance. The money that Long-Term spent going long (buying) matched the money it collected going short (selling). The collateral it paid equaled the collateral it collected. In other words, Long-Term pulled off the entire $2 billion trade *without using a dime of its own cash.* *

Now, normally, when you borrow a bond from, say, Merrill Lynch, you have to post a little bit of extra collateral—maybe a total of $1,010 on a $1,000 Treasury and more on a riskier bond. That $10 initial margin, equivalent to 1 percent of the bond's value, is called a *haircut*. It's Merrill Lynch's way of protecting itself in case the price of the bond rises.

The haircut naturally acts as a check on how much you can trade. But if you could avoid the haircut, well, the sky would be the limit. It would be like driving a car that didn't burn gas: you could drive as far as you wished. What's more, the rate of return would be substantially higher—*if* you didn't have that extra margin tied up at Merrill Lynch.

And from the very start, it was Long-Term's policy to refuse to pay the haircut or else to substantially reduce it. The policy surely flowed from Meriwether, who, for all his unassuming charm, was fiercely competitive at trading, golf, billiards, horses, and whatever else he

---

* Maintaining the position wasn't completely cost-free. Though a simple trade, it actually entailed four different payment streams. Long-Term *collected* interest on the collateral it paid out and *paid* interest (at a slightly higher rate) on the collateral it took in. It made some of this deficit back because it collected the 7.36 percent coupon on the bond it owned and paid the lesser 7.24 percent rate on the bond it shorted. Overall, it cost Long-Term a few basis points a month.

touched. Rosenfeld and Leahy, two of the more congenial and laid-back partners, were usually the ones who met with banks, though Hilibrand also got involved. In any case, the partners would insist, politely but firmly, that the fund was so well heeled that it didn't *need* to post an initial margin—and, what's more, that it wouldn't trade with anyone that saw matters differently. Merrill Lynch agreed to waive its usual haircut requirement and go along. So did Goldman Sachs, J. P. Morgan, Morgan Stanley, and just about everyone else. One firm that balked, PaineWebber, got virtually none of Long-Term's business. "You had no choice if you were going to do business with them," recalled Goldman Sachs's Jon Corzine, J.M.'s admiring rival.

Although Long-Term's trades could be insanely complex and ultimately numbered in the thousands, the fund had no more than a dozen or so major strategies.[9] Some, such as the Treasury arbitrage, involved buying and selling tangible securities. The others, derivative trades, did not. They were simply bets that Long-Term made with banks and other counterparties that hinged on the fate of various market prices.

Imagine, by illustration, that a Red Sox fan and a Yankees fan agree before the season that each will pay the other $1,000 for every run scored by his rival's team. Long-Term's derivative contracts were not dissimilar, except that the payoffs were tied to movements in bonds, stocks, and so forth rather than balls and strikes. These derivative obligations did not appear on Long-Term's balance sheet, nor were they "debt" in the formal sense. But if markets moved against the fund, the result would obviously be the same. And Long-Term generally was able to forgo paying initial margin on derivative deals; it made these bets without putting up any initial capital whatsoever.

Frequently, though not always, it got the same terms on repo financing of actual securities. Also, Long-Term often persuaded banks to lend to it for longer periods than the banks gave to other funds.[10] Thus, Long-Term could be more patient. Even if the banks had wanted to call in Long-Term's loans, they couldn't have done so very quickly. "They had everyone over a barrel," noted a senior executive at a top investment bank.

This was where Meriwether's marketing strategy really paid dividends. If the banks had given it a moment's thought, they would have realized that Long-Term was at *their* mercy. But the banks saw the

fund not as a credit-hungry start-up but as a luminous firm of celebrated scholars and brilliant traders, something like that New Age
"financial intermediary" conjured up by Merton. After all, it was
generally believed that Long-Term had the benefit of superior, virtually fail-safe technology. And banks, like some of the press, casually
assumed that it was so. *Business Week* gushed that the fund's Ph.D.s
would give rise to "a new computer age" on Wall Street. "Never has
this much academic talent been given this much money to bet with,"
the magazine observed in a cover story published during the fund's
first year.[11] If a new age was coming, no one wanted to miss it. Long-
Term was as fetching as a debutante on prom night, and all the banks
wanted to dance.

The banks had no trouble rationalizing their easy credit terms. The
banks did hold collateral, after all, and Long-Term generally settled
up (in cash) at the end of each trading day, collecting on winners and
paying on losers. And Long-Term *was* flush, so the risk of its failing
seemed slight. Only if Long-Term lost money with unthinkable
suddenness—only if, say, it was forced to dump the majority of its assets all at once and into an illiquid market—would the value of the
bankers' collateral be threatened and would the banks themselves be
exposed to losses.

Also, many of the banks' heads, such as Corzine and Merrill
Lynch's Tully, liked Meriwether personally, which tilted their organi-
zations in Long-Term's favor. But Long-Term's real selling point was
its connections to other powerful traders around the world. A firm
that did business with Long-Term might gain valuable inside knowledge—totally legal in the bond world—about the flow of markets.
"How do you get people to come to your party? You tell them that
every cool person in town is coming," said a banker in Zurich who
financed Long-Term with a zero percent haircut. "So everyone said,
'OK, I'll do it, but if anyone else gets a haircut, I get one too.'" This
was especially clever of Long-Term. The partners could say to each
new bank, "If we give you a haircut, we have to give it to everyone."
So they ended up giving it to nobody. (On a small number of riskier
trades they did agree to haircuts—but very skimpy ones.)

Since the banks, too, were doing arbitrage trading, Meriwether
viewed them, not unjustly, as his main competitors.[12] Long-Term resembled other hedge funds such as Soros's Quantum Fund less than
it did the proprietary desks of its banks, such as Goldman Sachs. The

Street was slowly shifting from research and client services to the lu-crative business of trading for its own account, fostering a wary ri-valry between Long-Term and its lenders.

Having worked at a major Wall Street bank, J.M. felt that invest-ment banks were rife with leaks and couldn't be trusted not to swipe his trades for themselves. Indeed, most of them were plying similar strategies. Thus, as a precaution, Long-Term would place orders for each leg of a trade with a different broker. Morgan would see one leg, Merrill Lynch another, and Goldman yet another, but nobody would see them all. Even Long-Term's lawyer was kept in the dark; he would hear the partners speak about "trading strategy three," as though Long-Term were developing a nuclear arsenal.

Hilibrand, especially, refused to give the banks a peek at his strate-gies or to meet them halfway on terms. He would call a dealer, pur-chase $100 million in bonds, and be off the phone in seconds.[13] "I'm just concerned about margin requirement, and I'm not putting up any margin," he bluntly told Merrill Lynch. Kevin Dunleavy, a Merrill Lynch salesman, sometimes called Hilibrand two or three times a day, trying to pitch strategies he had devised with the clever Hilibrand in mind. But Dunleavy was repeatedly frustrated by Hilibrand's obses-sive secrecy, which made it nearly impossible to service the account. "Rarely could you take your ideas and implement them into LTCM's strategy," noted Dunleavy, an unaffected New Yorker with a military brush cut. "It was very unusual, not to take input from the Street. Larry would never talk about the strategy. He would just tell you what he wanted to do."

The fund parceled out its business, choosing each bank for partic-ular services and keeping a distance from all of them. Chary of be-coming dependent on any one bank, Long-Term traded junk bonds with Goldman Sachs, government bonds and yen swaps with J. P. Morgan, mortgages with Lehman Brothers. Merrill Lynch was the fund's biggest counterparty in derivatives, but it was far down the list in repo loans. To be sure, there was something shrewd about this divide-and-conquer strategy, for Long-Term did each set of trades with the bank that boasted the most specific expertise. But Long-Term thus forfeited the benefits of a closer, ongoing relationship. J. P. Mor-gan, for one, was extremely curious about Long-Term and eager to de-velop a closer working alliance, but it couldn't get past the fund's unwillingness to share confidences. "How can you propose ideas to them without knowing what their appetite is?" wondered the head of risk management at a major Wall Street firm. As arbitrageurs, the partners tended to see every encounter as a discrete exchange, with tallyable pluses and minuses. Every relationship was a "trade"— renegotiable or revocable if someone else had a better price. The partners' only close ties were *within* Long-Term, mimicking the arrangement within their beloved group at Salomon.

They were a bred type—intellectual, introverted, detached, controlled. It didn't work to try to play one off against the other; they were too much on the same wavelength. Andrew Siciliano, who ran the bond and currency departments at Swiss Bank Corporation, was stunned by their uncanny closeness. One time, Siciliano called Victor Haghani, the head of the London office, and followed up in Greenwich with J.M. and Eric Rosenfeld a month or two later. The American-based partners didn't miss a beat; Siciliano had the eerie feeling that he was continuing the same conversation he'd had with Haghani.

Not that there weren't tensions within the firm. A small group— J.M., Hilibrand, Rosenfeld, and Haghani—dominated the rest. As at Salomon, compensation was skewed toward the top, with the inner circle garnering more than half the rewards. This group also had voting control. Lesser partners such as Myron Scholes were forever angling for more money, as well as more authority. But the inner circle had been together for years; as in a family, their exclusive and inbred alliance had became second nature.

If the firm could have been distilled into a single person, it would have been Hilibrand. While veteran traders tend to be cynical and insecure, the result of years of wrong guesses and narrow escapes, Hilibrand was cool and maddeningly self-confident. An incredibly hard worker, he was the pure arbitrageur; he believed in the models, stuck to his prices, was untroubled by doubt. Rosenfeld hated to hedge by selling a falling asset, as theory prescribed; Hilibrand *believed* and simply followed the form. Hilibrand's colleagues respected him immensely; inevitably, they turned to him when they needed a quick read. He was highly articulate, but his answers were like unrefined crystals, difficult for novices to comprehend. "You could refract the light with Larry's mind," said Deryck Maughan of Salomon Brothers. Like the other partners, but to a greater degree, Hilibrand saw every issue in black and white. He was trustworthy and quick to take offense at perceived wrongdoing but blind to concerns outside his narrow sphere. His Salomon colleagues used to joke that, according to the libertarian Hilibrand, if the street in front of your home had a pothole you ought to pave it yourself. But money probably meant less to him than to any of them. He found his passion in the intellectual challenge of trading. Aside from his family, he showed interest in little else. If anyone brought Hilibrand out of himself a bit, it was J.M. Hilibrand had a filial attachment to the chief, perhaps stemming from his close relationship to his own father. Rosenfeld had a similar devotion to Meriwether.

Outsiders couldn't quite explain J.M.'s hold on the group. He was an unlikely star, too bashful for the limelight. He spoke in fragments and seemed uncomfortable making eye contact.[14] He refused to talk about his personal life, even to close friends. After organizing Long-Term, J.M. and his wife moved out of Manhattan, to a $2.7 million, sixty-eight-acre estate in North Salem, in Westchester County—complete with a 15,000-square-foot heated indoor riding ring for Mimi.[15] The estate was set back three quarters of a mile on a private drive that the Meriwethers shared with their only neighbor, the entertainer David Letterman. As if to make the property even more private, the Meriwethers did extensive remodeling, fortifying the house with stone. J.M. liked to control his private life, as if to shelter it, too, from unwanted volatility.

Though he attended a church near home and made several visits to Catholic shrines, J.M. didn't speak about his faith, either. His self-control was implacable. Nor did he open up among his traders. At firm meetings he was mostly quiet. He welcomed frank debates among the partners, but he usually chimed in only at the very end or not at all.

The firm's headquarters were the ground floor of a glassy four-story office complex, on a street that ran from the shop-lined center of affluent Greenwich past a parade of Victorian homes on Long Island Sound. Several dozen of Long-Term's growing cadre of traders and strategists worked on the trading floor, where partners and non-partners sat elbow to elbow, cramped around a sleek, semicircular desk loaded with computers and market screens. The office had an elaborate kitchen that had been put in by a previous tenant, but the partners lunched at their desks. Food meant little to them.

J.M., Merton, and Scholes (the latter two because they didn't trade) had private offices, but J.M. was usually on the trading floor, a mahogany-paneled room that looked out through a full-length picture window to the water, resplendent and often speckled with sailboats. Aside from the natty Mullins, the partners dressed casually, in Top-Siders and chinos. The room hummed with trader talk, but it was a controlled hum, not like the chaos on the cavernous New York trading floors. Only occasionally did the partners revert to their past life for a few rounds of liar's poker.

Besides the Tuesday risk meetings, which were for partners only, Long-Term had research seminars on Wednesday mornings that were open to associates and usually another meeting on Thursday afternoons, when partners would focus on a specific trade. Merton, usually in Cambridge, would join in by telephone. The shared close quarters fostered a firm togetherness, but the associates and even some of the partners knew they could never be part of the inner circle. One junior trader perpetually worried that his trades would be found out by the press, which he feared could cost him his job. Associates in Greenwich, even senior traders, were kept so much in the dark that some resorted to calling their London counterparts to find out what the firm was buying and selling. Associates were never invited back to the partners' homes—there seemed to be an unwritten rule against partners and staff fraternizing. Leahy, a college hockey player, exchanged the normal office banter with the employees, but most of the partners treated the staff with cool formality. They were polite but interested only in one another and their work. The analysts and legal and accounting staffs were second-class citizens, shunted to a room in the back, where the pool table was.

Like everyone else on Wall Street, Long-Term's employees made good money. The top staffers could make $1 million to $2 million a year. There was subtle pressure on the staff to invest their bonuses in the fund, but most of them were eager to do so anyway—ironically, it was considered a major perk of working at Long-Term. And so, the staff confidently reinvested most of their pay.

■

Just as predicted, Long-Term's on-the-run and off-the-run bonds snapped back quickly. Long-Term made a magical $15 million—magical because it hadn't used any capital. As Scholes had promised, Long-Term had scooped up a nickel and, with leverage, turned it into more. True, many other firms had done the same kind of trade. "But we could finance better," an employee of Long-Term noted. "LTCM was really a financing house."

Long-Term preferred to reap a sure nickel than to gamble on making an uncertain dollar, because it could leverage its tiny margins like a high-volume grocer, sucking up nickel after nickel and multiplying the process thousands of times. Of course, not even a nickel bet was *absolutely* sure. And as Steinhardt, the fund manager, had recently been reminded, the penalty for being wrong is infinitely greater when you are leveraged. But in 1994, Long-Term was almost never wrong. In fact, nearly every trade it touched turned to gold.

Long-Term dubbed its safest bets *convergence* trades, because the instruments matured at a specific date, meaning that convergence appeared to be a sure thing. Others were known as *relative value* trades, in which convergence was expected but not guaranteed.[16]

■

The bond market turmoil of 1994 seeded the ground for a huge relative value trade in home mortgage securities. Mortgage securities are pieces of paper backed by the cash flow on pools of mortgages. They sound boring, but they aren't. Some $1 trillion of mortgage securities is outstanding at any given time. What makes them exciting is that clever investment bankers have separated the payments made by homeowners into two distinct pools: one for interest payments, the other for principal payments. If you think about it—and Long-Term did, quite a bit—the value of each pool (relative to the other) varies according to the rate at which homeowners pay off their loans ahead of schedule. If you refinance your mortgage, you pay it off in one lump sum—that is, in one giant payment of principal. Therefore, no further cash goes to the interest-only pool. But if you stand pat and keep writing those monthly checks, you keep making interest payments for up to thirty years. Therefore, if more people refinance, the interest-only securities, known as "IOs," will fall; if fewer people prepay, they will rise. The converse is true for principal-only securities, or POs. And since the rate of refinancings can change quickly, betting on IOs or POs can make or lose you a good deal of money.

In 1993, when Long-Term was raising capital, America was experiencing a surge of refinancings. With mortgage rates dropping below 7 percent for the first time since the Vietnam War, baby boomers who had never given their mortgages a second thought were suddenly delirious with the prospect of cutting their payments by hundreds of dollars a month. Getting the lowest rate became a point of pride; roughly two in five Americans refinanced in that one year—in fact, some folks did it twice. Naturally, the prices of IOs plummeted. Actually, they fell *too* much. Unless you assumed that the entire country was going to refinance tomorrow, the price of IOs was simply too low. Indeed, Meriwether, Hilibrand, Rosenfeld, Haghani, and Hawkins bought buckets of IOs for their personal accounts.

In 1994, as Long-Term was beginning to trade, IOs remained cheap for fear there would be another wave of refinancings. Bill Krasker had designed a model to predict prepayments, and Hawkins—an outgoing, curly-haired mortgage trader with backwoods charm—continually checked the model against the record of actual prepayments. The IO price seemed so out of whack that Hawkins wondered, "Is there something wrong with the model, or is this just a good opportunity?" The methodical Krasker carefully retooled the model, and it all but screamed, *"Buy!"* So Long-Term—once again with massive leverage—started buying IOs by the truckload. It acquired a huge stake, estimated at $2 billion worth.

Now, when interest rates rise, people aren't even going to *think* about refinancing. But when rates fall, they run to the mortgage broker. That means that IOs rise and fall in sync with interest rates—*so betting on IOs is like betting on interest rates.* But the partners didn't want to forecast rates; such outright speculation made them jittery, even though they did it on occasion. Because interest rates depend on so many variables, they are essentially unpredictable. The partners' forte was making highly specific relative bets that did not depend on broad unknowns.

In short, the partners merely felt that, given the present level of interest rates, IOs were cheap. So the partners shrewdly hedged their bet by purchasing Treasurys, the prices of which move in the *opposite* direction from interest rates. The net effect was to remove any element of rate forecasting. The partners excelled at identifying particular mispriced risks and hedging out all of the other risks. If Haifa oranges were cheap relative to Fuji apples, they would find a series of trades to isolate that particular arbitrage; they didn't simply buy every orange and sell every apple.

In the spring, when interest rates soared, Long-Term's IOs also soared, although its Treasury bonds, of course, fell. Thus, it was ahead on one leg of its trade and behind on the other. Then, in 1995, when interest rates receded, Long-Term's Treasurys rose in price. But this time people did not rush to refinance, so Long-Term's IOs held on to much of their former gains. Presumably, people who had gotten new mortgages in 1993 were not so eager to do it again. Long-Term made several hundred million dollars. It was off to a sizzling start.

Despite appearances, finding these "nickels" was anything but easy. Long-Term was searching for pairs of trades—or often, multiple pairs—that were "balanced" enough to be safe but unbalanced in one or two very particular aspects, so as to offer a potential for profit. Put differently, in any given strategy, Long-Term typically wanted exposure to one or two risk factors—but no more. In a common example—yield-curve trades—interest rates in a given country might be oddly out of line for a certain duration of debt. For instance, medium-term rates might be far higher than short-term rates and almost as high as long-term rates. Long-Term would concoct a series of arbitrages betting on this bulge to disappear.

The best place to look for such complex trades was in international bond markets. Markets in Europe, as well as in the Third World, were less efficient than America's; they had yet to be picked clean by computer-wielding arbitrageurs (or professors). For Long-Term, these underexploited markets were a happy hunting ground with a welter of opportunities. In 1994, when the trouble in the U.S. bond market rippled across the Atlantic, the spreads between German, French, and British government debt and, respectively, the futures on each country's bonds, widened to nonsensical levels. Long-Term plunged in and made a fast profit.[17] It also sallied into Latin America, where spreads had widened as well.[18] The positions were small, but Long-Term was pursuing every angle—you don't find nickels lying on the street. Then, Eric Rosenfeld found a few "coins" in Japan, arbitraging warrants on Japanese stocks against options on the Tokyo index—one of Long-Term's first excursions into equities.

By the mid-1990s, Europe had become a playground for international bond traders, who were hotly debating the outlook for monetary union. Its markets were increasingly unsettled by the prospect—still much in doubt—that France, Germany, Italy, and other age-old nation-states would really merge their currencies, abandoning their francs, marks, and lire for freshly minted euros. Every trader had a different view—just the sort of uncertain climate in which Long-Term thrived. Many investment banks were betting that bonds issued by the weaker countries, such as Italy and Spain, would strengthen relative to those of Germany, on the theory that if union did come about, it would force a convergence of interest rates all across Europe. Long-Term did some of these trades, but as usual, the partners were reluctant to risk too much on a broad economic theory. Long-Term's expertise was in the details. When it came to forecasting geopolitical trends, it did not have any apparent edge. What's more, the mostly American partners were Euro-skeptics. With Europe's highly regulated economies perennially trailing America's, the Continent seemed hopelessly rigid. A Swiss partner, Hans Hufschmid, tried to push the convergence theme, but the American partners, including Victor Haghani, the free-spirited London chief, resisted.

Haghani preferred to focus on strategies that were confined to single countries, where there would be fewer risk factors. For instance, he arbitraged two issues of gilts, the British equivalent of Treasurys, one of which was cheaper owing to an unfavorable tax treatment. When the U.K. government reversed its stance, Long-Term quickly made $200 million.[19]

Haghani frequently traded the yield curve of a country against itself. Thus, he might go long on Germany's ten-year bonds and sell its five-year paper, a subtle trade that required command of the math along with a keen appreciation for local economic trends. But at least it did not require comparing the trends in Germany with, say, the trends in Spain.

Newspaper accounts of Long-Term generally overlooked Haghani, who was intensely private. The press played up Meriwether's leadership and Merton's and Scholes's "models." But in fact Haghani was a critical player. While J.M. presided over the firm and Rosenfeld ran it from day to day, Haghani and the slightly senior Hilibrand had the most influence on trading. Similarly brilliant and mathematically adept, they spoke in a code that outsiders found impenetrable.

Although the two operated mostly as a team, Haghani was far more daring. A natural trader, Haghani had an intuitive feeling for markets and a volatile, impulsive streak. If a model identified a security as mispriced and if the firm felt it understood why the distortion had occurred, Hilibrand tended to go right ahead. Haghani, who trusted his instincts, might gamble on the security's becoming even more mispriced first. Barely thirty-one years old when Long-Term started (Hilibrand was thirty-four, Rosenfeld forty, and Meriwether forty-six), the swarthy, bearded Haghani routinely swung for the fences. Though a lively raconteur, he was less direct than Hilibrand: you could never tell if Haghani was challenging you in earnest or playing poker. He had a youthful impetuousness and belief in himself, perhaps the result of his privileged background.

The son of a wealthy Iranian importer-exporter and an American mother, Haghani grew up keenly aware of the political crosscurrents that often overwhelm the best-laid business plans. As a teenager, he had spent two years in Iran with his father, whom he adored; then the revolution had forced them to flee. At Salomon Brothers, Haghani had spent a lot of time in the London and Tokyo bureaus, where he had pushed the local traders to adopt the Arbitrage Group's model of markets and had exhorted the often bewildered staffers to trade in bigger size. He returned to London with Long-Term Capital Management just as the Continent was bubbling with talk of monetary union.

Haghani shunned the City, London's buttoned-down equivalent of Wall Street, and rented quarters in Mayfair, a lively fashion district. He ran the office informally, encouraging the staff to join him in give-and-take and spirited banter. His traders and analysts worked long hours, but they were motivated by the lure of Long-Term's growing profits and humbled by the sight of their boss trundling to the office on a bicycle. When the action abated, the traders would drift to a poolroom off the trading floor, where Haghani would issue challenges to visitors. (J.M., too, on his visits to London, would inevitably pick up the cue stick and take on all comers.) Less introverted than some of his partners, Haghani frequently invited traders home to dinner. After Long-Term's first big month, in May, he assembled the entire London staff, including the secretaries, and told them how the money had been made. This would have been heresy at the stiffer and more secretive Greenwich headquarters, where a rigid caste system prevailed.

Haghani's biggest trade was Italy—a bold choice. Italian finance was a mess, as was Italian politics. The fear that Italy might default on its loans, coupled with the still considerable strength of the Italian

ON THE RUN · 57

Communist Party, had pushed Italy's interest rates to as much as 8 percentage points over Germany's—a huge spread. Italy's bond market was still evolving, and the government was issuing lots of paper, partly to attract investors. For bond traders, it was fertile territory. Obviously, if Italy righted itself, people who had bet on Italy would make out like bandits. But what if it didn't?

The Italian market was further complicated because Italy had a quirky tax law and *two* types of government bonds—one of which paid a floating rate, the other a fixed rate. Strangely, the Italian government was forced (by an untrusting bond market) to pay an interest rate that was higher than the rate on a widely traded interest rate derivative known as "swaps." Swap rates are generally close to private-sector bank rates. Thus, the bond market was rating the Italian government as a poorer risk than private banks.

Haghani thought the market was seriously overstating the risk of the government's defaulting—*relative* to the price it was putting on other risks. With characteristic derring-do, he recommended a king-size arbitrage to exploit the supposed mispricing. It was a calculated gamble, because if Italy did default, Long-Term's counterparties might walk away from their contracts—and Long-Term could lose its shirt. To the American partners, who remained skeptical about Italy, this was a major worry. The risk-averse Bill Krasker was especially concerned, and the partners heatedly debated Italy for hours.

In simple terms, the arbitrage zeroed in on the market's utter lack of respect for Rome. But nothing at Long-Term was ever simple. Specifically, Haghani, who eventually prevailed, bought the fixed-rate Italian government bonds and shorted the fixed rate on Italian swaps. He also bought the floating-rate government paper, a coup for Long-Term because few others could get hold of this thinly traded security. Haghani balanced that with a short position, too. At first, Long-Term hedged the entire position, taking out a rather expensive Italian-default insurance policy (it even took out a second policy, in case the insurer went broke).[20] But as the Italian position got bigger, Long-Term couldn't afford to keep buying more insurance, and it simply took a chance. An insider judged that had Italy gone bust, the fund could have lost half of its capital.

The virtually unregulated hedge fund did not disclose its risk in Italy to investors; indeed, it didn't tell them anything about how and where their money was invested, save for broad generalities. J.M.'s letters were saturated with statistics on volatilities but mute on what the firm was actually *doing*. He covered for his shyness by adopting an aloof, impersonal tone, as though he were doing his investors a favor by disclosing anything. "It is our intent to maintain ongoing communications with you, our investors," he declared stiffly. Even the few dry nuggets that J.M. did disclose he asked investors to keep confidential, as if Long-Term's genius were a tender woodland plant that couldn't tolerate the glare of sunlight. The partners went to obsessive lengths to stay out of the press. They even repurchased the rights to photographs that had run in *Business Week* to keep their pictures from public view.

■

For all its attention to risk, Long-Term's management had a serious flaw. Unlike at banks, where independent risk managers watch over traders, Long-Term's partners monitored themselves. Though this enabled them to sidestep the rigidities of a big organization, there was no one to call the partners to account.

Traders needed approval from the risk-management committee to initiate a trade; however, Hilibrand and Haghani, who would fight relentlessly for what they wanted, had a way of getting it. Sooner or later, the other partners would defer, if only out of sheer exhaustion. Meriwether was largely to blame for this tolerant regime. If J.M. had a cardinal weakness, it was his failure to insert himself into the debates. And there was no one else who could have played the role of nanny, as there had been at Salomon—no Gutfreund. The traders were their own watchdogs.

The partners did go to considerable lengths to research their trades, the Italian trade being a prime example. Haghani recruited a network of intelligence sources to bolster his knowledge of Italy. He hired—first as a consultant, later full-time—Alberto Giovannini, a former official in the Italian Treasury and professor at Columbia University. Giovannini, who had also studied at MIT, would shuttle back and forth between London and Rome, where he could see his family and gossip with Italian officials. Still not satisfied, Haghani brought in Gérard Gennotte, yet another MIT grad, who was the son of Belgium's ambassador to Italy and was fluent in Italian. "Victor was always keen on Italy," an associate noted. And of course, Long-Term was plugged in to Italy's central bank, which had invested $100 million in the fund and lent it $150 million more.

However, Long-Term's approach was so mathematical, it's doubtful that all this intelligence made much difference. Its models said simply that Italy was "cheap" relative to historical patterns and anticipated risks. The partners assumed that, all else being equal, the future would look like the past. Therefore, in they went. Moreover, its models were hardly a secret. "You could pick up a *Journal of Finance* and see where someone was applying models," a London-based trader at Salomon Brothers noted with respect to the Italy trade. "Anyone who had done first-year math at university could do it." In truth, traders at other firms had been doing similar trades for years. By the time Long-Term started to trade, spreads in Italy had begun to narrow; rival firms were bidding *arrivederci*. Haghani got his first billion dollars' worth or so of Italian bonds from Salomon, which wanted out. The common notion that Long-Term had a unique black box was a myth. Other Wall Street firms had also found their way to MIT, and most of the big banks were employing similar models—and, what's more, were applying them to the same couple of dozen spreads in bond markets.

Long-Term's edge wasn't in its models but, first, in its experience in *reading* the models. The partners had been doing such trades for years. Second, the firm had better financing. During its first year, Rosenfeld sewed up repo financing with thirty banks and derivative facilities with twenty—all on liberal terms.[21] With financing so accessible—and with the partners so supremely confident—Long-Term traded on a greater scale, and it kept squeezing nickels long after others had quit. "We focused on smaller discrepancies than other people," one trader said. "We thought we could hedge further and leverage further."

At least one observer had grave doubts about the fund's seemingly cavalier approach to debt. Seth Klarman, the general partner of Baupost Group, a collection of smallish hedge funds based in Cambridge, Massachusetts, wrote to *his* investors that he had been offered a stake in a new fund run by former Salomon bond traders—obviously Long-Term—and had declined. Klarman was perturbed by a seemingly reckless trend on Wall Street. Investment banks possessed of the equivalent of financial Veg-O-Matics were slicing and dicing financial assets into potent, newfangled securities—IOs and POs—that investors were scooping up with reckless élan. What was worse, investors had rediscovered their thirst for leverage. With double-digit bond yields a thing of the past, investors—particularly the new hedge funds that were "popping up all over"—were resorting to borrowing to inflate their returns. How could investors be so certain that markets would always be liquid?, Klarman wondered. He feared that investors were turning "a blind eye to the consequences of 'outlier' events," such as the sudden disturbances and occasional crashes that, historically, have always upset the best-laid plans of investors. In general, Klarman warned, "Successful investors have positioned themselves to avoid the 100-year flood. Increasingly, that way of thinking has become passé." Turning to the former Salomon traders' fund—that is, to Long-Term—Klarman noted that, given its projected leverage, even a single serious mistake would put a "major dent" in the fund's capital. "Two major errors at the same time, of course, would be catastrophic."[22]

4

DEAR INVESTORS

*In a strict sense, there wasn't any risk—if the world
had behaved as it did in the past.*
—MERTON MILLER, ECONOMIST AND
NOBEL LAUREATE

L ONG-TERM EARNED 28 percent in 1994, its first year of operation. After fees to the partners, its investors' accounts rose by 20 percent. In a year in which the average investor in bonds had lost money, this was nothing short of phenomenal. In October, when it was clear that the fund would finish with impressive numbers, Meriwether warned his investors not to count on a repeat. Long-Term would very likely have years in which it lost money, J.M. stressed: "It is clear that significant losses can occur even over a one-year horizon." All good money managers write such letters. If they understand their business, they know they can have bad years. If they are honest, they let their investors know it or at least try to temper their expectations.

Yet J.M.'s letter went a good deal further. In an attachment penned by his two academic stars, Merton and Scholes, Long-Term did not merely concede the *possibility* of loss, it calculated the supposed *odds* of its occurring, and to precise mathematical degrees. Just as a handbook of poker might tell you that the odds of drawing an inside straight were 8.51 percent, the professors calculated that Long-Term would lose at least 5 percent of its money 12 percent of the time (that is, in twelve of every hundred years). The letter went on to state the precise odds of the fund's losing at least 10 percent, as well as 15 percent and 20 percent.[1]

Of course, Long-Term could jigger the odds by changing certain assumptions; thus the letter contained not just one column of numbers but multiple columns, like a page from the *Daily Racing Form*. The point was, Long-Term predicted the odds with *precision*. It was as if the professors had some secret knowledge or an altered view of the world, for no ordinary investor would hazard such forecasts. Most people, one hopes, know that their stocks can fall, but if asked to specify the odds, they would most likely blink in puzzlement. Indeed, Long-Term's letter betrayed a different way of *thinking* about the world. Imagine, for a moment, that a student at your child's school showed symptoms of a contagious and potentially dangerous disease. You would expect a warning, perhaps some advice on what precautions to take. But if a letter arrived from the principal stating that your child had a 19 percent chance of catching the sickness, a 12 percent chance of missing at least a week of school, and a 2 percent risk of fatality, you would find it a trifle odd, not to mention presumptuous. You would want to know more about the school's doctor and, in particular, about the kind of medicine he practiced.

In truth, Long-Term's letter told a great deal about the fund's philosophical "medicine." It mentioned no specific trades or investments; it didn't have to. It is enough to know that for each investment, Long-Term was chiefly concerned with two questions: What was the anticipated *average* return, and how much did the return in any typical year tend to vary from that average? With a pair of dice, for instance, the average roll is 7, and the variation from the average cannot be more than 5 (you can't roll more than 12 or less than 2). What's more, the odds in dice are such that two thirds of the time, you will roll either 7 or a number that is within two of 7.

Therefore, if a sensible investor was offered the chance to bet even money on rolling between 5 and 9, he would take it. Of course, you wouldn't *always* roll between 5 and 9, so you wouldn't, one hopes, wager too much. But what if you could make that bet on *1 million rolls* and settle up only at the end? In that case, you should bet the house. You might roll snake eyes once, maybe a second time, perhaps a third. But over a million rolls, the chance of losing is infinitesimally small. Try it.

It is much harder to calculate the odds in investing; indeed, very few aspects of life can be forecast so precisely (good fortune-tellers are scarce). We may deduce that if we buy a share of IBM at $80 we have a greater chance of making a profit than if we buy at $90, just as your child is at greater risk if two of his buddies are sick, rather than only one. But *how much* greater? We simply don't have enough facts to quantify either the risk of market loss or the risk of contagion.

Notice that there is a key difference between a share of IBM (or an infectious disease) and a pair of dice. With dice, there is *risk*—you could, after all, roll snake eyes—but there is no *uncertainty,* because you know (for certain) the chances of getting a 7 and every other result. Investing confronts us with both risk and uncertainty. There is a risk that the price of a share of IBM will fall, and there is uncertainty about how likely it is to do so. So many variables—political, economic, managerial, competitive factors—can affect the result that the uncertainty all but overwhelms us.

Seen in these terms, Long-Term's letter represented a dramatic leap. While it heartily acknowledged risk, it banished uncertainty by putting numerical odds on its likelihood of loss. To J.M. and his traders, money management was less an "art" requiring a series of judgments than it was a "science" that could be precisely quantified. "Roughly, over a long period of time," the letter stated, "investors may experience a loss of 5% or more in about one month in five, and a loss of 10% or more in about one month in ten." Only *one year in fifty* should it lose at least 20 percent of its portfolio—and the Merton-Scholes encyclical did not entertain the possibility of losing more.

The secret of this magical foretelling was breathtakingly simple. Just as the key number in the dice bet was the typical variance from 7, the key number for Long-Term was the usual variance, or volatility, in bond prices. By plugging tens of thousands of bond prices into its SPARC computers, Long-Term's traders knew the *historic* volatility—that is, how much bonds had fluctuated in the past. And that one number (calculated over thousands of daily, monthly, and yearly intervals and for numerous types of bonds) was the basis of their assessment of risk in the *future*. Peter Rosenthal, Long-Term's press spokesman, glibly explained, "Risk is a function of volatility. These things are quantifiable." Meriwether, Merton, Scholes, and company had no more earnest belief.

Their portfolio was like a hat holding thousands of pairs of numbers, each representing the volatility and return they expected in a given trade. "They were thinking all the time about the numbers in the hat," noted Robert Stavis, who worked in the group at Salomon. They were looking at the individual pairs—the IOs, the Italys, and so on—but they were also thinking about the correlations between the pairs. Would the results in mortgages tend to mimic those in Italy? Would one trade be up when the other was down? The partners adjusted the weighting of each trade according to its effect both on return and on volatility, singly and for the entire portfolio, Stavis said. "And they'd constantly be tuning the mix."

■

Meriwether's traders were profoundly concerned with limiting risk. The idea that they could do so by targeting a specific level of volatility was central to how they ran the fund. If the portfolio was a little too quiet, they'd borrow more, raising the "vol"; if it was too volatile, they'd reduce their leverage, calming the fund down. Rather than target a specific return, they engineered the "hat" so that (they believed) it would fluctuate during most years about as much as the stock market did. With any more volatility, the risk would be too high. With less, they would be leaving money on the table. "To anyone with their theoretical background," noted Merrill's Dale Meyer, who helped sell the fund, "volatility and returns were the same thing. Increased volatility *meant* increased returns."

If this seems unremarkable, it is only because, by the 1990s, this approach had permeated most of Wall Street. Trading rooms had adopted the academics' faith in numeric certainties; risk managers at banks monitored volatilities as though they contained the Holy Grail. A senior executive at J. P. Morgan, when asked how he defined risk, breezily replied, "As volatility around the mean." The conceit of modern Wall Street was that the closing prices printed in each day's *Wall Street Journal* were as reliable and predictive about the future as the actuarial tables of life insurance companies or the known and cer-

tain odds in shooting craps. And the conceit stemmed largely from
Merton and Scholes. Every investment bank, every trading floor on
Wall Street was staffed by young, intelligent Ph.D.s who had studied
under Merton, Scholes, or their disciples. The same firms that spent
tens of millions of dollars per year on expensive research analysts—
i.e., stock pickers—staffed their trading desks with finance majors
who put capital at risk on the assumption that the market was efficient, meaning that stock prices were ever correct and therefore that
stock picking was a fraud.

Some of Long-Term's investors had learned this credo practically
in the crib. Terence Sullivan, who kept notes on his meetings with
Long-Term, believed it would take a rare, "calamitous" event—
maybe a once-in-a-hundred-year flood—for Long-Term to go seriously wrong. There would be times, Sullivan knew, when prices
would deviate from the norm and when markets would move against
Long-Term, costing it money. But for the markets in *all* of their trades
to *consistently* depart from the norm would be a statistical freak, like
rolling seven consecutive snake eyes or being hit by lightning twice.
Sullivan had learned this long before, in business school at the University of Pittsburgh—which, like all such schools, was steeped in the
teachings of Merton and Scholes.

■

Neither Merton nor Scholes was involved in trading at Long-Term
except in a minor, advisory sense. Nor, as some investors believed, did
the professors create the "models" that detailed the cases for various
trades. But Merton and Scholes were the fund's philosophical fathers.
As Scholes remarked at its inception, "We're not just a fund. We're a
financial-technology company."[2] More specifically, Long-Term was
an experiment in managing risk by the numbers. At the center of this
experiment was the notion of volatility, which had supplanted leverage, in the partners' minds, as the best proxy for risk. Indeed, many
of Long-Term's trades were attempts to exploit spreads that, in its
view, reflected an inaccurate estimate of future volatility risk—the
one risk that (to Long-Term) really counted. Such strategies had
evolved directly from the Black-Scholes formula.

The formula had built on discoveries in the physical sciences. Stat-
isticians had long been aware of the "law of large numbers." Roughly
speaking, if you have enough samples of a random event, they will

tend to distribute in the familiar bell curve, with the most occurrences around the average and a sharp drop-off at either extreme. This is called the *normal distribution* or, in mathematical terms, the *log-normal distribution*. A basketball coach knows that, given the usual distribution of heights, on a block with one hundred school-age boys he is likely to find sixty to seventy boys of roughly average height, a few who are short and a few who are tall, and maybe one who could play starting center. If the coach is lucky, he might find two centers. But he would never find, say, *twenty* seven-footers on that single street—assuming, of course, that the families are unrelated, for otherwise the selection would not be random. As Peter Bernstein has written, nature's pattern emerges only from the chaotic disorder of many *random* events.[3]

To Black, Scholes, and Merton, price changes in financial markets were random, too.* No one could predict any *particular* change, but over a long enough period, they assumed that the distribution of all such prices would mirror the pattern of other random events, like coin flips, dice rolls, or the heights of high school students. The market for Italian bonds and on-the-run Treasurys would also describe a bell curve, with many days in which prices changed only a little either up or down and a very few observations at the extremes, representing sudden upswings or market plunges.

If the amount of the typical change—the "volatility"—were known, they believed, the odds that a stock, bond, or any other asset would rise or fall by some proportion over time could be derived as well. The differential equations used to solve the Black-Scholes formula were adapted from physics equations that describe, among other phenomena in the physical world, the way cream spreads through a cup of coffee.[4] Any *one* molecule's trip is random, but as a group, the molecules distribute themselves in predictable fashion, from the center out. The cream will never go all to one side.

Black-Scholes says that prices don't (predictably) go to one side either. In valuing an option, which is the right to buy a security at a stated "strike price" in the future, all that matters is the volatility, or

---

* The Black-Scholes formula explicitly states, "We will assume ideal conditions in the market for the stock and for the option. . . . The stock price follows a random walk in continuous time."

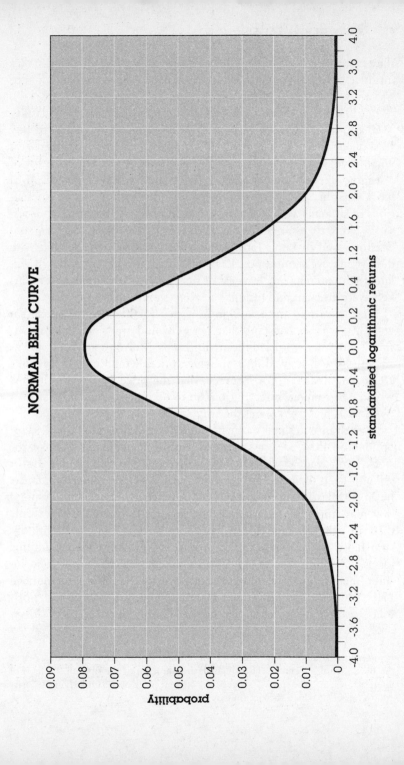

NORMAL BELL CURVE

standardized logarithmic returns

probability

the rate at which the underlying security jumps around.* This makes intuitive sense: the more a security fluctuates, the more likely it is to rise above the strike price.

But Black-Scholes makes a very key assumption: that the volatility of a security is *constant*. To say that the value of an option to buy IBM depends on its volatility is meaningless unless you can agree on what its volatility is. Therefore, the professors treated the volatility of a security like an inherent, unchanging trait. You have blue eyes; IBM has a volatility of X. You or I might assume that the market fluctuations of so many yesterdays are so much noise—arbitrary, not necessarily likely to recur, and best forgotten. But to Black, Scholes, and Merton—and to Long-Term—these fluctuations were invested with deep predictive significance. Each tick of the market up or down was latent with an unerring forecast of future risk. This implied that markets were efficient and rational at every step.

Merton carried the assumption a step further. He assumed that volatility was *so* constant that prices would trade in "continuous time"—in other words, without any jumps. Merton's markets were as smooth as well-brewed java, in which prices would indeed flow like cream. He assumed, for instance, that the price of a share of IBM would never plunge directly from 80 to 60 but would always stop at $79^3/_4$, $79^1/_2$, and $79^1/_4$ along the way.

At each infinitesimal moment, traders would readjust the price of options on IBM, keeping them in synchrony with the price of the stock. And traders who owned both could—by nimbly buying or selling—keep their portfolio in an Edenic, risk-free state of balance. In short, Merton assumed a perfect, risk-free arbitrage. This assumption may approximate real markets when they are calm—but only then. In 1987, so-called portfolio insurance was marketed (with absurd ballyhoo) to institutional investors as a technique of limiting losses via continuous selling when markets fall. These portfolio insurers helped to exacerbate a market crash that was later dubbed Black Monday. That day, the market was highly *discontinuous*. Portfolio insurers who had counted on nimbly limiting their losses

---

* The other factors that determine an option's price were known long before the Black-Scholes formula. They include the duration of the option, the level of interest rates, and the spread between the current price of the underlying security and the price at which the option can be exercised.

couldn't keep pace with the panic that broke out on Wall Street and, indeed, lost their shirts.

Merton's perfect-arbitrage assumption was an essential building block in Long-Term's (and many other firms') hedging strategies. The partners, of course, had worked with the same risk assumptions at Salomon Brothers and had racked up phenomenal profits—albeit with the occasional nasty loss. This gave them tremendous confidence. Their trades usually *were* sensible, meaning that they were aligned with the odds. Nonetheless, the fact that the group's ship hadn't capsized in the past didn't guarantee that the group had properly calculated the odds of a tidal wave—just that such waves were relatively infrequent.

Merton's theories were seductive not because they were mostly wrong but because they were so nearly, or so nearly often, right. As the English essayist G. K. Chesterton wrote, life is "a trap for logicians" because it is almost reasonable but not quite; it is usually sensible but occasionally otherwise:

> It looks just a little more mathematical and regular than it is; its exactitude is obvious, but its inexactitude is hidden; its wildness lies in wait.[5]

Merton was prey to this very trap. His "continuous-time finance" seemed to wrap the financial universe in a tidy ball. On paper it solved, or pointed to the solutions for, virtually every problem in finance: how to value junk bonds, how much to pay for deposit insurance, you name it. His theories seemed to behold the elegance and order he had always craved. "Not all that is beautiful in science need also be practical," he wrote with satisfaction. "But here we have both."[6]

Eric Rosenfeld, who had studied at MIT in the 1970s, looked up to Merton as an "unbelievable mathematician." He noted that a single unpublished paper of Merton's had triggered a host of dissertations by a cadre of inspired disciples. Of course, Merton's entire oeuvre depended on his assumptions about random walks, with their close tie-in to the physical world. As the unassuming Rosenfeld described it, he and his fellow Merton protégés used to run to the physics library looking for formulaic solutions that they could "jam into finance."

While studying with Merton, Rosenfeld played a cameo role in developing financial software, which was the bridge that brought the math to Wall Street. He and a friend, Mitchell Kapor, were early devotees of the Apple II, at a time when little software existed for it. Kapor thought computers were cool, and Rosenfeld was using quantitative systems for investing as well as for betting on football. In 1978, Rosenfeld, who was writing his thesis and spending gobs of time at the university computer center, asked Kapor if he could write a program that would run on the Apple. Kapor did—and realized they were on to something. The two became partners in a tiny company called Micro Finance Systems. They published a desktop graphics and statistics program known as Tiny TROLL that was just powerful enough to do useful work. It sold thousands of copies, and Kapor and Rosenfeld made hundreds of thousands of dollars on it.

Kapor, a former disc jockey and teacher of transcendental meditation, thought he had discovered the next wave. He hatched plans for a second venture and invited Rosenfeld to join him. But Kapor had also caught the finance bug. He was so intrigued by his friend's account of how stocks mimicked molecules that *he* enrolled at MIT. But after Kapor took Merton's finance course, he decided that quantitative finance was less a science than a faith—a doctrine for ideologues "blinded by the power of the model." It appealed to intellectuals who craved a sense of order but could lead them disastrously astray if markets moved outside the model. Kapor went on to form Lotus Development Corporation and became an icon of the software industry. Rosenfeld, who had gotten a job teaching at Harvard, staked his royalties from Tiny TROLL on two other ventures—one of which, a chartered sailboat, almost sank on its maiden voyage—and lost a lot of money.[7]

Kapor wasn't the only one who wondered if Merton's model might be too tidy for the real world. Paul Samuelson, Merton's mentor at MIT, had doubts when Long-Term was organized. Samuelson, the first financial economist to win a Nobel Prize, recognized that "continuous time" was merely an ideal state; in real time, traders took seconds, minutes, or even hours to analyze events and react. When events overwhelmed them, the markets gapped. Heat molecules didn't jump out of line; IBM most certainly did. "This is very important to the Long-Term story," Samuelson noted. "The essence of the Black-Scholes formula is that you know, with certainty, not what the deal of the cards will be but what kind of universe is being sampled, which gives you the assumption of the log-normal process. I wondered back then [when Long-Term started]."[8]

The beauty of cards is that the universe is known; there are fifty-two cards in a deck, and only fifty-two. Life insurance is a bit different: since new people are always being added to the universe, actuaries rely on samplings. They aren't perfect, but they work, because the sample of people is very large and mortality rates change only very slowly. But in markets, we are never sure that the sample is complete. The universe of all trades looked one way throughout the 1920s and another way after the Great Depression. The pattern changed again during the inflationary 1970s, yet again in the effervescent 1990s. After which of these periods was the picture "normal," and how do we know that the next new period won't change the story again? To focus on a single company, IBM lives in a dynamic, ever-changing world, in which managers perpetually confront new possibilities, new problems, and novel products, the risks of each of which would seem impossible to quantify. If a manager at Big Blue proposed to rely on the past as an accurate gauge of future risk, he would probably be fired.

Eugene Fama, Scholes's thesis adviser, wondered what *his* old student was up to as well. Fama had all the admiration in the world for the option formula *as a model.* But trusting people's money to such models was different. In the early 1960s, Fama had written his thesis on the price movements of the thirty Dow Jones Industrial Average stocks and discovered a remarkable pattern: for every stock, there were many more days of *extreme* price movements than would occur in a normal distribution. Fama's stocks were like a world in which most people were average height but every twentieth person was either a giant or a dwarf. There were too many extreme readings, or "outliers," that random distribution could not explain. As Fama put it:

> If the population of price changes is strictly normal, on the average for any stock . . . an observation more than five standard deviations from the mean should be observed about once every 7,000 years. In fact such observations seem to occur about once every three to four years.[9]

Graphically, Fama's stocks depicted a bell curve with the ends swollen, representing too many incidents at the extremes (known as the "tails"). Fama's thesis, which he undoubtedly discussed with Scholes, was rife with implications for the future Long-Term Capital. In contrast to the idealized markets in models, Fama warned, real-life ones experienced "discontinuous" price changes (those nasty jumps) and a higher probability of large losses; indeed, "such a market is inherently more risky."[10]

By the time Long-Term was formed, it was well documented that virtually *all* financial assets behaved like the stocks that Fama had studied.[11] Mortgage securities might usually behave as the model predicted, but there would come a day when—with no warning at all—they would leap off the charts. As Fama put it, "Life always has a fat tail."[12] A few months after J.M.'s letter, the Mexican peso collapsed and investors panicked, setting off a chain reaction from Texas to Tierra del Fuego. The markets in Argentina and Venezuela were not independent dice; they collapsed simultaneously. Confidence wasn't restored until Robert Rubin, the Treasury secretary and former Goldman arbitrageur, organized a bailout.

If you follow the market even casually, you probably have a gut feeling that stocks (or bonds) are often inexplicably volatile; they do an awful lot of bouncing around. The most obvious example was Black Monday, when, on no apparent news, the market plunged 23 percent. Economists later figured that, on the basis of the market's historic volatility, had the market been open every day since the creation of the Universe, the odds would still have been against its falling that much on any single day. In fact, had the life of the Universe been repeated *one billion times,* such a crash would still have been theoretically "unlikely."[13] But it happened anyway. Obviously, past volatilities do *not* prepare investors for shocks that lie in wait—nor do they signal in advance just when such shocks might choose to occur.

There is a reason why financial markets run to extremes more often than coin flips—and more often than the "hundred-year storm" that Long-Term's partners would later cite as the culprit behind their disaster. A key condition of random events is that each new flip is *independent* of the previous one. The coin doesn't remember that it landed on tails three times in a row; the odds on the fourth flip are still fifty-fifty.

But markets have memories. Sometimes a trend will continue just because traders expect (or fear) that it will. Investors may slavishly fol-

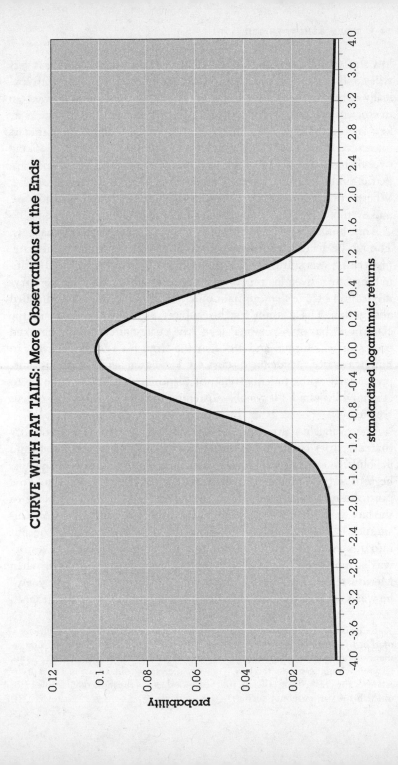

CURVE WITH FAT TAILS: More Observations at the Ends

low the trend for no other reason than that they think enough others will do likewise. Such momentum trading has nothing to do with logically appraising securities; it doesn't fit the ideal of rational investors in efficient markets. But it's human. After three bad "flips" in the market, the fourth flip may no longer be completely random. Some traders may have taken losses and be forced to sell; other investors, looking over their shoulders, may panic and decide to beat them to it—as happened with Treasury bonds during Long-Term's inaugural spring. Wherever the human spirit is present, the little runs that Fama noticed, and even big, Black Monday–sized runs, are possible.* [14]

This human spirit was totally absent from Merton's markets. Though he acknowledged that his models represented an ideal state, his writing was suffused with the notion of perfect prices and rational investors. Even his prose was wooden and dry, as if he were trying to boil off life's emotional content and reduce it to a controlled abstraction. His passion for his subject electrified students in the classroom, but on a personal level, the curly-haired, plump-cheeked professor was formal and aloof. Aside from his Ferrari, Heaven, to him, was a deep academic discussion. He was generous with his time, particularly with students, but not disposed to give-and-take or to changing his mind. "It was like listening to Billy Graham," a student recalled.

The evangelical Merton showed disdain for the very possibility that investors could be anything but calculating automatons, and he blithely ignored the times when their emotions ran riot. Thus, he took credit for the contribution that his theories made to "the portfolio-insurance products of the 1980s"—as if he were blind to the fact that, when real people had tried those products, portfolio insurance had miserably failed. [15] Even the word "speculative" he put into quotes, as though the notion that it might apply to real investors was so unpleasant he had to handle it with forceps. Indeed, when Merton referred to "well-known and colorful passages by Keynes," he was knocking the English economist and man of letters for the sin

* Curiously, Fama devoted the rest of his career to justifying the efficient-market hypothesis. He argued that Black Monday had been a rational adjustment to a (one-day?) change in underlying corporate values. On the other hand, Lawrence Summers, now the U.S. Treasury secretary, told *The Wall Street Journal* after the crash, "The efficient market hypothesis is the most remarkable error in the history of economic theory."

of letting a vivid, human adjective or two slip into his copy. He had the disease of perfect belief, which makes compromise impossible. When Robert J. Shiller, an American economist, dared to suggest that markets were too volatile to fit the model of perfect markets, you could sense that for Merton, to entertain any doubt at all was to risk seeing the entire edifice crumble: "We need hardly mention the significance of such a conclusion. If Shiller's rejection of market efficiency is sustained, then serious doubt is cast on the validity of this cornerstone of modern financial economic theory."[16]

The traders at Long-Term knew the models were imperfect, of course. "We know this doesn't work by rote," said Robert Stavis, the former member of the Arbitrage Group at Salomon. "But this is the best model we have. You look at the old-timers who went with their gut. You had this model, you had these numbers, and in the end you thought they were a lot more powerful than a guy's gut."

Long-Term's traders were *not* automatons. They debated, sometimes hotly, for hours every week, about what the models implied and whether to do what the models recommended. They were also aware of the "fat tail" criticism—the idea that unexpected disaster should be expected—and they tried to adjust the models for it. But can one ever program for the unexpected? Most of Long-Term's trades were low risk, but they were not *no* risk. Nor was the degree of risk precisely quantifiable. The problem with the math is that it adorned with certitude events that were inherently *uncertain*. "You take Monica Lewinsky, who walks into Clinton's office with a pizza. You have no idea where that's going to go," Conseco's Max Bublitz, who had declined to invest in Long-Term, noted. "Yet if you apply math to it, you come up with a thirty-eight percent chance she's going to go down on him. It looks great, but it's all a guess."

By the mid-1990s, this distinction was as hopelessly lost on Wall Street as it was in Greenwich. Banks from Merrill to Morgan to Bankers Trust were computing, to the tiniest fraction, the supposed amount by which their trades could fall in any day, month, or year. Even the Federal Reserve was endorsing such programs, which went by the generic name "Value-at-Risk." Beneath the programs' sophisticated veneer, they amounted to asking, "If markets behave as they have in the past, how much will we lose?" But what if markets did something different? History, Mark Twain noted, rhymes; it does not repeat.[17]

Such programs worked until they failed to work—as they did in Mexico in 1995. And they failed precisely at moments of unexpected turbulence—when they were needed most. They were like insurance for all the days when it didn't storm; they predicted what one would lose on a *normal* day but not when the peso collapsed. David DeRosa, a currency trader who teaches at Yale, dubbed Value-at-Risk "a lighthouse for the soon-to-be-shipwrecked." J. P. Morgan, which pioneered the methodology (under the brand name RiskMetrics), candidly admitted its flaws. In a document dated October 1994, the same month as Meriwether's letter, Morgan admitted that markets did not appear to be random or independent in the way of coin flips and that volatilities "are themselves quite volatile." Nonetheless, the firm, and its imitators all over Wall Street, continued to use Value-at-Risk. Morgan couldn't find any "persuasive alternatives,"[18] the bank explained—as if that would make up for its shortcomings.

Of all the firms that subscribed to Value-at-Risk, Long-Term was the archetype.[19] The professors' addendum read like the notes from one of Merton's lectures; it confidently informed investors that returns in the stock market were, indeed, independently (randomly) distributed. What's more, they stressed that Long-Term expected its returns to be negatively correlated from one period to the next, meaning that a down month would likely be followed by a good month and so on, thus making sustained losing streaks even less likely. "A low return in any one quarter may be more likely to be followed by a higher return in the subsequent quarter," Merton and Scholes argued. Over time, that was logical, because over time markets do correct their mistakes. Otherwise, there would be no point in buying mispriced securities. But what if, before prices corrected, they got further—drastically further—out of line, as had happened to Eckstein in the 1970s? That was a possibility the letter didn't mention.

A central tenet of the partners' philosophy was that markets were steadily getting more efficient, more liquid, more "continuous"—more as Merton had envisioned them.[20] With more investors hunting for mispriced securities and with market news traveling faster, it seemed logical that investors would take less time to correct mistaken prices. And on most days, they probably did. An efficient market is a less volatile one (it has no Black Mondays) and, from day to day, a less risky one. Spreads should therefore contract. This boosted the partners' confidence that spreads would narrow. Indeed, they were confident enough to leverage such bets many times over.

∎

Although global investors were burned by the Mexican fiasco, Long-Term was unaffected, and its stirring success continued. In fact, in 1995, as earlier trades bore fruit, the firm's results improved. Italy, no longer looking like the Continent's problem child, was being hailed as the design capital of Europe, more creative than Germany and less hobbled by tradition than France. As other traders grasped Italy's potential for growth, the bond market in Rome began to percolate, and Long-Term's profits swelled.[21]

Thanks to Italy and the IO mortgage trade in particular, Long-Term in 1995 earned an astounding 59 percent before fees and 43 percent after. A little over half of the gains came from Europe. During its first two years, in which Long-Term had earned a remarkable $1.6 billion, Italy contributed an estimated $600 million in profits. All told, it was the fastest, most impressive start by any fund ever. For an investor who had started on day one, each original dollar had swelled by 71 percent, even after the partnership group had taken its robust cut. It did not hurt J.M.'s mood that Salomon Brothers was struggling in his absence. The bank had suffered wrenching losses in 1994 and was widely rumored to be up for sale.

Meriwether's only nagging worry was that Long-Term hadn't been volatile *enough*. The fund had told investors to expect an accordion, with pockets of losses tucked between its bellows, but over the first two years, in only one month had Long-Term lost more than 1 percent. "Where's the accordion?" one investor wondered. To William F. Sharpe, a Nobel Prize–winning economist and an adviser to one of Long-Term's investors, the returns seemed surreally smooth. "We distinctly asked, 'What's the risk?'" Sharpe recalled. "Myron [Scholes] said, 'Well, our goal is to get the risk level [the volatility] of the S&P 500.' He said, 'We're having trouble getting it that big.'"

With such a stellar start, Long-Term, again with Merrill Lynch, had no trouble raising an additional $1 billion of new money. Meriwether almost allowed himself a note of pride. Writing to investors, he noted that Long-Term had swelled to sixteen partners and ninety-six people overall, about half of them involved in trading and strategy.[22] He stressed the firm's elite character—its bilingual staffers, its many Ph.D.s, its sophisticated "financial technology." J.M. had been parsing the odds all his life: Long-Term was to be the pinnacle of his work—a grand, supremely orchestrated symphony of risk taking.

Including the money from new investors, the firm's equity capital had, in less than two years, virtually tripled, to a total of $3.6 billion. Long-Term's assets had also grown, to the extraordinary sum of $102 billion. Thus, at the end of 1995, it was leveraged 28 to 1. Of course, its return on *total* assets—both those that it owned and those that it had borrowed—was far, far less than the gaudy return cited above. This return on total capital was approximately 2.45 percent.[23] This minuscule figure is what Long-Term would have earned had it invested only its own money. But even this figure is too high because it doesn't reflect Long-Term's derivative trades, which, as noted, weren't recorded on its balance sheet. But derivatives most certainly increased Long-Term's exposure. (Whether you buy a bond or simply bet on its price, you are exposed to the same potential gain or loss.) And these off-balance-sheet trades most definitely increased Long-Term's riskiness.

Taking its derivative trades into account, its cash-on-cash return was probably less than 1 percent.[24] The exact number is unimportant. The point is that almost all of its heady 59 percent return was due to the remarkable power of leverage. Seen in this light, Sharpe's question—What was the risk?—would be difficult to answer. A cash investor risks his out-of-pocket investment, but Long-Term didn't make such an up-front commitment. Its derivative trades, in particular, required *no* capital up front. The fund simply settled with its banks each day, paying or receiving cash depending on which way a trade had moved. In lieu of working capital, Long-Term designated a hypothetical slice of its equity as standing behind each trade. This so-called *risk capital* represented the capital that Long-Term figured it needed to keep in the vault, just in case. Rosenfeld recalled,

> Even though we didn't get charged a haircut, we had a risk management process where we calculated our hypothetical working capital. We went through every trade and said, "Suppose we are in a really stressful time, how much would the haircut be?"

As Long-Term's strategies grew more diverse, the fund felt comfortable taking bigger positions. It focused on its portfolio *as a whole,* and thus it was willing to pile bigger trades onto each of its "risk" dollars back in the vault. The theory, of course, was that the likelihood of many leveraged trades collapsing simultaneously was slim, just as an insurer does not expect that all of its clients will file claims simultaneously.

Indeed, Long-Term thought of itself in exactly those terms: as an insurer of financial risk. In effect, the fund pocketed premiums for the hazard of owning less liquid and generally riskier bonds—the premiums being the spreads that it earned on off-the-run Treasurys, mortgage IOs, Italian bonds, and so forth. Of course, the rub with insurance is that it takes a while before one can tell whether the premium is adequate. A property and casualty insurer will always make money in a year without serious storms. But after such a year or even several good years, it is fair to ask, Was the insurer that good, or was it merely lucky? Were the premiums adequate, or was it writing too many inexpensive insurance policies for seaside homes on wooden stilts—with little thought to the potential for claims? And if each of Long-Term's bonds was, in effect, a "policy," the number of policies it insured—and the level of losses it could someday face—would grow with each added dollar of leverage. The question the partners could have asked themselves was, how hard had they stretched to make that 59 percent, and what sort of claims might they face after a storm?

5

TUG-OF-WAR

This small group . . . attempted to marry the best of finance theory
with the best of finance practice.
—ROBERT MERTON

THE RANDOM BAD MONTH, the season of storms, seemed never to come. Long-Term was not only phenomenally profitable, it was eerily consistent, as though defying a law of nature. The fund resembled a batter who hit for power but never struck out. The partners strode to the plate and rapped hit after hit, day after day. More confident than ever, they lengthened their swing, which is to say they leveraged further. By the spring of 1996, Long-Term had an astounding $140 billion in assets, thirty times its underlying capital. Though still unknown to 99 percent of Americans, Long-Term was two and a half times as big as Fidelity Magellan, the largest mutual fund, and four times the size of the next largest hedge fund.[1] Meriwether, Hilibrand, Haghani, and company now controlled more assets than Lehman Brothers and Morgan Stanley and were within shouting distance of Salomon. Though they had only a couple dozen traders, their fund—barely two years old—was bigger than some of Wall Street's age-old institutions. A stealth missile trusted to the care of supposed experts, it had a fearsome potency unimaginable to the man on the street.

However, Long-Term was not a secret to its banks. After the event, it was widely reported that Wall Street had somehow been ignorant of Long-Term's swollen asset total and leverage ratio. Merrill Lynch would go so far as to state in a press release, "On September 21, [1998,] this was the first time that we learned the overall size and scale of the positions and extent of leverage."[2] Komansky personally declared that Long-Term's lack of "transparency" had kept him in the dark, and various other Wall Street CEOs professed to be shocked at Long-Term's leverage.[3]

In a strict sense, this may have been true. Komansky and Corzine may have not known. But people beneath them knew. Long-Term disclosed its total assets and liabilities to its banks on a quarterly basis and to investors every month. Long-Term also reported those numbers to the Commodity Futures Trading Commission. It reported its derivative totals only annually—too infrequently to give an accurate picture of such a fast-growing firm. Still, the numbers indicated (to anyone who cared to look) that something big was brewing. Long-Term disclosed derivative bets as of the end of 1995 on a total of $650 billion of securities—not exactly chicken feed.[4] As Brooksley Born, chairwoman of the CFTC, would candidly admit, "We didn't see any major warning bells and we knew [the information] was fairly widely available."[5] Thomas Bell, Long-Term's outside counsel, was more right than most when he observed, "People got statements. It was a failure to connect the dots."

But this was not the whole picture either. On their own, Long-Term's vaguely worded disclosures were next to meaningless. Aside from broad generalizations such as "interest rate swaps" or "government securities," it was impossible to tell what its assets were. The derivative disclosures were especially opaque. Imagine asking your local bank for a personal loan on the basis of your "real estate assets" without bothering to say whether the real estate was in Appalachia or in Beverly Hills.

With regard to *particular* assets—say, mortgage securities or Italian bonds—each bank knew only its own exposure to Long-Term. Goldman Sachs had no idea that Salomon might be financing a similar trade; J. P. Morgan would not have known that Merrill Lynch was duplicating Morgan's loans. So in theory, each bank had no notion of how big Long-Term was in any particular trade. But in practice, the banks were in a good position to estimate. The world of bond arbitrage is relatively small. Certainly, the banks knew enough to ask for more specific disclosure. And of course, they could have declined to do business with Long-Term if satisfactory answers were not forthcoming.

But the banks were fighting to do more hedge fund business, not less. Five years into a bull market, the banks were awash in liquidity, and the hedge fund trade was a lucrative way for Wall Street to employ its surplus capital. The banks accomplished this by a practice known as "renting out the balance sheet"—literally, transferring their enormous borrowing power to hedge funds with lesser credit ratings, a service for which they charged mere pennies on every $100 of credit. Long-Term, which was easily the Street's biggest hedge fund customer, was reputed to be throwing off $100 million to $200 million in fees to Wall Street each year, and each of the banks wanted as big a share of the money as possible.[6] "Banks were tripping over themselves to make twenty basis points [$20/100$ of a percent]"—a trifle given the implied risks, noted John Succo, then a trading manager at Lehman Brothers.

As many as fifty-five banks were giving Long-Term financing.[7] Dazzled by the partners' air of infallibility, the banks raced to top one another's offers. "People were lending them money at LIBOR [a private-sector bank rate] plus fifty basis points when it should have been LIBOR plus two hundred points," said Andrew Siciliano, the bond manager at the Basel-based Swiss Bank, which specialized in derivative trading. Siciliano worried that the Greenwich fund was getting the better of Swiss Bank. The firm squeezed every counterparty to the max.

Long-Term deftly exploited the banks' hunger for fees, pushing them to do business on the most advantageous of terms. The fund traded on razor-thin margins, cutting out the normal profit the banks could expect from servicing such a behemoth. But the banks didn't stop dreaming that Long-Term would deliver them a profit at the end of the rainbow; like frustrated but hopeful parents, they kept favoring their incorrigible child with treats. Merrill Lynch and Salomon Brothers were Long-Term's biggest sugar daddies, at least in terms of financing. Salomon counted Long-Term as its biggest customer, especially in European swaps,[8] but the two firms' intertwined histories kept them at a wary distance.

Merrill Lynch, on the other hand, was increasingly eager to nuzzle up to Long-Term. And the hedge fund was happy to reciprocate—on its own terms. J.M. quickly befriended Daniel Tully, the Merrill Lynch chairman, and the Tullys and Meriwethers became a foursome. J.M. even made Tully a partner in Waterville, J.M.'s golf course in County Kerry, Ireland. To Tully, who was so devoted to his ancestral homeland that he signed his name in green, this cemented an already fast business alliance. Underlings at Merrill quickly grasped that the chairman considered Long-Term to be a special client. "It was incumbent not just on the salesperson but on the entire organization to get behind the relationship," Tully stressed.⁹

J.M. also nuzzled up to Komansky and Herb Allison, who were waiting in the wings to take the reins from Tully. Always comfortable in betting fraternities, J.M. took the Merrill bosses to Belmont, a racetrack where he boarded horses. Typically, J.M. asked a lot of questions and let his guests do the talking, and Allison noticed that he remembered the answers—even little things, such as the name of Allison's wife—just as he remembered trades. J.M. was always a good listener. In such a sharp-elbowed business, he stuck out as essentially decent. "You couldn't help but like him," Allison thought.¹⁰

The high point of Long-Term's seduction of Merrill was an annual three-day golf competition at Waterville, an internationally renowned course that had been host to, among others, Tiger Woods. About a dozen attended from each firm, with the Merrill executives escorting some of the Long-Term partners in private jets, though each company paid its own way. Waterville was an enchanting place, carved from lush natural grasses, adjacent to a quaint seaside Irish village. Invitations to the elite affair, held each September, were hot items at Merrill, which printed "Waterville International Cup" shirts bearing checkerboards in green, white, and orange, the Irish colors. In their off-hours the golfers fished and feasted on sumptuous dinners; then they retired to an intimate bed-and-breakfast. Early risers enjoyed the solitary splendor of lofting drives into the ocean at dawn.

For Meriwether, Waterville symbolized the distance he had come from caddying at Flossmoor. He was an animated host, thriving on the competition and taking note of every shot, but not neglecting to give Allison pointers on his release. Led by J.M., a four-handicap player, Long-Term won the Waterville Cup year after year, prompting the bankers to whistle at Long-Term's competitive spirit. The Merrill team was impressed with the arbitrageurs, who golfed with as much élan as they traded. Daniel Napoli, Merrill's risk manager, quipped,

"If they could have earned a Ph.D. at golf, they would have." Stephen Bellotti, who ran foreign currency trading at Merrill, turned to Myron Scholes at one of these weekends and playfully demanded, "Myron, what do you have more of—money or brains?" Scholes shot back: "Brains, but it's getting close!"

As the business relationship grew closer, Long-Term began to push Merrill Lynch for more financing. Leahy, who managed the relationship for Long-Term, would say, "If you want us to trade, you got to give us more balance sheet." Gradually, Merrill opened the spigot. By 1996, it was providing $6.5 billion of repo financing (roughly equal to Merrill's total equity) and proportionately more on the derivative side. But aside from pleasant weekends in Ireland, it wasn't clear what Merrill was getting in return. Long-Term simply shaved too much from the bid and asked prices to leave a normal profit for its broker. The broker might squawk, but Long-Term wouldn't budge.

At one point, citing Merrill's growing exposure to the high-risk hedge fund, a person on Merrill's repo desk refused to approve more credit. But shortly before the firms' next golf weekend, the repo man heard from an anxious salesman: "I'm going to see Dick Leahy! We don't want to be embarrassed. How about putting on another five hundred million dollars?" When the repo man resisted, the salesman added, "You *gotta* do these trades, or we lose the business."

Merrill salesmen, eager to promote their prize account, rationalized that financing Long-Term was the key to being able to trade with the firm and that trading would enable Merrill to see Long-Term's order flow. Of course, since Merrill saw only one side of each trade, the information was of dubious value. The usually healthy tension between the financing and sales desks was tilted in Long-Term's favor, because people at Merrill knew the account was "special." Long-Term felt free to tap friends at every level of the firm and did so. This started with Tully, the chairman, a former broker who was "damn proud" that Merrill had won so much of Long-Term's business. Even Allison, whom some derided as a hard-edged bean counter, got caught up in Long-Term's glamour and urged his underlings to expand the relationship. "Everybody was enamored with their intellect," Dunleavy, the salesman, recalled. "It was like Kennedy's inner circle—Camelot! They had the best and the brightest."

However, the Merrill executives eventually grew uneasy—not because of Long-Term's leverage, but because Merrill was making only

$25 million a year off the account, peanuts considering the two firms' level of business. The financing desk began to fight back: Since Merrill's balance sheet was a precious resource, why squander it on a chintzy client?

Allison, who was in charge of Merrill's business with big institutions, including Long-Term, finally took J.M. aside, suggesting ironically that it might be nice for Merrill to make a little money on its trades, too. Like others who dealt with Long-Term, Allison felt that the partners analyzed every deal in terms of the profit and loss on discrete trades rather than in terms of the overall relationship. And he said as much to Meriwether.

J.M. replied sympathetically, but Long-Term kept squeezing Merrill all the same. The firm seemed willfully tone-deaf, even at the risk of souring key alliances. One time, it took advantage of a technical loophole in a loan document to make $7 million at Merrill's expense. When an executive protested, J.M. frowned and said, "I didn't realize." But he didn't back down.

"He was sincere," the Merrill executive said. "It was how he looked at the world: someone wins, someone loses."

Insultingly, the partners refused to trust Merrill with the firm's secrets but expected to get big slugs of Merrill Lynch bond underwritings, a plum that investment banks reserve for the choicest clients. Even more galling, Long-Term tried to sell Merrill on an unusual warrant that had been concocted by Myron Scholes. The warrant would have been a cheap way for the partners to bet more money on their own fund—while exposing Merrill to serious risk. Merrill quickly refused. By now, the famous bull was growing restless. Merrill began to take back some of its balance sheet, though it remained one of Long-Term's biggest bankers.

Merrill was dying to clear Long-Term's trades, but Long-Term refused, because it got this service from Bear Stearns, where J.M. had a friend, Vincent Mattone, who had formerly been with Salomon. Clearing brokers perform many vital functions, such as record keeping and settling trades. Though clearing is usually a lucrative business, Bear had agreed to give Long-Term attractive terms because it, too, hoped to get more of Long-Term's trading business. Bear also lent money to six or seven of the partners so they could raise their personal investments in the fund. However, Long-Term quickly discovered that Bear could not be pushed around.

For one thing, Bear refused to do much financing on Long-Term's usual no-haircut basis. The street-savvy Bear had once turned down a similar request from a prince of Liechtenstein who was eager to trade foreign currencies, and it wasn't about to relax the rules for a hedge fund. "Our decision was very clear," one executive recalled. "We don't do business without initial margin." What's more, Bear was wary about risking too much of its capital on Long-Term. The most important clearing function is providing intraday credit. For Long-Term, which might do hundreds of trades in a day, Bear in effect acted as a bank, holding many of Long-Term's assets and paying and receiving monies on Long-Term's behalf to and from counterparties around the world.

Without a clearing broker, Long-Term would not have been able to operate—at least not with anything like its customary flexibility or speed. Moreover, a prime broker typically has the right to stop clearing without notice, and it is difficult to get a new clearing broker in a hurry. Therefore, Long-Term was dependent on Bear Stearns to a greater extent than on any other firm. And for a Wall Street brokerage, Bear was an unconventional place. Alan Greenberg, the nearly septuagenarian chairman, despised the bureaucratic airs of the Morgans and the Merrills. He still sat on the trading floor and answered his phone with a gruff hello. He was famous for exhorting employees not to waste paper clips. Greenberg's partner, James Cayne, the chief executive, had made his name by daring to make a market in New York City bonds in the difficult 1970s, when a young J.M. had been pursuing a similar strategy. Under Greenberg's and Cayne's unflinching management, Bear was informal, pragmatic, and relentlessly focused on its own self-interest. This worried Long-Term.

In 1994, as Long-Term was getting off the ground, Askin Capital, the hedge fund that had suffered crushing losses in the mortgage market, had collapsed after Bear had issued a margin call. The realization that Bear held all the cards had been gnawing at Long-Term ever since. In 1996, the partners began to agitate for a change.

What Long-Term wanted was a contractual promise from Bear that it would continue to clear Long-Term's trades, even if the hedge fund encountered serious problems. But the broker was worried about its own security. If Bear continued to clear a fund down to "dollar zero," it could be forced to make good on eleventh-hour desperation trades should the fund eventually collapse. In short, Long-Term and Bear were each worried about the other's ability to do it harm.

Over many meetings, the two sides came to a rough agreement. Basically, Bear was willing to promise to keep clearing for Long-Term as long as the hedge fund kept $1.5 billion on call at Bear. Though this was acceptable to Long-Term, the partners wanted to resolve some other issues before they signed; chiefly, and with uncanny prescience, they were anxious to protect Long-Term's flexibility during a crisis. Hilibrand, having read reports of the Askin debacle, realized that if Long-Term ever did stumble, Bear would be able to force a liquidation, perhaps at fire-sale prices. Bear would also be in a position to divulge Long-Term's positions, potentially setting off a wave of selling. Thus, Hilibrand wanted to nail down Long-Term's right to hold Bear liable for any abuses, such as breaching Long-Term's confidentiality.

In typical Hilibrand style, he relentlessly hammered away at Bear. Michael Alix, a senior credit executive at Bear, thought Hilibrand extremely difficult and a trifle paranoid, though some of his concerns would turn out to have merit. The winsome Eric Rosenfeld, who also took part in the talks, seemed able to see Bear's point of view; Hilibrand couldn't. The discussions were like a legal case in which Hilibrand never ran out of arguments. The parties negotiated in mounting frustration, but nothing was signed. Hilibrand was pushing the much-sought-after clearing agreement out of sight.

The failure to secure an agreement with Bear was a persistent concern, and JM regularly revisited the matter. Just as Long-Term massaged its relationship with Merrill over golfing weekends, JM and some of "the boys" regularly played poker with Cayne and his colleague Vinny Mattone, either at Long-Term's offices in Greenwich or at Cayne's Park Avenue apartment. The witty, wry Rosenfeld would have Cayne in stitches, but when JM would pipe up, "Jimmy, you got to do something on the clearance agreement," Cayne would unflinchingly reply, "No—*you* gotta."

Long-Term was also pressing Chase Manhattan. The fund seemed to want to draw all of Wall Street into its web, and the partners were shrewd enough to realize that the time to line up banks was now, when results were good. Chase had declined to become a counterparty in 1994, feeling that Long-Term was too new. But when J.M. returned in 1996, the reception was warmer. J.M. had a contact at

Chase, too: David Pflug, the portly head of global credit, who handled loans to clients on Wall Street. The suspendered, blunt-spoken Pflug (pronounced "Fluge") had advised J.M. during the Mozer crisis, when he had convinced the beleaguered Salomon Brothers to arrange for emergency credit. Now, in 1996, Pflug agreed to finance Long-Term on interest rate swaps—in which, typically, one side agrees to pay the other a fixed rate of interest in return for receiving a rate that floats with the market. Chase also backed Long-Term on yield-curve trades—again, a standard sonata in the fixed-income trader's repertoire. Long-Term deepened its new alliance by selling Chase a $20 million investment in the fund.

But what Long-Term really wanted was a *partner*—a bank that would give it cash on demand when special needs (or even emergency needs) arose. In the partners' endless negotiations with Merrill, Bear, and now Chase, they seemed to be looking for a firm that would support them as resolutely as Salomon had. Pflug was sympathetic and arranged for a $500 million revolving loan from a large syndicate of banks—in other words, a standby facility that Long-Term could tap as needed. The bank syndicate demonstrated unusual faith in the hedge fund by agreeing to fund the revolver without the fund's having to put up any collateral.

Then, with the revolver in its pocket, Long-Term turned up the heat on Chase. Various of the partners began to push the bank to sell them a peculiar warrant. Of course, this was the same warrant they had sought, without success, from Merrill. A warrant is an option; the partners wanted a warrant on their own fund to add a layer of personal leverage to the enormous leverage already in the portfolio. Even though they had virtually all of their personal assets in the fund, the partners, especially Hilibrand, were hot for more exposure. They suffered from a curious blind spot; though they fought like tigers for a clearing agreement that would protect them during a crisis, when it came to investing their own capital, they seemed not to consider the possibility of failing.

The warrant would have exposed Chase to untenable risks. Under Scholes's plan, the partners would pay the bank about $15 million a year, give or take, depending on interest rates. In return, Chase would pay the partners whatever they would have earned on a $200 million slice of the fund. For relative peanuts, Chase would be committing to a huge potential liability if the fund continued to skyrocket. In theory, Chase could hedge its risk by buying some of the fund for itself.

Then, if the value of the fund rose, Chase would make a profit on *its* investment.

But what if the fund fell? According to options theory, which Merton and Scholes had of course devised, as the value of the fund decreased, Chase would need less of a hedge. In other words, if Long-Term fell, Chase would want to gradually sell assets that mimicked those in the fund.

But that would not be so easy, because Long-Term's assets were secret. And the partners pointedly refused to disclose them. Pflug was stunned by Long-Term's arrogance: the partners wanted Chase to shoulder all of the risks in this dubious deal without divulging what the risks were. "How the hell are we supposed to hedge it?," Pflug wondered. The head of Chase's hedge fund practice was skeptical as well.

But Long-Term would not give up on the warrant. It was rich with tax sweeteners—always alluring to Hilibrand—because the partners could claim any profits from the warrant as capital gains and defer them until the warrant expired. The concoction was Scholes's finest hour—an option that would leverage the partners' interest at the expense of Uncle Sam.

Long-Term pitched the warrant scheme all over the bank; J.M. even took it to Walter Shipley, Chase's chief executive. Hilibrand finally offered to dispatch Scholes to give the bank a lesson on option pricing, but Pflug was too smart to go head-to-head with the guy who had invented the formula. "You can overintellectualize these Greek letters," Pflug reflected, referring to the alphas, betas, and gammas in the option trader's argot. "One Greek word that ought to be in there is *hubris*."

What hubris did Pflug divine? The partners were not arrogant in their mannerisms or even in their speech; it was more deep-seated. It was the arrogance of people who had been to Harvard and MIT—of people who really believed that they were more intelligent than others. "Do you know why we make so much money?" Greg Hawkins once asked an old friend from Salomon. "It's because we're smarter." Once the Hawk even tried to lecture a colleague's wife about molecular biology, her longtime specialty. "You're full of shit," she finally replied.

■

By 1996, Long-Term had grown to well over a hundred employees and the partners were building immense fortunes. All along, they had been deferring the 25 percent of the outside investors' profits that they took as fees, thus leaving the money in the fund, where, untouched by the tax man, it could compound all the faster. As their third year drew to a close, the partners collectively had a stake in the fund of $1.4 billion, nine times their initial $150 million investment. It was an incredible fortune to have made in so little time—and all from bond spreads! The partners' nervy decision to keep redoubling their bets had vaulted them into the ranks of the superrich overnight. Unlike corporate titans, who hedged their bets by continually peeling off shares, J.M., Hilibrand, Rosenfeld, and the rest left every nickel on the table. When they needed spending money, they simply redeemed a bit of the fund, which they treated like a personal checking account.

By the standards of Wall Street moguls, most of the partners were not lavish spenders, and they frowned on ostentation. They kidded the free-spending Hawkins for flying in decorators to his country home in Saratoga, near the track where Hawkins kept thoroughbreds. When Hawk suggested they buy a company jet, the others wouldn't hear of it. But each of them had their moments. J.M. had his horses and memberships in three tony golf clubs—Winged Foot and Shinnecock in New York State and Cypress Point in California—in addition to Waterville.[11] He also had a taste for pricey automobiles, including a Ferrari Testa Rossa. Rosenfeld, who lived in a spacious waterfront home in Westchester, indulged a passion for wine. He had a photographic memory for vintages and stocked his ten-thousand-bottle cellar directly from France. As if to add a twinkle to his soft-spoken demeanor, the former professor scarcely went visiting without toting along one of his cherished Clos de Vougeots or other choice Burgundies. For Hilibrand, the money meant added seclusion. He bought a fifteen-acre, $2.1 million plot in a wooded private community in Greenwich and was spending $4 million to build a lavish thirty-thousand-square-foot house.[12] But even such indulgences could hardly make a dent in the partners' bank accounts. The pursuit of money may have been central to their lives, but as is often the case, it went far beyond any conceivable lifestyle needs. The money was a scorecard, a proof of their superlative trading skills. For Merton and Scholes, it added a worldly validation to their academic successes.

Fights over shares were common; as at Salomon Brothers, compensation was the natural turf for venting internal tensions. The casual air at Steamboat Road was deceptive, for it masked latent tensions that emerged every time issues of control, shares, or big portfolio moves surfaced. The fiery Scholes, who was eager to edge his way up the ladder, was prickly with Mullins, each academic thinking he was smarter than the other. Hawkins, an easygoing southerner, deeply resented the secretive, domineering Hilibrand. Even Rosenfeld, who was in charge of operational details, came under subtle pressure from Meriwether, who would periodically grouse, "Eric has got to find a way to make some money," as if running the firm wasn't enough.

The arbitrageurs were blind to the value of contributions that didn't drop straight to the bottom line; only financial points counted. Perhaps this was one reason they were so intent, well after they had any need, on maximizing their personal net worths. They simply wouldn't give up on Scholes's warrant idea, the main point of which was to leverage their personal fortunes. And the warrant became an obsession with them.

Just as the partners had browbeaten Merrill, Bear, and Chase, they began to lobby Union Bank of Switzerland for the warrant. It was a curious choice, because UBS had already snubbed Long-Term twice. UBS had declined to invest in the hedge fund in 1994, when the fund was taking off. A little later, J.M. and Haghani had gone calling again, hoping to enlist UBS for bond and swap trading. But UBS feared the leverage in such trades and once again declined.

However, Long-Term continued to press the Zurich-based bank. What's more, the hedge fund had a key ally within UBS, a Brooklyn native and former Salomon salesman named Ron Tannenbaum. Affable and rugged-looking, Tannenbaum had joined Salomon in New York a year after Hilibrand. He had later moved to Tokyo, where he had been a sort of local distribution agent for the Arbitrage Group. Then he had transferred to London, where he had seen a lot of Meriwether. At first, Tannenbaum had been intimidated by J.M. and probably awed by J.M.'s traders. But over the years, Tannenbaum became the group's friend and steadfast admirer.

At UBS, Tannenbaum covered hedge funds. He kept urging his bosses to give the boys from Greenwich a chance. Meanwhile, the bank was going through unsettling changes. Long the premier bank in Switzerland, UBS had epitomized the country's tradition-bound banking establishment. Steeped in Swiss culture, it recruited gnomelike bankers from the national army rather than from MIT and offered each vice president a choice of three polished woods— mahogany, walnut, or pine—to panel his office with.[13] The complacent bank had been startled to discover that international finance no longer moved at such a leisurely, Alpine pace. It had been shocked when Swiss Bank, a rival much quicker to modernize and, in particular, to embrace derivatives, had overtaken UBS. By the mid-1990s, UBS had begun to fight back, hiring a slew of aggressive traders. Mathis Cabiallavetta, a debonair prince of Swiss banking who had risen to chief executive, gave his gunslinger traders free rein in a desperate bid to regain UBS's perch at the top. With the bank eager to grow, in September 1995, Tannenbaum persuaded the board to approve Long-Term as a counterparty. The bank also hired a Malaysian-born trader from Merrill, T. J. Lim, and gave him marching orders to gin up its derivative business. Thus, by 1996, the stage was set for Long-Term to finally gain a foothold in the Alps.

Overnight, the hedge fund became UBS's biggest account, netting the bank $15 million in revenue in its first year.[14] But as always with Long-Term, the business was low margin—typically half of 1 percent. On one trade involving Japanese equities, Long-Term shaved the margin to 22.5 basis points, less than one quarter of a percent. Ramy Goldstein, UBS's freewheeling head of equity derivatives, took the low-margin trade under protest. "Ronnie, they're not customers, they're *competitors!*," Goldstein, a silver-haired former Israeli paratrooper with a doctorate from Yale University, exclaimed to Tannenbaum. "Lose my number," he added. "I don't want to do more LTCM deals!"

But UBS's LTCM deals had only begun. With controls at UBS growing ever looser, the bank began to swing for the fences. In fact, the charismatic Goldstein, who had a cowboy's thirst for adventure, led the way, pursuing a raft of risky stock-option trades. Meanwhile, Tannenbaum began to think about elevating the Long-Term relationship to higher-margin products. UBS started assisting Long-Term on tax-related proposals, which reunited Tannenbaum with a good friend from his Salomon days: Myron Scholes.

With Long-Term showing such sexy profits, UBS was regretting its earlier failure to invest. "God, that's the biggest mistake we ever made," moaned Hans-Peter Bauer, head of fixed-income, currency, and derivatives, who had rejected Long-Term before. Long-Term had stopped taking new money, so the window for investors apparently was closed. Indeed, wealthy Swiss were paying 10 percent premiums to buy out old investors. But in July 1996, knowing that Tannenbaum was tight with the boys from Greenwich. Bauer asked the salesman to see if his friends might, perchance, let the bank invest.

Long-Term was now getting *very* interested in UBS, and turned the charm on in its eager salesman. The fund broke with its no-new-money stance and offered Tannenbaum a slice of the fund for himself, personally, though UBS wouldn't let him accept it. At the time, Long-Term was thinking of forming a splinter fund—LTCM-X, it was dubbed—to invest in especially high risk trades and also to focus on Latin America. The frustrated Scholes saw LTCM-X as a way to get out from under Hilibrand's control, which he increasingly resented. With LTCM-X in mind, the firm offered a partnership to Roberto Mendoza, a Harvard-educated vice chairman at J. P. Morgan and the son of a former Cuban ambassador to Great Britain. With these plans percolating along, Scholes dangled before Tannenbaum the prospect of working for LTCM-X—presumably part of an effort to ingratiate Long-Term with Tannenbaum's employer. In October, Scholes offered the ultimate carrot, telling Tannenbaum that the fund would agree to let UBS make a large investment in the fund—*if* the bank also agreed to write a warrant on the fund for the Long-Term partners.

In the fall, Cabiallavetta, the bank chairman, and Goldstein paid a call on the partners in Greenwich. By now, the UBS brass, though eager to cement the tie to Long-Term, had started to worry that Tannenbaum might be getting a little too cozy with his account. "We aren't sure if Ronnie is our man or yours," one of them noted. J.M. brushed off their concern, saying, "Ron's a good man."

The partners treated Cabiallavetta like a long-lost cousin. Almost all the partners attended the meeting, except for Merton, who was at Harvard, and Haghani, who, though in from London, was dashing in and out of J.M.'s office to handle some emergency. When Cabiallavetta asked about the outlook for European monetary integration, J.M. had Mullins give a little lecture, which impressed the Swiss. Only Long-Term had a resident central banker. Little was said at the meeting about the warrant, but Tannenbaum spent November writing a proposal to show to his superiors. The basic pitch was right out of the Black-Scholes model. The key determinant in the option-pricing formula is volatility. And Long-Term had been exceptionally steady. In fact, 1996 had been its steadiest year yet. Thus, a Black-

Scholes trader would be willing to write a call option on the fund for a relatively small premium. Sportingly, Scholes had offered a premium that was somewhat higher. In other words, *under the assumption that Long-Term's results would remain steady,* UBS could book an immediate $25 million profit. Goldstein was aghast. "Ronnie, we could lose multiples of that!" he protested. The deal hinged on the Achilles' heel of Black-Scholes: the assumption that volatility is a constant. If Long-Term should encounter a skittish patch over the warrant's seven-year life, UBS could face a massive loss.

Tannenbaum wrote a masterly sales report. He portrayed the benefits of the warrant largely in relational terms, citing what UBS would gain from being Long-Term's partner, from seeing its trading flow, and so forth. "The Principals of LTCM will help accelerate UBS' learning process in portfolio management, risk management, and dynamic capital allocation," the salesman wrote. Presuming Tannenbaum believed that, he was the only one left on Wall Street who did. But then, he had nourished a wish to be part of the Long-Term gang for a decade. He was still fond of recalling how he had started out with Hilibrand, "the biggest brain in the business." Of course, Tannenbaum was only a salesman and scarcely had authority to approve major deals. But by year-end, although nothing had been signed, Scholes's warrant was getting a hearing from UBS senior traders and managers.

The fund earned 57 percent in 1996 (41 percent after the partners' fees) thanks to leveraged spread trades on Japanese convertibles, junk bonds, interest rate swaps, and—again—Italian bonds. Also, when French bonds began to trade above German bonds (implying, curiously, that France bore less inflation risk than Germany), the partners cleverly, and successfully, bet on Germany to make a relative comeback. Their total profits in 1996 were an astounding $2.1 billion.[15] To put this number into perspective, this small band of traders, analysts, and researchers, unknown to the general public and employed in the most arcane and esoteric of businesses, earned more that year than McDonald's did selling hamburgers all over the world, more than Merrill Lynch, Disney, Xerox, American Express, Sears, Nike, Lucent, or Gillette—among the best-run companies and best-known brands in American business.

And they had done it with stunningly little volatility. Not once in 1996 did Long-Term suffer a monthly loss of 1 percent.[16] To Hilibrand, Haghani, and Hawkins, the results proved convincingly that diversification worked. The fund's diverse trades were blending with symphonic perfection, like the independent dice or the random cards from a model by Merton.[17] "We can't get the risk [read: volatility] high enough," the traders told a friend, as if awed by their own doctrine. "We're seeing the power of diversification."

Only Meriwether, who had lived through more ups and downs than his partners, was circumspect. At a year-end luncheon in London, Costas Kaplanis, one of J.M.'s old traders from Salomon Brothers, tipped his hat to Long-Term's spectacular first three years, but J.M. refused to accept congratulations. He humbly replied that one would need at least six years of results to say for sure that Long-Term's formula was working. Perhaps he sensed that the partners had enjoyed some luck—an unusual stretch of balmy weather. As if to batten down the hatches, Long-Term asked its investors—now about a hundred in number—to agree to stagger the dates on which they could take out money in the future. People who did not agree could take their money home (none did). This gave Long-Term added protection should its investors ever want to withdraw en masse.

In fact, money was pouring into the arbitrage business via rival banks and competitor funds—an added reason for J.M.'s dour mood. This new money, he knew, was forcing spreads tighter—indeed, it was one reason for Long-Term's recent profits. But it would make new opportunities tougher to find.

Writing to investors just before the year closed, J.M. was the model of prudence. Long-Term's results reflected "greater than expected convergence in a number of important strategies," he noted. As a result, "1996 net returns to date have substantially exceeded the expectations of the Management Company as of the beginning of the year."

This did not augur well. Since spreads on Long-Term's existing trades had already narrowed, such trades offered less potential for profit in the future. Moreover, the fund had not been able to find new trades quickly enough to keep pace with the growth in its capital. Rather humbly, J.M. all but predicted that the rocket would return to earth: "Our current, but necessarily imprecise, judgment is that the net return for 1997 is likely to be materially below the 1996 return, although actual results may be considerably above or below our expectations including potential for loss."[18]

6

A NOBEL PRIZE

*Despite its scientific pretensions, economics still remains
more of an art than a science.*
—ROBERT KUTTNER

WHETHER LONG-TERM wanted to admit it or not, the secret of
bond arbitrage was out. By the late 1990s, almost every investment bank on Wall Street had, to some degree, gotten into the
game. Most had separate arbitrage desks, with traders specifically assigned to look for opportunities in every nook and cranny of the business. Lured by the scent of the fantastic profits being earned in
Greenwich, other banks were reaching for the same nickels as Long-
Term. Inevitably, they whittled away the very spreads that had attracted them; thus do free markets punish success. Long-Term had
always been dogged by imitators, but now the imitators were piling
on faster than ever. No sooner did a spread open up than rival traders
plugged it. "Everyone else was catching up to us," Rosenfeld complained. "We'd go to put on a trade, but when we started to nibble,
the opportunity would vanish."[1]

Characteristically, Meriwether encouraged the firm to explore new
territory. Even at Salomon, the troops had always sought to extend
their turf. Hadn't they moved from swap spreads to mortgage-backed
securities? Hadn't they branched into junk bonds and European
debt? In retrospect, such moves had been baby steps, not bold new

departures. But the partners' experience—to them, at least—seemed to belie the adage that it is dangerous to try to transport success to unfamiliar ground. Trusting their models, they simply rebooted their computers in virgin terrain.

By 1997, the plans for the high-risk splinter company, LTCM-X, had faded. (Mendoza, the Morgan official, had decided not to accept Long-Term's offer of a partnership.) Instead, the partners were toying with ways of broadening the mother fund, even of going beyond public markets. From Long-Term's point of view, the trouble with the securities business was its inherent accessibility. Anybody could buy a bond or mimic someone who did. The partners' reclusive style ill fitted the rough democracy of markets. They were increasingly intrigued with the idea of making less liquid, more permanent investments in financial businesses, beyond the reach of hated copycats.

Merton was exploring a joint venture with Banca Nazionale del Lavoro, an Italian bank with a big money management operation, to peddle mutual funds to retail investors. The idea was to combine BNL's institutional clout with Long-Term's academic pedigree and offer a product to the everyday *signore*. Merton, with his naive belief in perfect markets, was pushing the notion of "optimum portfolios" for the little man. Giovannini, Long-Term's resident Italian, was deputized to coordinate the effort, and Gennotte was dispatched to Rome, where he took up temporary residence to work out details with BNL. Meanwhile, J. P. Morgan was urging Long-Term to diversify further. Morgan executives felt that the partners should "leverage" their intellect—in effect, apply their brains and methodology to businesses outside the normal scope of hedge funds. Quietly, the partners began to explore setting up an insurance operation.

While such grand ventures were progressing slowly, Long-Term was under immediate pressure to park its capital *somewhere*. By 1997, it had more than $5 billion in equity. If Long-Term was to sustain its splendid rate of return, that capital would have to be invested. But Long-Term's computers were failing to find opportunities. In one new foray, Long-Term boldly crashed the market for securities backed by *commercial* mortgages—wholly different from the market for IOs and POs, which, of course, were backed by familiar home mortgages. Long-Term's appetite was so stunningly large that it transformed the commercial market, which soared from $30 billion of new issues a year to $60 billion almost overnight. Hilibrand made no pretense of having expertise in commercial real estate; predictably, he felt the firm could find an edge in financing. "They could earn the carry [the spread] with very little risk," a mortgage banker recalled. "The spread was thin, but Long-Term had a *huge* ability to leverage." This was the firm's standard formula; the partners were determined to drag their cookie cutter wherever they could.

But commercial mortgages were relatively small potatoes. Equities—that is, traded stocks—loomed as a far larger and more tantalizing new frontier. It was an open frontier because most traders with Long-Term's mathematical bent had naturally left equities alone. Although pricing a bond can largely be reduced to math, valuing a stock is far more subjective. Wall Street (and academe) had devised many a formula to forecast the market, but none, no matter how esoteric or rigorous, had worked. Over the short run, stocks are subject to the whim of often emotional traders. Over the long run, they vary with business performance, which is subject to great uncertainty and is notoriously hard to forecast. It requires judgment—not merely math—of the sort that no computer has ever mastered. As the economist Burton Malkiel once observed, "God Almighty does not know the proper price-earning multiple for a common stock."[2] But Long-Term Capital did know—or at least, it boldly reckoned that it could transport its models to equities.

Haghani had been researching equities, particularly in Europe, and he thought the field was ripe for a firm with the necessary quantitative skills but—importantly—without the need to get enmeshed in the messy details of specific-stock analysis. Rosenfeld, too, had been thinking about equity arbitrage since his days at Salomon. One attractive point was that equity arbitrage would (he supposed) be *uncorrelated* with bond arbitrage. Ever Merton's disciple, Rosenfeld wanted *random* investment dice, and it was hard to imagine that the spreads between stocks would widen at the same moment as the spreads between mortgages or the spreads between European bonds.[3] Equities seemed of a different world. By definition, this would not be a small extension of the business but a radical, risky experiment.

Haghani focused his research on so-called paired shares. Various European stocks were doubly listed. Volkswagen, for instance, listed a "preference" share and an ordinary share, the latter with superior voting rights. BMW was another. Haghani also looked at pairs of stocks with related (but not identical) assets, such as Telecom Italia, the Italian phone company, and Telecom Italia Mobile, its subsidiary, or Louis Vuitton and Dior. For various reasons, one side of a given pair often traded at a discount to its partner. Hence, Haghani spotted the potential for arbitrage. David Modest, yet another MIT-trained economist, did the modeling on equity trades. But Haghani ran the show. "Modest did what Victor told him," one insider noted. "Victor said, 'Go short this,' and Modest would work out how to do it."

The paired-share trades weren't perfect arbitrages, because the two sides of each trade were never precisely equivalent. An ordinary share of Volkswagen was *worth* a premium over a preference share, especially as, in Germany and elsewhere in Europe, managements did not feel the same obligation as in the United States to treat all stockholders fairly. No one could say precisely what the "right" premium was, only that the 40 percent premium in VW's case, for example, seemed excessive. But the spread could persist or even widen—the models be damned. Given such uncertainties, most players limited paired-share trades to moderate size. But with its coffers burgeoning, Long-Term was developing a sense of proportion all its own; like a man who pays for dinner with hundred-dollar bills and never asks for change, it had lost the habit of moderation.

Haghani and Modest found about fifteen paired-share trades, and Haghani bet on them in staggering size. His favorite was Royal Dutch/Shell, the huge Anglo-Dutch oil consortium. Royal Dutch/Shell was owned by two listed companies, Royal Dutch Petroleum of the Netherlands and Shell Transport of England. Although Royal Dutch and Shell got their income from the same source—that is, from dividends on Royal Dutch/Shell—the English firm had historically traded at an 8 percent or so discount to its Dutch cousin. The stocks were owned by distinct pools of investors, and the Dutch stock was typically more liquid. But there was no good reason for the price differential. With Europe becoming a single economic unit, Haghani reckoned that national differences would matter less and less, and the spread between Royal Dutch and Shell would contract. This was a popular view.

But the size of Haghani's position was stunning. Long-Term bet $2.3 billion—half of it long on Shell, the other half short on Royal Dutch—without, of course, any assurance that the spread would contract. In practical terms, a position that large was totally illiquid.

Contrary to common supposition, there is nothing wrong with being illiquid—unless you are vulnerable to being forced to sell in a hurry. But Long-Term, being highly leveraged, was in that very spot—for, as we have seen, leveraged investors can accumulate losses with terrifying speed. Ignoring this oft-proven verity, Haghani struck a gargantuan trade with borrowed money. He was under stress due to the ill health of his father, who died later that year, and he felt pressure due to the deteriorating landscape in bond arbitrage. Still, there is no explaining the size of the Royal Dutch/Shell trade, other than to accept that Haghani was beginning to believe in his own invincibility. "It was ridiculously big," said an executive at a Wall Street bank. Goldman Sachs had the same trade on. They believed it was a good trade. But Long-Term's trade was ten times the size of Goldman's.

On the American side of the Atlantic, Hilibrand also was busy in equities. As early as 1995, Long-Term had started to dabble in merger arbitrage, also known as "risk arbitrage," or betting that announced acquisitions would actually close. In 1995, when Westinghouse agreed to buy CBS, for example, the price of CBS vaulted 20 percent, to $78 a share. But that price was still below the deal price of $82 a share. Thus, anyone who bought CBS after the announcement stood to make a 5 percent profit—if the deal closed. Of course, if the merger fell through, the stock could give back the entire 20 percent gain. And many mergers do fall through.

Since any number of events can sabotage a deal, merger arbitrageurs have to be canny jacks-of-all-trades—knowledgeable about the companies, their industries, the financing, antitrust and other regulatory issues, and the condition of markets in general. Because of the range of experience required, a small group of specialists does nothing *but* merger deals. The best of them are highly selective; their skill resides in being able to choose the very few deals that are most likely to close. Long-Term's approach was altogether different. Since its professors claimed no expertise in individual stocks—indeed, they assumed that the future course of stocks was random—the fund made no attempt to pick the winners. It simply bought a market basket, or virtually every deal stock that it deemed a safe bet.

The partners debated hiring a risk-arbitrage specialist but didn't. Meanwhile, Hilibrand bought deal stock after deal stock. And he confidently bought them in very big size, despite the growing discomfort of a half dozen of his partners. Scholes and Merton argued that merger arbitrage—particularly on such a scale—was excessively risky for the obvious reason that Long-Term was playing in a field in which it had absolutely no expertise. Meriwether and his traders knew the bond world inside out. In merger arbitrage, J.M. had no edge; indeed, it was Long-Term's rivals who had the advantage.

Within Long-Term, the debate over merger arbitrage was fierce. Meriwether ran the debate like a seminar, tolerating all points of view. In a sense, this was a mistake: J.M. never put his foot down. After such a long and fruitful partnership, he was disinclined to intervene against his two enfant terrible traders, Hilibrand and Haghani. J.M.'s personal loyalties weighed on portfolio considerations, a serious flaw in a risk manager.

"This trade was by far the most controversial in our partnership," Eric Rosenfeld admitted. "A lot of people felt we shouldn't be in the risk arb business because it is so information sensitive and we weren't trying to trade in an information-sensitive way."[4]

The firm would most likely have steered clear of risk arbitrage had the generally popular Rosenfeld opposed the trade (Meriwether, in particular, rarely made a decision without consulting his trusted protégé). However, Rosenfeld, too, tended to side with Hilibrand and Haghani, and the others finally went along.

Veteran arbs quickly realized that somebody new had entered the game and that the somebody was both very big and indiscriminate— or, as Rosenfeld put it, not "information sensitive." By buying in such volume, Long-Term was boosting deal stocks across the board, squeezing spreads to unprofitable levels. As usual, Long-Term was content to earn relatively tiny spreads because it intended to multiply its returns with leverage. Still, one marvels at Long-Term's audacity, sauntering into a corner of Wall Street—one in which savvy veterans had been working for years—and rewriting the economics of the field overnight. Long-Term was the gorilla that announces the rules wherever it goes.

One night, Hilibrand, J.M., and Mullins had dinner with Daniel Tisch, a prominent risk arbitrageur. Tisch, son of the investor Larry Tisch, had the impression that Long-Term was thinking about the business solely in mathematical terms. Indeed, Hilibrand expressed every financial puzzle in terms of a spread. In risk arb, spreads were roughly 4 percent to 10 percent, much greater than bond spreads. "Our business looks very attractive next to their business, where they trade to make a couple of basis points," Tisch noted. "The only trouble is, if you're wrong on a government bond the spread may change by a half a point. If you're wrong on risk arb, you can lose half your position." In short, the reason that deal spreads were so much wider than bond spreads was that you could lose a lot more money on merger arbitrage. Tisch left feeling that Long-Term didn't know what it was doing. It was both inexperienced and highly leveraged—a potentially explosive combination. Terence Sullivan, the Long-Term investor from Shaker Heights, heard of its risk-arb involvement through the grapevine and was shocked that the fund was straying so far from its ken.

Apart from CBS, Long-Term's biggest position was MCI Communications, which in 1996 agreed to be acquired by British Telecommunications. Both CBS and MCI had to clear regulatory thickets, and each deal dragged on for longer than expected. In the case of CBS, Long-Term continued to snap up shares even when CBS stock had inched to within 62 cents of the deal price. Long-Term's leverage on the trade was 20 to 1—without its having any specialized knowledge of the merger. "You're picking up nickels in front of bulldozers," a friendly money manager warned Rosenfeld, alluding to the risk that one deal or another would collapse. Eventually the CBS merger was completed, which only emboldened Long-Term to do more such trades. Its portfolio would grow to thirty deals.

Readers may be excused for wondering how Long-Term could borrow so much toward the purchase of stocks. The Federal Reserve Board, under a statutory provision known as "Regulation T," sets a limit on broker loans for stocks, also known as "margin." For the past twenty-five years, the Fed has set the maximum margin loan at 50 percent of the total investment.

When Long-Term purchased stocks, it of course was subject to Reg T. But for the most part, Long-Term built its equity positions *without buying actual securities*. Rather, the fund entered into derivative contracts that mimicked the *behavior* of stocks. If, for instance, Long-Term wanted to earn the return on $100 million of CBS stock over a three-year period, it would strike a "swap" contract with, say, Swiss Bank. Long-Term would agree to make a fixed annual payment, calculated as an interest rate on $100 million. And Swiss Bank would agree to pay Long-Term whatever profit would have been earned had Long-Term actually purchased the stock. (If the stock fell, Long-Term would pay Swiss Bank.) Most likely, Swiss Bank would hedge its risk by buying actual shares. But that was no concern of Long-Term's.

What mattered to J.M. and company was that they could make a huge investment in CBS *with no money down* and without having to make all of the usual disclosures. And despite Reg T, it was perfectly legal. The Fed, after all, merely restricted loans toward the *purchase* of stocks. Long-Term wasn't purchasing anything; it was making side bets on the *direction* of stocks—which amounted to the same thing.

The Street had been using equity swaps to get around Reg T for about a decade, but in recent years the scale of the business had soared. Moreover, banks had become increasingly blunt about helping firms skirt the margin rules. Derivatives had not started out this way; in fact, the premise behind them had been innocuous. Investment bankers in the late 1970s and early 1980s had had the idea that simple agreements—contracts, derivatives, call them what you like— would be a more efficient way of transferring risk than actually buying and selling assets. For example, in the prederivative era, most families were stuck with fixed-rate mortgages. Even a homeowner who would have preferred to roll the dice (i.e., assume a little risk on future rates) had no practical way to act on his sentiments. The bank offered him, and everyone else, the same conventional fixed-rate loan. That was understandable, as the mortgage bank was also paying a fixed rate for its money. But by using derivatives (a favorite example of Merton's) the bank could convert a fixed-rate loan into a floating-rate one. The genius behind the idea is that, for every customer, there is always some other party with the opposite need. Perhaps a company planned to make annual borrowings for many years and would prefer the predictability of a fixed rate. If only a family that had a fixed-rate mortgage, and the company, which was facing varying borrowing costs, could swap loans! Thanks to derivatives, they could. (Not that they knew it; banks, naturally, acted as intermediaries.)

The first modern swap was engineered in 1981. IBM had bonds denominated in Swiss francs and German marks and wanted to convert this debt to dollars. David Swensen, a Yale Ph.D. newly arrived at Salomon, suggested that perhaps some other borrower could be persuaded to issue debt that, aside from being denominated in dollars, was identical to IBM's. One obvious choice was the World Bank, which had an appetite for holding debt in a variety of currencies. As an inducement to borrow, Salomon gave the bank a slightly lower-than-market interest rate. Then the two borrowers switched—IBM winding up with dollar debt, the World Bank with the foreign stuff—and voilà! the world of swaps was born.

The business grew—at first slowly, then exponentially. Soon, banks were swapping obligations for currencies, interest rate payments, equities, any future stream of cash that could be traded for another. In 1990, there were $2 trillion worth of interest rate swaps (just one type of derivative) outstanding. By 1997, the total had soared to $22 trillion.[5] One offshoot—largely unintended—of this tremendous growth was that banks' financial statements became increasingly obscure. Derivatives weren't disclosed in any way that was meaningful to outsiders. And as the volume of deals exploded, the banks' balance sheets revealed less and less of their total obligations. By the mid-1990s, the financial statements of even many midsized banks were wrapped in an impenetrable haze.

The bankers were too busy making money to bother about the risks or the shoddy disclosure in this fast-growing business. The few who did voice caution, such as Henry Kaufman, a noted economist who worked at Salomon in the 1980s, were ignored. Kaufman recalled:

> I still remember when Meriwether's group came in and we started doing interest-rate swaps. There was always a question of what type of limits we would set. It just kept mounting and mounting. After we had a billion it went to two billion. Then it went to five billion. There was never an analytical framework for saying how far we should go.

By 1995, when Meriwether's traders were happily ensconced at Long-Term, the group had a total derivative book worth $650 billion. Within two years, the total doubled, to an astounding $1.25 trillion. Given the opaque nature of Long-Term's (and everyone else's) disclosures, it was impossible to pinpoint the fund's derivative risks according to specific trades. And since many of its contracts were hedges that tended to cancel each other out, it was impossible to calculate Long-Term's true economic exposure. One could say only that it appeared to be growing very quickly—as were exposures up and down Wall Street. Almost imperceptibly, the Street had bought into a massive faith game, in which each bank had become knitted to its neighbor through a web of contractual obligations requiring little or no down payment.

Regulators became increasingly worried. By the mid-1990s, Wall Street had become accustomed to one or two derivative "shocks" a year. Banks or institutions considered healthy one day would go up in smoke the next due to hidden derivative exposures. One by one, Orange County, Bankers Trust, Barings Bank, Metallgesellschaft, Sumitomo Corp., and others revealed sudden and massive losses. As the list of individual traumas grew, regulators began to fret about the possibility of a shock to the entire *system:* pull on the right thread, and the entire ball of string would unravel, they feared. But was there such a thread, a firm so intertwined with Wall Street that its failure could undo the system? Such fears may have been unfocused, but they were not unreasonable. In the words of Nicholas Brady, the former Treasury secretary, "Every time there's been a fire, these guys [derivative traders] have been around it."[6]

As early as the spring of 1994, just when Long-Term was starting to trade, the New York Fed was becoming uneasy about hedge funds' easy access to credit, including derivative credit. In April, in a letter to the CEOs of every bank in the New York region, Chester Feldberg, executive vice president of the New York Fed, admonished the bankers not to eschew their historic duty to prudence. "Credit limits for customers are an *essential* tool for credit risk management," Feldberg warned.[7] Following up such concerns, Fed regulators met with managers at several large New York banks in 1997 to discuss the banks' relationships with hedge funds.[8] The Fed examiners urged the banks to step up their monitoring of hedge fund accounts but, surprisingly, reported that the banks were already improving their supervision.[9]

With regard to derivatives, the policy-making arm of the Fed took a laissez-faire approach—starting with Greenspan, who was enamored with the seamless artistry of the new financial tools. In public debates, Greenspan repeatedly joined forces with private bankers, led by Citicorp's John Reed, who were fighting tooth and nail to head off proposals for tougher disclosure requirements. Even as hedge funds increasingly used swaps to dodge the Fed's own margin rules,

Greenspan cast an approving eye. Incredibly, rather than trying to extend some form of margin rule to the derivative world, Greenspan proposed to eliminate the margin rules entirely. His 1995 testimony to Congress read like a banker's brief. At its heart was a beguilingly simple idea: that more trading (and hence more lending) was always and inherently good because it bolstered "liquidity."

> Removal of these financing constraints would promote the safety and soundness of broker-dealers by permitting more financing alternatives and hence more effective liquidity management. . . . In the case of broker-dealers, the Federal Reserve Board sees no public policy purpose in it being involved in overseeing their securities credit.[10]

A bit of liquidity greases the wheels of markets; what Greenspan overlooked is that with too much liquidity, the market is apt to skid off the tracks.[11] Too much trading encourages speculation, and no market, no matter how liquid, can accommodate all potential sellers when the day of reckoning comes. But Greenspan was hardly the first to be seduced by the notion that if only we had a little more "liquidity," we could prevent collapses forever.

Save for the Fed, the only ones who could restrain derivative lending were the banks. But Wall Street never polices itself in good times. The banks' own balance sheets were steadily ballooning; by the late 1990s, Wall Street was leveraged 25 to 1.[12] Awash with liquidity if not quite drowning in it, the banks *had* to find an outlet for their capital. The most tempting targets were hedge funds. "People were looking at the good side of the world," noted Steve Freidheim, a trader and hedge fund manager at Bankers Trust. "I could borrow any amount I wanted, and the rates kept coming down. I'd get calls from banks saying, 'Hey, we got another fifty million for you—we got a hundred million!'" As banks relentlessly chased the fund business, they silently relaxed their standards, marking down the risk of possible negative news. By 1996, Wall Street was trading $500 billion in repos and $200 billion in currency and interest rate swaps every day.[13]

No borrower had to account for its total exposure; no lender asked. Each bank knew the extent of its *own* exposure to an individual client, in particular to Long-Term. None bothered to think about whether the hedge fund might be similarly exposed to a dozen other banks. "You'd be doing big chunks of business with them," recalled Siciliano, the manager at Swiss Bank. "You'd assume you were their number one provider, but really you were number ten. You couldn't believe they were doing that much volume."

Swiss Bank had a subtle but powerful impact on Long-Term. Too sophisticated in derivatives to be easily impressed by the superstars in Greenwich, its history had paralleled Long-Term's. In 1977, when commodity traders had begun to apply the options formula that Merton and Scholes had invented, Edward and William O'Connor, two brothers who traded soybeans, had founded a new firm to invest in options. O'Connor & Associates became one of the savviest of the new derivatives firms. In 1986, the firm hired David Solo, a terse, precise-spoken electrical engineer from MIT and a brilliant quantitative trader. After the 1987 stock market crash, when options traders suffered massive losses, O'Connor realized it needed deeper pockets. Citicorp, Bankers Trust, and UBS all had a chance to acquire O'Connor but passed. Finally, in 1991, Swiss Bank bought it. This was a bold move. Swiss banks were cloistered bureaucracies in which only Swiss nationals could hope for employment and promotion. Of Switzerland's big three banks, Swiss Bank was the most traditional. Marcel Ospel, the head of Swiss Bank's international division, meant to change this. Though he had started as a sixteen-year-old apprentice, splitting his time between banking and school, Ospel had done a stint at Merrill Lynch and realized that Switzerland's banks would have to modernize or go the way of the cuckoo clock. He used O'Connor to shake up the parochial culture in Basel, injecting Yankee ideas such as an incentive system that rewarded traders for long-term performance. In 1995, Ospel engineered the purchase of S. G. Warburg, Britain's largest investment bank, and Swiss Bank was cloistered no more.

Too late, Cabiallavetta, Ospel's counterpart at the rival UBS, realized that Swiss Bank was building a powerhouse in derivatives that outclassed his own. Charismatic and loud where Ospel was quiet and shy, Cabiallavetta panicked and became desperate to overtake the upstart. He was especially keen on building the relationship with Long-Term, which he idealized as the perfect partner in derivatives. The best way to do that, he decided, was to approve Myron Scholes's warrant. At Swiss Bank, the warrant had been flatly rejected, but at UBS, it had percolated toward the highest echelons of the bank. Lim, the trader, and Bauer, the derivatives boss, who still regretted not having made an investment in Long-Term, had both embraced the warrant. Steven Schulman, the risk manager at UBS, had given it a favorable nod. So had Werner Bonadurer, who oversaw trading. That left it to Cabiallavetta. In June 1997, a hungry UBS agreed to sell Long-Term its long-sought warrant. In a companion part of the agreement, UBS, assuming a massive risk, became the single biggest investor in the fund.

The terms called for a group of the partners to pay UBS a premium of $289 million. In return, UBS promised to pay the partners any profits (more or less) that an investor with $800 million worth of Long-Term would make over the next seven years. As a hedge against this obligation, UBS bought an $800 million interest in the fund. Finally, as a sweetener, the bank was permitted to invest an additional $266 million in Long-Term. That was the "basic idea," according to Tannenbaum, the salesman: "If we wrote them calls on their own stock, they would let us invest a third again as much in the equity of the fund."

Tannenbaum's superiors regarded the warrant as a coup. UBS's managers were so ecstatic that they fought over which division of the bank should book the transaction. Bonadurer claimed it for the fixed-income division—an odd choice, except that Bonadurer and Cabiallavetta were close friends. Then, part of the deal was shifted to the bank's treasury department, which paid a 5 percent premium.[14] UBS's managers figured that eventually they could repackage their Long-Term investment and sell it to wealthy clients; in the meantime, they chortled about their new strategic relationship to Meriwether. Cabiallavetta toasted their alliance in Hong Kong, where he and J.M. were attending the annual meeting of the World Bank, always a hot attraction for international financiers.

At Long-Term, Hilibrand and Scholes stormily debated how big a share of the warrant would be allotted to each. Scholes had put his brains into it, but Hilibrand had the most money and, characteristically, wanted the lion's share. By switching the partners' prospective income to capital gains, the warrant would lower their tax rate, but the more significant motive seemed to be the hope of further gains. Assuming the fund rose, the warrant would work on their fortunes like rocket fuel. Of course, if the fund should falter, the partners would lose the $289 million. But there is nothing like success to blind one to the possibility of failure. At the very time when the outlets for their narrow skills were closing, the partners tossed off their innate caution, which had served them so well, like an old suit.

Many put their entire net worth into the fund. Mullins, the former Fed official, was an exception; he stuck to his characteristic banker's prudence and opted out of the warrant.[15] Otherwise, Siciliano noted, "These guys believed in what they were doing with every ounce of their being." The partners also forged a similar, though smaller, warrant deal with Crédit Suisse, another Swiss investment bank.

But even that was not enough. To leverage even further, LTCM, the partners' management company, borrowed a total of $100 million from a trio of banks—Chase, Fleet Bank, and Crédit Lyonnais of France—which money the partners plowed right back into the fund.[16] Their hunger to turn millions into billions knew no bounds, nor did it recognize any risks. For men who prided themselves on being disciples of reason, their drive to live on the edge seemed inexplicable, unless they believed that becoming the richest would certify them as also being the smartest.

As if to tempt the fates, Hilibrand personally borrowed $24 million *more* from Crédit Lyonnais, which set up a program to let the partners borrow against their interests in the fund. Hans Hufschmid, who specialized in currency trades, borrowed $15 million, and two other partners borrowed lesser amounts.[17] In addition, some of the partners had leveraged personally with Bear Stearns, their broker. Considering that the fund itself was so heavily leveraged, the partners, Hilibrand in particular, were dangerously adding leverage to leverage, as if coating a flammable tinderbox with kerosene. As opposed to a poor man who bets the limit on a single horse, the already rich Hilibrand had little to win and everything to lose.

The UBS warrant raised $1 billion of equity for Long-Term at the worst possible moment—when the fund was struggling to find places to invest the money it already had and when it was fighting off more and more competitors in arbitrage. In the first half of 1997, it earned only 13 percent before fees—still impressive, though well below its prior average. Its leverage (again, not counting derivatives) fell from 30 to 1 to 20 to 1, evidence that opportunities had grown scarce. A group of skeptical partners, including Scholes, were growing increasingly uncomfortable with the fund's portfolio.

One bright spot was Japan, where Long-Term was extremely profitable, thanks in part to David Modest, a graying, forty-three-year-old former scholar. Modest, Rosenfeld, and a young trader named Carl Huttenlocher devised a series of equity arbitrages to exploit the Japanese lack of familiarity with, and mispricing of, options. Long-Term's models made this an "obvious" and, indeed, highly lucrative trade. Modest, a droll theoretician from Berkeley, and a handful of others would work the graveyard shift, staying until 1 A.M., when the next day's Tokyo market finally closed. Shortly after, while Greenwich slept, a skeleton crew would arrive in time for the opening in London, where Japanese warrants traded. "We had a couple of traders like David [Modest] just killing themselves," Rosenfeld recalled. In June 1997, the traders were able to revert to normal hours, as Long-Term opened a Tokyo office. It was run by Chi-fu Huang, a prized MIT mathematician and expert in modeling whom Long-Term snatched away from Goldman Sachs, and Arjun Krishnamachar, a former swaps trader at Salomon.

J.M., who had been traveling to Japan for years, liked having an institutional presence there. For a Western hedge fund in Tokyo, Long-Term had remarkable cachet. Mullins, who had informally advised Japanese government officials when he had worked at the Fed, continued to do so at Long-Term. Wherever it operated, the fund's tentacles penetrated to the highest reaches. The partners' circle of contacts was a major asset.

Even in Japan, the partners pursued a controversial trade. In 1997, Japan's long bond was yielding only 2 percent, seemingly rock bottom. Long-Term placed a naked, unhedged bet that this rate would rise—a so-called directional trade in that it was betting on a single rate as distinct from a spread. Many of the partners had doubts about the trade, which for Long-Term was unusually speculative. But Hilibrand and Haghani were increasingly running the firm irrespective of the weaker partners' wishes. With the results so good, it was easy to dismiss the naysayers as worrywarts.

■

At Long-Term's 1997 annual meeting, in July, the partners admitted they were concerned about the shrinking spreads in bond arbitrage. The meeting had to be held outside the United States, so as not to jeopardize Long-Term's legal status as an offshore fund. It was hosted in a hotel by the Toronto airport so that the partners could jet in and out in a day. Only four of them (Leahy, Mullins, Rosenfeld, and Scholes) and about twenty-five investors attended. The mood was downbeat: spreads had converged more quickly than the partners had expected, squeezing potential profits. Though typically taciturn, Rosenfeld did reveal that Long-Term was getting involved in equity trades. The small crowd of investors suddenly livened. One investor demanded, "We hear you're the biggest player in risk arbitrage. Are you?" Rosenfeld responded evasively. The investors sensed that Long-Term was approaching a denouement. "Do you have any plan to return the money?" an investor asked. Again, Rosenfeld was vague. "Well, whatever you do, don't return mine," the investor said.

■

Coincident with the dour outlook for arbitrage, two prominent finance professors published a paper arguing that arbitrage was far riskier than its adherents claimed—the first shot at Long-Term's model fired from within academe. Writing in the prestigious *Journal of Finance*, Andrei Shleifer of Harvard and Robert W. Vishny of Chicago presciently warned that an arbitrage firm of Long-Term's type could be overwhelmed if "noise traders" (meaning uninformed speculators) pushed prices away from true value. With uncanny foresight, they predicted that, in such a case, arbitrageurs would "experience an adverse price shock" and be forced to liquidate at market lows.[18] Merton read an early version prior to publication but was not convinced; at a conference of scholars in Cambridge, he pooh-poohed the notion that markets could ever be overwhelmed.[19]

Then, in July, just weeks after the warrant deal, international markets were badly shaken. Thailand, beset by financial defaults, allowed its currency to float. It promptly fell 20 percent. The weakness spread to currencies in the Philippines, Malaysia, and South Korea. Responding to the sharp declines, Karim Abdel-Motaal, an emerging-markets guru at J. P. Morgan, declared, "We think the sell-offs have been exaggerated."[20] They continued anyway. Singapore's dollar came under heavy selling. Only Indonesia, by far the largest of the Asian "Tigers," seemed resistant. Then, on a single day, the rupiah fell 5 percent. In less than a month, pundits had stopped talking of Asia's miracle; now it was Asia's "crisis." Glass-walled skyscrapers erected during the boom were suddenly going vacant, and factories stood idle. Mahathir Mohamad, the prime minister of Malaysia, blamed "rogue speculators" from overseas, specifically George Soros, for selling the Tigers out.

Mahathir had some of the right culprits but the wrong crime. Foreigners could hardly be blamed for deserting a listing ship; their sin was having provided the too-easy short-term credit that had launched the ship at flank speed. Comforted by Treasury Secretary Robert Rubin's bailout of Mexico, Western banks and investors had shoveled money at Asia, fueling speculative investments and underwriting the region's corrupt behavior. Rubin had paved the way by urging Asian governments to lift controls on capital and thus to allow the money to pour in—despite the area's appalling lack of corporate disclosure and regulatory oversight. "The simple fact is that very sophisticated banks loaned to Indonesian companies, without any real knowledge of their financial condition," noted James Wolfensohn, president of the World Bank.[21]

Though Western investors had repeatedly made the same mistake—today romanticizing the developing world, tomorrow coming to rue their naïveté—the bankers never learned. In 1996, $93 billion of foreign capital had flooded Indonesia, Malaysia, the Philippines, South Korea, and Thailand even as their economies were slowing. Now that same money was draining out, unnerving markets around the world. From Long-Term's point of view, both Asia's uphill and downhill slopes were instructive. Easy credit, which hedge funds also enjoyed, had led to ill-advised and excessive investments. Then, when the tables had turned, Greenspan's much-vaunted liquidity was nowhere to be found, and the damage spread almost at random. Once a typhoon breaks loose in markets, there is no telling where it will go.

■

In late summer, the fund received a bit of bad news: the MCI merger was renegotiated at a lower price. MCI's stock price collapsed, and Long-Term lost $150 million overnight—the first sign that it had been fishing in dangerous waters. In Asia, where Long-Term's investments were primarily in Japan, the fund was weathering the storm. September, in fact, was one of Long-Term's best months: it earned $300 million.

But the firm's prospects were steadily dimming. When the partners returned from their annual golfing party in Waterville with Merrill Lynch, they announced a shocking diktat: outside investors in Long-

Term would have to take back about half of their money, just as the investor at the annual meeting had feared. "The fund has excess capital," Meriwether explained. The capital account was close to $7 billion, almost as much as at mighty Merrill Lynch. Accenting the positive, J.M. added, "This has occurred primarily because of a substantial increase in the capital base from the larger-than-expected, past realized rates of return, and high reinvestment rates elected by the fund's investors."[22]

Still, there was no getting around the harsher truth that spreads had narrowed and opportunities had diminished. With a common European currency now a fait accompli, the easy money on convergence in Europe had already been made. With borders disappearing, the spread between Italian and German bonds had shrunk from 2 percentage points to three quarters of a point in just six months.

Long-Term's plan was to return, at the end of 1997, all profits on money invested during 1994, its first year, and to return *all* money (principal and profits) invested after that date. It excluded the partners and employees and partially excluded some big strategic investors such as the Bank of Taiwan. Jimmy Cayne, chief executive of Bear Stearns, Long-Term's clearing broker, got an exception, too. Others demanded to stay in, but Long-Term turned them down. They were naturally angry that Meriwether and his boys, supposedly charged with watching out for their investors' interests, were giving themselves preferential treatment. "This is outrageous!" one investor thundered to Merrill Lynch. "We were there when they needed us."

The plan was controversial within Long-Term, too. Jim McEntee, J.M.'s friend, thought simple conservatism weighed in favor of not returning capital. Scholes and Merton, an inseparable pair, were strongly opposed to giving it back as well. They felt the firm was souring its franchise as a money manager. What's more, since the academics owned a bigger proportional share of LTCM, the management company, than they did of the portfolio, they had a personal interest in seeing the total of funds under management grow. On the other hand, Hilibrand and Haghani, who owned so much of the fund, didn't want to dilute their stakes by including outside owners. As usual, the latter two carried the day. Scholes was furious at Hilibrand, a control freak who gave little apparent thought to his partners.

In retrospect, the outside investors' pleas to stay in the fund would seem ironic, and the forced redemption of their money would come to seem a godsend. It was the partners who would suffer the most. But without the benefit of hindsight, the partners' obsessive pursuit of wealth carried more than a whiff of greed. Now that they had the scale to operate worldwide, they had no interest in managing money for others and largely froze them out. They added an unusually self-serving touch, tacking on fees, for the first time, to the bonus money invested by some of their own employees!

The partners justified the forced redemption as a sensible response to diminished prospects. Myron Scholes said it was ironic that Long-Term was giving money back at the same time that newcomers were piling into the field.[23] The implication was that Long-Term was prudently scaling back in the face of shrinking spreads. Yet the fund was not going to shrink by one iota. Returning capital only reduced the equity *supporting* its assets, which weren't, in fact, shrinking at all. Indeed, at a time when opportunities were drying up and the portfolio was bloated with 7,600 positions, the fund was defiantly and ill-advisedly leveraging itself further, like an Icarus chasing the sun.[24]

Moreover, by forcing outsiders to sell, the partners were, once again, increasing their personal leverage in the fund. The personal debt, on top of the leverage in the management company and the debt in the fund itself, made for three levels of debt precariously pyramided one atop the other.

Six days after Meriwether informed investors that they would have to take money back, the firm's cradle, Salomon Brothers, dropped a bombshell of its own. Salomon had never fully regained its footing after the Mozer scandal, the exit of Meriwether, and the defections of Rosenfeld, Haghani, Hawkins, and Hilibrand. It had tried to build its investment bank, but the bank hadn't been profitable. Now its arbitrage unit was facing the same pressures as Long-Term was. Earlier in the year, its executives had agreed that Salomon would need a significant infusion of capital or risk becoming a second-class firm.

Warren Buffett, who, through Berkshire Hathaway, was Salomon's biggest shareholder, was constitutionally opposed to investing more money in failing enterprises, which time and again he had equated with throwing good money after bad. Deryck Maughan, the chief executive of Salomon, made it clear that the only other option was to sell the company. "Warren wanted to sell so badly," a director of the company said.

But to whom? Maughan sounded out Chase, but the bank rebuffed him. Then he had lunch with Sanford I. Weill, chairman of Travelers, the insurer and parent of broker Smith Barney. Weill was one of the great second acts in American business. The son of a Brooklyn dress manufacturer, Weill had founded a humble four-man brokerage firm and, via mergers, stitched together the giant Shearson Lehman. Eventually, he had sold to American Express, lost out in a power struggle and resigned. Then, in the late 1980s and early '90s, he had done it again, getting control of a small credit company and using it to take over Smith Barney and also Travelers. He disliked arbitrage, which he considered too volatile, but he had dreams of building a premier investment bank, a rung above the ragtag brokerage business in Wall Street's social hierarchy. Perhaps Smith Barney and Salomon could put their two second-class banks together, Weill proposed.

After the lunch with Maughan, Weill called back to insist that *he* would have to be in charge if Travelers and Salomon merged. Buffett didn't care who ran the new company, he just wanted to sell the old one—at a good price, naturally. Weill offered $9 billion in stock, bailing the Omaha sage out of one of his most troubled investments. Ever diplomatic, Buffett praised Weill as a "genius" at building shareholder value.[25] Weill's underlings were aghast that he had paid so much for a second-rate firm, particularly one in which the primary source of profits was arbitrage, which the chairman detested. One house jester snickered, "Sandy spent nine billion dollars to get a piece of paper from Warren Buffett saying what a great investor he was. He was running around showing it to people like a kid in a candy store."

It is interesting to contrast Long-Term and its mother firm as each crossed a threshold. Meriwether had successfully overtaken his old employer in every way that counted. In capital, Long-Term boasted $7 billion to Salomon's $5 billion. In profits, the hedge fund had earned $2.1 billion in its last full year, compared with $900 million for the investment bank. Salomon still had a profitable arbitrage unit, but its attempt to build a broad bank had failed. Long-Term, while toying with the idea of diversifying, had remained focused, a smart decision thus far. But as both firms well knew, arbitrage was entering a tougher period. Their responses were 180 degrees apart. By merging Salomon with a more diversified partner, Buffett had diluted the Salomon shareholders' interests in arbitrage and in the rest of Salomon's business. Now they would own pieces of a much larger Travelers. Long-Term's partners had made the *exact opposite* decision: to a great extent, they had bought out their partners, thus redoubling their bets on arbitrage. The irony was that Buffett had converted a chronic loser into $9 billion while Long-Term's partners had converted a consistent winner into a giant—and still unrealized—bet on the future.

■

In October, the fund got a positive jolt: Merton and Scholes won the Nobel Memorial Prize in Economic Science. Merton, who was teaching a class at Harvard, got a three-minute ovation from his students. He humbly warned, however, "It's a wrong perception to believe that you can eliminate risk just because you can measure it."[26] Scholes, sitting for a celebrity profile with his hometown *Ottawa Citizen,* was brusquely reminded of how skeptical the outside world was of derivatives. The *Citizen* had the temerity to inquire, "How responsible do you feel for the 1987 stock market crash?" The stunned Nobel laureate sputtered, "Not at all. Not really at all. It's the same as asking [Alfred] Nobel if he is responsible for the First World War because he invented dynamite." Pressed, Scholes admitted that people trading on his theory— meaning dynamically hedging, or selling on the way down—had exacerbated the crash, though he blamed a lack of "liquidity," the familiar scapegoat. Always good at reducing high finance to everyday English, Scholes described Long-Term in refreshingly plain terms: "What we do is look around the world for investments that we think are, because of our models, undervalued or overvalued. And then we hedge out the risk of something we don't know, like a market factor."[27]

From their colleagues in academe, Merton and Scholes got effusive praise; the rule that six economists have seven opinions on every subject did not apply to the Black-Scholes theorem, which was hailed as a towering contribution to theory as well as practice. Gregg Jarrell, a Chicago School economist at the University of Rochester, called it "one of the most elegant and precise models that any of us has ever seen."[28] But was reality so precise? No matter. *The Economist* intoned, "What Mr. Merton and Mr. Scholes did, back in 1973, was to put a price on risk."[29] A writer in *The Wall Street Journal* found proof in the award of the newspaper's most cherished belief, succinctly opining, "The Royal Swedish Academy of Sciences has made a clear statement: Markets work."[30]

It was an odd time to express one's faith. All across Asia, currency and stock markets were imploding. One day the epicenter was Thailand, the next Malaysia, then Indonesia. On a single day, October 1, Indonesia's rupiah plunged 6.5 percent, the Malaysian ringgit fell 4.5 percent, the Philippine peso 2.2 percent. Two days later, the rupiah plunged 8.5 percent more. Though Asians had sown the seeds of their own crisis, no one was prepared for the market's brutality or for the random way in which the contagion spread. Even Latin American markets were pounded. In the age of the Internet, markets seemed connected by an invisible plasma linking the fate of bourses oceans apart. By late October, companies across Asia were defaulting, raising the specter of recession. Speculators then turned their guns on the Hong Kong dollar. The government, still under the British Crown, retaliated, raising overnight interest rates to a staggering 300 percent. The island's stock market gave up 23 percent in a week.

By now, U.S. investors, fearing that Asia's agony would trigger a global slowdown, were in full retreat. The Dow, which had reached a high of 8,300 during the summer, had fallen through most of October. On the Friday before Halloween, it fell more than 100 points, to 7,715. Then on Monday, October 27—yet another miserable Monday—Asia's flu finally landed at America's door. The day's losses began in Hong Kong, where the market fell 6 percent. As America awoke, the New York Stock Exchange was hit with heavy selling. It shut down twice, trying to forestall panic, but to no avail. Option writers, who had sold insurance against a market drop, were desperately selling stocks, similar to Black Monday a decade earlier.[31] Merton and Scholes's genie had escaped from the bottle again. As always, this chain-reaction selling—the dynamic hedging that Merton had envisioned in his model—made a bad day worse. The Dow fell a record 554 points, a drop of 7 percent. Around the world, from the United States to Asia to Europe to Latin America, markets lost an estimated $1.2 trillion, or 6 percent of their total value.[32] In a speech to the Brookings Institution just two days later, Nick Brady blamed the leverage implicit in derivative markets for worsening the damage:

I have heard all the arguments about how derivatives and dynamic hedging decreases transaction costs and increases the depth of markets. But certainly carried to extremes they are not worth what they cost. . . . Excess leverage's part in last week's sell-off is well worth a lot of thought.[33]

Long-Term Capital dodged the bullet again. The fund broke even in October and November, quite an accomplishment. Indeed, for Long-Term, Asia was an opportunity. With markets whipped up (more "volatile," as traders would say), Long-Term began to place hefty derivative bets that stock trading would settle down—or that the volatility of stocks would fall. This was risky stuff. Salomon had made this bet before October and had lost $110 million. But shorting volatility was the most natural of bets for Long-Term. In a sense, every one of its spread trades was a bet on lessened volatility. When markets are jumpy, the premium for safety is greater; when markets settle down, spreads tend to contract. "A lot of our trades were 'vol' trades," Rosenfeld noted.[34] In one form or another, the fund was always betting on calmer or more convergent markets.

UBS, Long-Term's new big investor, also had gambled on equity volatility, and that and other exotic trades were turning into a disaster for the bank. Rumors were circulating of massive losses in the derivatives unit, run (with total autonomy) by Goldstein, who had pocketed an $11.5 million bonus for 1996.[35] When toted up, UBS's losses in 1997 would reach $644 million. Among other bad trades, UBS lost heavily on Japanese convertibles, which Long-Term had understood better. Cabiallavetta, the bank's chief executive, had long protected Goldstein. Now he finally realized that his pet trader was destroying the bank. In November, Cabiallavetta fired Goldstein.

Then, in December, Cabiallavetta admitted that his bank was bereft of leadership and humbly struck a merger with the archrival Swiss Bank. Although Cabiallavetta would stay as chairman and the bank would keep the UBS name, Swiss Bank was clearly the winner. Basel filled most of the important jobs and imposed its more conservative culture on the gunslingers in Zurich. Ironically, by merging with its flamboyant rival, Swiss Bank had become a party to the Long-Term warrant that it previously had spurned.

■

In Stockholm, Merton and Scholes put up at the Grand, a sumptuous hotel with a curving staircase, overlooking the old city. At the Nobel banquet, a black-tie affair for 1,200, the laureates sat with a few friends and family members, the king and queen, various princes, and the queen's mother. Waiters and waitresses who had auditioned from all over Sweden served smoked fish on silver platters. The laureates were in a bubbly mood. Merton, as if to reassure himself that he was really there, kept inquiring of his guests, "Are you having a good time?" He gave a brief toast, expressing gratitude and also regret that Fischer Black hadn't lived to share the award.

Merton's lecture to the academy focused on the applications spawned by his option theory, ranging from adjustable-rate mortgages to student loan guarantees to flexible health care plans. " 'Option-like' structures were soon seen to be lurking everywhere," Merton asserted, though it seems unlikely that cause and effect were so direct. His own principal contribution, Merton noted—this being two months after the Dow's 554-point one-day spill—had been to show that "dynamic trading prescribed by Black and Scholes . . . would provide a perfect hedge in the limit of continuous trading."[36]

■

Despite the festive mood, both laureates were deeply concerned about Long-Term's future. Though Scholes confidently told Eugene Fama, his old adviser, that Long-Term Capital was safely making a thousand small bets, Scholes decided not to invest his half of the million-dollar Nobel bounty in the fund.[37] Ironically, the ivory-tower academics had a keener sense of the risks than the seasoned traders did. Scholes and Merton were both leading the good life. Scholes drove a white BMW; Merton, the car buff, sported a dark Jaguar. Scholes had rented a spacious home overlooking the water in Greenwich. Merton had dyed his hair red, left his wife, and moved into a snazzy pad in Boston. But their fortunes were relatively small, and neither felt as invulnerable as their multimillionaire partners did. As outsiders, not traders, they had a perspective not shared by Hilibrand. The laureates could see that the fund was moving away from its sphere of expertise and adding risk at the worst possible moment. Moreover, Merton was highly agitated about the fund's compensation structure, which was top-weighted toward Hilibrand and Haghani. As an options expert, he knew that the senior partners had an added incentive to shoot for the moon—a "moral hazard," as economists say. The hunger the traders had shown at Salomon to make as much as possible, no matter what the scale, was still alive and still disfiguring their relations with their partners. Krasker, the cautious modeler, was worried, too; he took money out of the fund at the end of 1997. Randy Hiller, who had been part of the group at

Salomon, ominously told a friend that he thought Long-Term was an accident waiting to happen.

At year-end, when Long-Term returned $2.7 billion to investors, its leverage ratio skyrocketed from 18 to 1 to 28 to 1 (as always, not including derivatives). Thus, though the firm's prospects looked bleaker than ever, the partners had raised their leverage back to the level prevailing during the business's salad days. With derivatives, it may have been even higher.

Long-Term managed to earn 25 percent (17 percent after fees) in 1997—its worst year yet but still a remarkable achievement, given the deteriorating market. The original investors got $1.82 back for each $1 they had put into the fund and still had their original dollar in. Thanks to their exorbitant fees and tax deferrals, the partners did even better—much better. Their capital soared 36 percent to an exalted $1.9 billion, some 40 percent of the fund's total of $4.7 billion. Now the partners were on the brink of amassing dynastic fortunes.

Though it was an odd time to be expanding, at the end of the year Long-Term moved into plush new headquarters. The site, overlooking a car wash, was pedestrian for Greenwich, but the office bespoke the firm's inflated self-image as a fixture among Wall Street banks. It had a large trading floor sporting three double rows of ergonomically adjustable desks and room to accommodate a planned expansion. It also had a three-thousand-square-foot gym with separate locker rooms for men and women and a full-time trainer. Two pool tables were ceremonially housed in a big room in the back. J.M. had a large office off to the side, and conference rooms and a library were slung around the perimeter. Like a miniversion of Salomon, the firm it had surpassed, Long-Term had a (quite large) data center as well as a backup generator under the building that supposedly could light all Greenwich for a day. But the partners cut back on the office Christmas party in deference to their modest year. The mood was noticeably subdued.

Mullins felt the firm had done a good job of heading off trouble in 1997. "We anticipated Asia—or had a strategy for it," he said.[38] But the professors had overlooked the larger truism of Asia: In times of trouble, markets become more closely linked, and seemingly unrelated assets rise and fall in tandem. They barely noticed a seemingly remote news item that moved over the wires just before Christmas: Standard & Poor's, the rating agency, had downgraded Russia's debt.

THE FALL OF
LONG-TERM
CAPITAL
MANAGEMENT

7

BANK OF VOLATILITY

Markets can remain irrational longer than you can remain solvent.
—JOHN MAYNARD KEYNES

EARLY IN 1998, Long-Term began to short large amounts of equity volatility. This simple trade, second nature to Rosenfeld and David Modest, would be indecipherable to 999 out of 1,000 Americans. But more than any other, "equity vol" was Long-Term's signature trade, and it set the fund ineluctably on the road to disaster. Equity vol comes straight from the Black-Scholes model. It is based on the assumption that the volatility of stocks is, over time, consistent. The stock market, for instance, typically varies by about 15 percent to 20 percent a year. Now and then, the market might be more volatile, but it will always revert to form—or so the mathematicians in Greenwich believed. It was guided by the unseen law of large numbers, which assured the world of a normal distribution of brown cows and spotted cows and quiet trading days and market crashes. For Long-Term's professors, with their supreme faith in markets, this was written in stone. It flowed from their Mertonian view of markets as efficient machines that spit out new prices with all the random logic of heat molecules dispersing through a cloud. And when the models told them that the markets were mispricing equity vol, they were willing to bet the firm on it.

■

There is no stock or security known as "equity vol," no direct way of making a wager on it. But there is an indirect way. Remember that, according to the Black-Scholes formula, the key element in pricing an option is the expected volatility of the underlying asset. As the asset gets jumpier, the price of the option rises. Therefore, if you knew the price of an option, you could infer the level of volatility the market was expecting.

An analogy may be helpful. There is no direct way to bet on the weather in Florida—but in certain seasons, the price of orange juice futures fluctuates according to the likelihood of a frost. Indeed, an experienced trader could infer, if the price of juice was unusually high, that the market was expecting a chilly winter and thus a scarcity of oranges. And if the trader believed that the market's weather forecast was wrong, he could try to profit on his opinion by shorting orange juice.

In a similar manner, Long-Term deduced that the options market was anticipating volatility in the stock market of roughly 20 percent. Long-Term viewed this as incorrect, because actual volatility was only about 15 percent. Thus, it figured that option prices would sooner or later fall. So Long-Term began to short options—specifically, options on the Standard & Poor's 500 stock index and on the equivalent indices on the major exchanges in Europe. In their own argot, the professors were "selling volatility."

The people on the other side of the option trade may not have realized it, but they, in turn, were buying volatility. Let's think about them for a moment. Typically, the buyers of options were equity investors who wanted insurance against a market decline. They were willing to pay a small premium against the risk of a crash. Long-Term, on the other side, collected the premium but was committed to paying out if the market swooned. In fact, it sold insurance (options) both ways—against a sharp downturn and against a sharp rise.

The buyers, not being as sophisticated as Long-Term, didn't know whether option prices were right or wrong, but, like a man with a beautiful beachfront home who fears a nasty hurricane season, they wanted insurance at whatever the going rate. With Asia still in turmoil and with stocks at nosebleed levels, investors were understandably jittery. One could scarcely pick up the paper but that some pundit was predicting the crash to end all crashes. So it was hardly surprising that people were paying more for protection, driving up the price of options. Institutions in Europe were capitalizing on people's fears by marketing equity products with downside protection—that is, equities that "couldn't" go down! To protect themselves in case stocks did fall, these institutions, too, were buying insurance, which in Long-Term's view was artificially inflating option prices.

If Long-Term was right—if the price of options was too high—then in effect it was charging a premium price for insurance, and over the life of its option contracts, which was five years, it should expect to come out ahead. Many other hedge funds were doing the same trade. These financial firms were providing market insurance to ordinary investors. This was not necessarily stupid. The funds were saying, "If people are willing to pay foolish prices for insurance, why shouldn't we sell it to them?"

But the trades were quite risky nonetheless. For one, forecasting the market's volatility is notoriously dicey—*unless you believe that the past is a reliable predictor of the future.* Who could predict when a crisis in Asia might develop—or how jittery markets would become if one did? Who could say how volatile the market "should" be? It was like forecasting a frost in Florida.

What's more, Long-Term could still lose money on the equity vol trade, even if it later turned out that its judgment about volatility had been correct. Since long-dated options don't trade on exchanges, Long-Term had to tailor private options contracts, which it sold to big banks such as J. P. Morgan, Salomon Brothers, Morgan Stanley, and Bankers Trust. The market for such arcane contracts was thin, with only a handful of players who traded on a "by appointment" basis. And the market was inherently imbalanced. Banks such as Morgan were eager to "buy" volatility from Long-Term, because the banks, in turn, were selling insurance to retail investors. In short, there was a natural pool of people and institutions on the buying side. That's why the price of volatility was often a bit higher than the mathematicians deemed was logical. But on the selling side, there were very few players. If no one came to sell or if equity investors suddenly became more desperate for insurance, the price of volatility could go even higher.

And Long-Term would have to settle up—paying or receiving monies according to how option prices moved—*every day.* It might be right on equity vol in the long run, but only if it could stand the pain in the short run. And over five years, the pain suffered on such a large trade could be considerable. On a given day, it was possible that *no one* would want to sell, in which case Morgan could mark up the asset to whatever higher price it decided was reasonable. Therefore, Long-Term wasn't betting only on the extent of ultimate realized volatility, it was betting on day-by-day *inferred* volatility, as determined by what other investors would pay for options. In effect, it was betting that these other, and presumably less rational, investors wouldn't bid up prices further. This was—so unlike the partners' credo—rank speculation. By putting themselves at the mercy of short-term fluctuations, the partners had abandoned whatever advantage lay in their precise mathematical models.

Long-Term shorted options at prices that implied a market volatility of 19 percent a year (traders refer to this as "selling volatility at 19 percent"). As option prices rose, Long-Term continued to sell. Other firms sold in tiny amounts. Not Long-Term. It just kept selling. Rosenfeld, Hilibrand, and Modest worked the trade in Greenwich; Haghani and Hufschmid did it in London. Eventually, they had a staggering $40 million riding on each percentage point change in equity volatility in the United States and an equivalent amount in Europe—perhaps a fourth of the overall market. Morgan Stanley coined a nickname for the fund: the Central Bank of Volatility.

Indeed, equity vol was Long-Term's archetypal trade. In many of its spread trades, the firm was indirectly expressing an opinion on volatility. The partners believed that, over time, investors would become more rational, more steady, more efficient—more like *they* were—and thus that credit spreads would narrow. "We've always had that belief," Rosenfeld noted.[1] The equity vol trade was an explicit articulation of this doctrine; it underscored the central role that volatility played in Long-Term's Mertonian universe. "The MIT types always want to short volatility," noted Andrew Hall, an oil trader who had worked at Salomon in the 1980s. "Academics have embedded in their minds the Black-Scholes models that assume the normal distributions. They think these models are the Holy Grail."

In the first months of 1998, markets were smooth. The International Monetary Fund worked out a bailout of South Korea, capping a stabilizing trend in Asia. In Europe, where the launch of the euro was less than a year away, investors were bathing in a spirit of optimism. In the United States, the Dow broke into record territory. As investors regained confidence, bond spreads narrowed. At the start of 1998, A-rated bonds (those issued by strong corporations, such as Ford Motor) yielded 75 basis points more than Treasurys; by February, the spread had narrowed to 70 points.

Such balmy currents, though apparently unrelated, reflected a generalized feeling that the crisis of the previous fall had passed even though a certain edginess lingered. In October 1997, after the debacle in Asia, Merrill Lynch had ordered its bond traders to downsize their positions. They had in fact pulled back, but by the beginning of 1998 they were reverting to business as usual. The world had gotten past so many crises; it had seen the United States and the IMF rescue Mexico, Thailand, Korea. "No one believed that Asia would spread," noted Dan Napoli, Merrill's risk manager, referring to the traders who put the firm's capital on the line. As such sanguine attitudes percolated up from the trading desk of bank after bank, credit spreads inevitably narrowed.

The mood at Long-Term was relaxed, too. Though the fund's leverage was up, and though the partners had taken out huge personal loans, their exposure seemed tolerable. According to one estimate, Hilibrand alone was worth half a billion dollars and Meriwether was in the low hundreds of millions. And the partners had seemingly tailored the fund's portfolio to control the risk. According to their models, the maximum that they were likely to lose on any single trading day was $45 million—certainly tolerable for a firm with a hundred times as much in capital.[2] According to these same models, the odds against the firm's suffering a sustained run of bad luck—say, losing 40 percent of its capital in a single month—were unthinkably high. (So far, in their worst month, they had lost a mere 2.9 percent.) Indeed, the figures implied that it would take a so-called ten-sigma event—that is, a statistical freak occurring one in every ten to the twenty-fourth power times—for the firm to lose all of its capital within one year.[3]

If the partners were anxious, it was not about losing; it was that they wouldn't find enough investments where they could win. As the pressure to find suitable trades mounted, they increasingly strayed into more exotic tundra, such as Brazilian and Russian bonds and

Danish mortgages. Martin Siegel, who handled Brazil and other emerging markets, was a misfit at Long-Term. An old-time trader, he knew nothing about models. Siegel had made money for Meriwether at Salomon by investing in the Mexican telephone company, and J.M., typically, had given him a job at Long-Term out of loyalty.

Long-Term also began to make more directional bets, abandoning (for a fraction of its portfolio) the cautious hedging strategy that had been its trademark. Scholes was deeply upset by such trades, particularly its big position in Norwegian kroner. He argued that Long-Term should stick to its models; it did not have any "informational advantage" in Norway.[4] A year or so before, Haghani had exploded at the suggestion that Long-Term invest in Greece. "How can you trust this economy?" he had demanded. But when challenged himself, he cast such quibbles aside. Haghani felt he could never lose; he pushed and pushed his partners until he got his way.

The fund went deeper into equities, too. Knowing that many high-tech companies issued puts (options) cheaply to manage their employee stock-option programs, Long-Term bought heaps of these puts, issued by companies such as Microsoft and Dell, and hedged them by selling puts on the S&P 500. Modest was the engineer in these trades, but Haghani, invariably, was the architect. An associate was stunned to find that Modest had even shorted big-company stocks—reportedly including Microsoft, Dell, and General Electric—seemingly on Haghani's whim. Modest explained to the associate, "Victor blew into town, he liked this trade and told me to do it." Modest added, unnecessarily, "Victor is Victor—what am I going to do?"

By now Long-Term was succumbing to the fatal temptation to put its money *someplace*. In a clear speculation, it bet on the U.S. stock market to decline, via options.[5] Then, a young, statistically minded equity researcher named Alain Sunier proposed buying stocks that, according to a model, were likely to be added to the S&P index (when a stock is added to the index, many portfolios are compelled to buy it). Hilibrand got very interested in this trade. He ignored Sunier's model, discarding Sunier's companies and adding new ones. And Hilibrand insisted on buying hefty stakes in every one of them. Long-Term's notional investment in the trade soared to an astronomical $2 billion. A colleague asked what had happened. Sunier threw up his arms and replied: "He [Hilibrand] turned off all my stocks."

Hilibrand also shorted Berkshire Hathaway, the holding company run by Warren Buffett, believing that Berkshire was overpriced relative to its individual parts. But since many of Berkshire's assets were private, Hilibrand couldn't buy the parts, making it a poorly conceived arbitrage. Though usually coldly calculating, Hilibrand was being a bit too clever—trying to profit at the billionaire's expense—and dangerously moving the fund afield of its expertise. This was plainly unwise. Even on well-conceived trades, the partners had lost all sense of scale. In one trade that would lose them money, Long-Term bought a huge 15 percent share, worth $480 million, of a junk-bond issue from Starwood Hotels & Resorts, a real estate operator that itself had a tendency to overreach.

Though their trades wanted for scrutiny more than ever, the partners' weekly risk meetings became increasingly scripted. They no longer had the patience to research and analyze trades quite as they had done with Italy. Though their debates were heated, the results seemed preordained. Scholes protested about the size of the firm's various positions. After all, the firm had had trouble exiting from some of its large trades—an obvious red flag.[6] Merton, Mullins, and McEntee made protests, too. But the dissenters stopped short of threatening to quit, the one step that might have prompted J.M. and Rosenfeld to confront their two top traders.

And Hilibrand and Haghani weren't really listening. Younger colleagues espied an impulsive streak, not so surprising in Haghani, perhaps, but totally baffling in the case of Hilibrand. The intellectually curious Modest was deeply resentful of having to be, as a colleague teased him, "Larry's execution slave." The rare Long-Term man with Renaissance interests, Modest, who was raised in Boston, loved the arts, literature, and opera. His interest in finance was more academic than entrepreneurial; he had never liked the senior partners' autocratic reign and control over his time and had been thinking of bolting until 1998, when he had been made a junior partner. When he saw his partners departing from their trademark prudence, the firm lost all its meaning for him. Totally dominated by the two senior traders, Long-Term had become a lopsided firm; it was a partnership only in name.

Wall Street knew nothing of these internal tensions; indeed, the banks continued to give the fund a free ride. Merrill Lynch happily financed the fund in Brazil—a risky market—on the slimmest of haircuts. Becoming anxious, people on Merrill's repo desk squawked to

Robert McDonough, the Merrill credit officer responsible for hedge funds, about Long-Term's exposure in emerging markets. McDonough just laughed. "We're in bed with these guys," he noted. "If they go down, we go down!"

Few possibilities could have seemed more remote. Indeed, so strong was Merrill's confidence in Greenwich that on April 1, 123 starry-eyed Merrill executives purchased (in individual, separate stakes) most of Merrill's investment in Long-Term for the executives' personal deferred compensation plans. Komansky, who had succeeded Tully as Merrill's chairman, put in $800,000; in total, the executives invested $22 million. Ironically, Merrill, Long-Term's midwife, got out closer to the top than anyone else, leaving its own executives to take the downhill ride.

Merrill's willingness to finance its client was part of a pervasive climate of financial laxity, palpable in Wall Street's eagerness to underwrite emerging markets. Russia was commonly touted as the next capitalist nirvana. "People were saying 'Asia was isolated, let's move on.' The amount of money pursuing these areas was tremendous," noted Merrill's Richard Dunn, then head of debt markets in Europe and the United Kingdom. At such times, it took uncommon courage to refuse to lend, for it would have meant squandering business to the competition. "We misread the haircuts that we needed to be protected," Dunn admitted. "It wasn't a mistake we made singly for Long-Term. The whole market was pressuring us. To suffer the organization telling you that you are losing business—it takes a tremendous amount [of courage] to stand up and say, 'I'm not going to do it.' The Street all got that collectively wrong."

In April, Sandy Weill, still trying to digest his ill-considered acquisition of Salomon, announced the biggest financial merger in history: Travelers and Citicorp. The deal was emblematic of the Street's Panglossian mood. Thirty-year Treasury yields had dipped below 6 percent, reminiscent of the stable and innocent bond markets of Meriwether's youth. The belief in a brighter tomorrow, coupled with the general willingness to lend, pushed down rates for even the least creditworthy of borrowers. Spreads fell to their lowest levels in years. A-rated bonds fell to 60 points (down from 75 at the start of the year). The shrinking spreads worked like a tonic on Long-Term's profit-and-loss statement. Having been flat in the first quarter, the fund earned almost 3 percent in April. The end of April, approximately, was the low point for spreads, the high point for confidence, and the high point for Long-Term Capital, which boasted $134 billion in assets. In just over four years, an investment in the fund had quadrupled, before accounting for the partners' fees. After deducting this tithe, the value of a single dollar invested at the start had risen to $2.85—a phenomenal 185 percent profit in barely fifty months.

Far from resting on their laurels, the partners, led by Dick Leahy, set up a Bermuda-based reinsurance subsidiary, christened Osprey Re. Osprey, which was capitalized with $200 million, reflected Long-Term's self-image as an insurer of financial risks. Now the partners were planning to reinsure tangible risks, such as losses from severe storms, earthquakes, hurricanes, and the like. Their mutual fund venture with BNL, the Italian bank, had been tabled by the Italians and dropped. But the partners were exploring another new front: private equity ventures.[7] Would nothing ever shake them?

In the manner of markets, the first hints of trouble were scattered, small, and seemingly unrelated. John Succo, who ran the equity derivatives desk at Lehman Brothers, was among those who felt that the Street was playing with fire, specifically with the unseen leverage in derivatives. At the end of April, Succo was speaking at an investors' conference sponsored by the maverick newsletter publisher James Grant. In response to a question, Succo declared that the senior managements at some—possibly all—Wall Street firms had no idea of the risks being run by their twenty-six-year-old traders. He hedged a bit, adding that *his* management was better informed. But the heresy was accomplished. For suggesting that Wall Street's top brass was uninformed, the prophetic Succo was forced to resign from Lehman.

Lloyd Blankfein, a partner at Goldman Sachs, was worried by leverage in the system, too. He mentioned to Peter Fisher, who ran trading activities at the New York Fed, that people were wasting their time trying to figure out whether somewhere there lurked a Mexico that could trigger another financial crisis. Blankfein thought the next big problem would be a *credit problem*, not a problem specific to any one market. People weren't distinguishing among risks, Blankfein complained, alluding to vanishing credit spreads. For the moment, everything was a Treasury bill.

For Steve Freidheim of Bankers Trust, the alarm sounded during a spring trip to Singapore and Hong Kong. Cognizant of Mexico's rapid recovery, he was hopeful that Asia, too, would be back on its feet in no time. But what Freidheim saw in Asia shook him: "a lot of big players" were taking money off the table. During a lunch at a private club in Hong Kong, a major banker suddenly changed the terms of a deal to reduce the banker's exposure to Asia. Freidheim returned to the United States in a pessimistic mood. "We began to short the market after that," he recalled. Credit spreads at home had never been tighter. There was only one way for them to go, he felt, especially if the still fragile condition of Asia should become apparent.

Imperceptibly at first, other Wall Street traders started to reach similar conclusions. Banks and securities firms began to cut back their inventories of riskier, less liquid bonds—which, of course, were the very types of bonds in Long-Term's portfolio.[8] The selling was not coordinated, but the effect was much as if it had been, for the various trading desks generally owned the same securities. Meriwether may have felt a shudder of doubt, for in a visit with Siciliano, the Swiss Bank manager, J.M. said he was looking for ways to invest the partners' capital outside the fund, perhaps in stocks or real estate. They were too concentrated, J.M. added, as if forgetting that his partners had recently passed up the chance to take back some of their capital.

By far, the firm where unease lay heaviest was Travelers. The firm's bosses had been shocked to learn that the fixed-income arbitrageurs at Salomon Brothers, their newly acquired subsidiary, routinely took home year-end bonuses of $10 million and more. Weill and his top lieutenant, Jamie Dimon, were hostile to the star system pioneered by Hilibrand, under which traders at Salomon (now Salomon Smith Barney) took home a percentage of their profits. Since the traders were not penalized for losses, they had a perverse incentive to bet as much of the company's money as they could. Essentially, Weill and Dimon viewed arbitrage as a dressed-up form of gambling. Not surprisingly, they took a dim view of Long-Term, a major Salomon client. Shortly after the merger, Dimon asked Long-Term for more information. Meriwether reflexively replied that such information was private. Dimon, who had no allegiance to Greenwich, threatened to cut Long-Term off, and J.M. meekly complied with Dimon's request.[9] A new breeze was blowing.

Robert Stavis, the co-head of arbitrage at Salomon, was trying to branch into equity trades, just as Long-Term was doing, but Stavis's new bosses, particularly Steven Black, head of global equities at Salomon Smith Barney, blocked him. Stavis was eager to get bigger in equity vol, but Black put his foot down. Always Long-Term's alter ego, the Arbitrage Group at Salomon was turning into the more prudent firm that Long-Term might have been had J.M. steered it with a firmer hand.

By April, Salomon's group was down $200 million, prompting serious discussions about its future. Stavis told Weill that he should be prepared for further losses, which was not what Weill, who knew that Wall Street focused on short-term earnings and was himself obsessed with Travelers' stock price, wanted to hear. Aware that spreads had diminished, the Travelers executives made a logical decision—but one that had somehow eluded Meriwether—to scale the business back. The only good news at Salomon was that Travelers' pending merger with Citicorp made Arbitrage seem less important. In discussing the possibility of trading losses, Weill was fond of saying, "I'd like to be big enough so that when we get these explosions they will feel like pinpricks." As part of Citicorp, he would be. Still, as a check, a Salomon official put in a call to Long-Term to find out how much capital the hedge fund was using in its trades. Its answer: "Almost none." Salomon, which hadn't analyzed its arbitrage business quite so intently, was unnerved. It was obvious that both firms had been relying too much on leverage, and Salomon Smith Barney, at least, began to cut back.

In May, contrary to the forecasts of Long-Term's models, arbitrage spreads began to widen. Bond arbitrageurs suffered losses, setting off a modest but hard-to-break cycle of selling. Firms such as Salomon, which had less capital as a result of the losses, now were in violation of their own computer-determined guidelines regarding the proper ratio of capital to assets. Thus, they sold a bit more. "As people liquidated, volatility moved up," a Salomon trader in London recalled. "That forced more people to liquidate."

It was still just a pinprick, but there were more pins than Weill had reckoned on. One of them punctured the mortgage market, where the bond market trouble of 1994 had started, too. Mortgage-backed securities declined, prompting hedge funds to pare other exposures, such as in emerging markets.[10] Suddenly, Asia was not so calm. In Indonesia, the biggest of the Asian Tigers, the IMF bailout ran into snags. Then, in May, street rioting forced President Suharto to resign after thirty-two years in power. The real revolutionaries had been the currency traders, who had forced a currency devaluation and exposed a corrupt autocrat's nepotistic program as a failure.

Everyone knew the speculators' next target; ominously, it was Russia. Sergei Dubinin, chairman of the Russian central bank, said the ruble was safe. Hoping to have the definitive word, he added, "There will be no devaluation of the ruble."[11] By the end of May, he had tripled interest rates to halt the flight of capital. Russia's financial system, already teetering, was now on the verge of collapse. In the United States, meanwhile, the economy was slowing—always bullish for bond prices. Yields on Treasurys fell, and thus the spread between Treasurys and other types of bonds, such as corporate issues, began to widen. This trend being the opposite of what Long-Term was betting on, the fund had its worst month ever, losing 6.7 percent.

Though Swiss Bank, which would be Long-Term's biggest investor after merging with UBS, knew nothing of the losses, it was getting nervous. After reviewing the warrant package, Tim Fredrickson, the head of derivatives at Swiss Bank, called the bank's Siciliano and warned him, "This thing isn't too pretty." The basic problem was that the investment was unhedgeable: Swiss Bank was completely exposed on the downside. "At that point," Siciliano recalled, "it was like a benign tumor. If things were to go bad we'd have a problem, but they had never had a problem."

■

In June, Ron Tannenbaum, the UBS salesman who had pitched the warrant, left the bank—a footnote in the unfolding drama. Of greater import, credit spreads continued to widen. More frightening still, they widened in *every* market in which Long-Term was active. The trouble wasn't specific to any security; it was a general pulling back of credit, a pervasive sense that markets had been undercharging for risk. Investors wanted safety; now they would pay any amount to buy a Treasury (meaning that they would accept any lower yield, as long as they got out of riskier bonds).

Jim McEntee, J.M.'s friend and the one partner who relied on his nose, as distinct from a computer, sensed the trade-winds changing. He repeatedly urged his partners to lower the firm's risks, but McEntee was ignored as a nonscientific, old-fashioned gambler. Since moving to Connecticut, the partners, who no longer had to jostle with the throngs on Wall Street every day, had become even more isolated from the anecdotal, but occasionally useful, gossip that traders pass around. They found it easy to brush off McEntee's alarums, particularly since the Sheik's own trades had been losing money. Increasingly frustrated, McEntee met James Rickards, Long-Term's general counsel, after work one night at the Horseneck Tavern in Greenwich. Rickards was leaving the next morning on an expedition to climb Mount McKinley in Alaska. "By the time you get back, the world will have completely changed," McEntee predicted darkly.

All over Wall Street, McEntee's fellow traders were now speaking of a "flight to quality"—that is, to Treasury bonds. By mid-June, the yield on the thirty-year Treasury had fallen to 5.58 percent, the lowest since the government had started issuing thirty-year bonds in 1977. "Everyone in the [Treasury] market is afraid to go home short," Matthew Alexy, a strategist with Credit Suisse First Boston, told *The Wall Street Journal*.[12] Except for Long-Term Capital, which went home short on Treasurys every day. Treasurys were the basic bond that the fund sold short to hedge the riskier bonds it owned. And as Treasurys rallied, spreads between them and other bonds widened. Mortgage-backed securities jumped from 96 basis points over Treasurys to 113 points. Corporate bonds rose from 99 to 105, and junk issues rose from 224 to 266. Even those safe-seeming off-the-run Treasurys climbed from 6 points over to 8 points over.[13] In every market, the premium demanded for riskier bonds increased. In every market, Long-Term was losing money.

Why this all-consuming fear of risk? Once again, Asia was the spark. In Japan, the yen was plummeting, accentuating the country's already deep recession. Japanese bond yields were plummeting— exactly the opposite of Long-Term's bet. And Japan was the cornerstone of the East Asian economy. With Japanese importers scaling back their purchases, there was talk of a regional depression. In Indonesia, the rupiah had lost 85 percent of its precrisis value. In South Korea, stocks plunged 8 percent in a single day. The fear was pervasive, but every day, it emerged in a different place.

The drumbeat from Russia grew steadily louder. In June, Goldman Sachs managed to sell $1.25 billion in five-year Eurobond notes for the Russian government at a modest (for Russia) 12 percent interest rate. Goldman's issue, truly a triumph of salesmanship, briefly persuaded investors that Russia's problems were abating. But Goldman's motives may have been a trifle impure. Naturally, the bank pocketed tens of millions of dollars in fees. Moreover, Goldman had $250 million in Russian loans outstanding; the new bonds enabled Russia to pay Goldman back at a most convenient time. The century-old investment bank was preparing to sell stock to the public, and it preferred to have the Russian loan off its books. And Goldman, which was hoping to go public in the fall, did not wait long to see if the optimism it had generated in Russia lingered. It quickly unloaded its inventory of Russian bonds so as not to be stuck with the paper it had floated to investors.[14] By the end of June, thanks to bonds issued by Goldman as well as J. P. Morgan and Deutsche Bank, foreign markets were beginning to choke on Russian paper. Interest rates on one-year Russian bills skyrocketed to 90 percent.

Even in America, there were hints of a slowdown. The stock market was suddenly volatile, and option prices jumped. Of direct significance to Long-Term, implied volatility rose to 27 percent. Having shorted equity vol at far lower levels, Long-Term was showing a substantial loss. Overall, in June, the fund lost 10 percent, by far its worst month ever. Long-Term was now down 14 percent for the first half of 1998—its first sustained losing streak.

Salomon Smith Barney's Arbitrage Group had losses, too. Weill had promised he would be able to live with volatile trading results, but he couldn't. Before June was out, he decided to close the firm's U.S. bond arbitrage operation, a business he had never liked. One might well ask why Weill had acquired Salomon, since Arbitrage had been its chief moneymaker. In any case, Salomon began to liquidate assets in earnest. Of course, there was a substantial overlap between Salomon's positions and Long-Term's trades. Thus, Salomon's selling helped to tip Long-Term's portfolio into negative territory; arguably, it triggered the fund's downhill spiral. Meriwether had outlasted his creator, but it would haunt him from the grave.

Like Salomon, Long-Term had shorted a simple swap spread, a number that is derived from the interest rate on a standard, widely used trade. The swap rate is, at any given moment, the fixed rate that banks, insurers, and other investors demand to be paid in exchange for agreeing to pay the LIBOR rate, a short-term bank rate. The twist is that the LIBOR rate floats; no one knows *where* it will go in the future. Typically, swap rates in each country trade at a slight spread above the interest rate on the country's government debt. Thus, this swap spread is a basic barometer of credit market anxiety; it is the premium that investors demand for taking the risk of being exposed to rate fluctuations in the future.

In the United States, in April 1998, the swap spread was 48 basis points. In recent historical terms, this number was high (it had been below 35 points for most of the 1990s, although, during the last recession, in 1990, it had briefly spurted to 84). Long-Term, seeing no recession on the horizon, had bet on this spread to narrow. In Europe, Long-Term's position was more nuanced. The swap spread was 45 points in England and only 20 in Germany, an unusually wide gap. There was an economic reason for this disparity, but it seemed to be a temporary, unnatural quirk.* Thus, in Europe, Long-Term bet that *the spread between the two spreads* would narrow.

Both of Long-Term's swap trades were intelligent convergence plays, though not, as history had shown, sure things. The swap market was deep and had a history that was very suitable for modeling. But as had been the case in so many other trades, the size of Long-Term's swap positions was unreasonably large. And as Salomon began to liquidate its (quite similar) swap positions, Long-Term began to lose both ways. The spread in the United States widened— to 56 points—and so did the gap between the United Kingdom's and Germany's.

What was worse, in July, word of Salomon's exit from U.S. arbitrage became public. A memo from the brass, leaked to *The Wall Street Journal,* ominously declared, "Opportunity for arbitrage profits has lessened over time while the risks and volatility have grown."[15] Naturally, traders at diverse firms began to unload interest rate swaps as well as other arbitrage trades, for fear of being trampled by Salomon's steamroller.

The Long-Term partners badly underestimated the seriousness of the second biggest player in their business calling it quits. They expected other arbitrageurs to fill the void. When a junior trader voiced concern to Eric Rosenfeld, the latter brushed him off, insisting that the partners were on top of the situation. In July, after Swiss Bank and UBS merged, Siciliano visited Meriwether, who stunned Siciliano with the news of Long-Term's recent losses. But J.M., too, seemed

*In England, the government had done little borrowing, leading to lower government rates and wider spreads. In Germany, conversely, heavy government borrowing had led to narrower spreads.

confident—almost relieved. Finally, the one or two bad months he had long been expecting had come. The only disconcerting note was that Long-Term had lost money on *all* of its trades, something J.M. hadn't expected. But he coolly added that now the fund would take advantage of lower prices and load up on some favorite trades. Siciliano, who had already been uneasy about Long-Term, promptly advised Felix Fischer, the chief risk officer at UBS, that the bank would be seriously exposed if Long-Term's losses continued. Neither man warned the bank's senior management.

Bear Stearns, the fund's clearing broker, also took a strong interest in Long-Term's losses. But in July, the fund recovered. "Since we could see the daily P&L [profit-and-loss statement], we knew in early July there was a significant recovery," noted Bear's Mike Alix. "The story was, they had gone back and retested all their models and come to the conclusion that June was an expected aberration. That was the party line."

J.M. was careful to personally notify Allison at Merrill Lynch and other of the fund's big partners about the losses. He generally sounded relaxed. Writing to investors, J.M. reported that "future expected returns are good."[16] Meriwether was his old self on the golf course, too; the losses hadn't damped his spirits. A golfing friend said he seemed "at peace with himself."

The surest sign of Long-Term's continued confidence was that the fund continued to recruit new people. Always infatuated with new technology, the partners hired eight new software whizzes over the summer. The staff hit a peak of 190.

Long-Term did pare back its assets, intending to bring them into line with its now-depleted reserves. But the total selling was slight. While Long-Term sold some directional trades, the partners were keen on holding on to their big convergence positions, such as equity vol, swaps, and Royal Dutch/Shell; they also added to some positions.[17] Overall, their assets declined only to $128 billion from $134 billion, and their leverage actually rose, to thirty-one times. According to the fund's models, Long-Term had reduced the amount it was likely to lose on a typical trading day, from $45 million to $34 million.[18] But this was a highly mechanistic way of evaluating risk. It relied on past volatilities as a gauge of the future: as usual, the partners driving Long-Term had their eyes on the rearview mirror.

In July, the markets continued to be edgy. In Russia, where fears of devaluation had not been put to bed, yields on short-term bonds soared to a dizzying 120 percent annual rate. However, the attitude of global investors—the plugged-in traders who were forever checking CNN or Bloomberg and who seemed never to sleep—was that Russia was a problem, but a contained one. As one Russia hand nonchalantly observed, the central bank could easily shut the dollar window and halt the flight of money. "People won't care," he added. "Just some hedge funds will get hosed!"[19]

If people did not care, it was because the monetary policemen had been so quick to patch any sign of trouble. In July, at Secretary Rubin's urging, the IMF and various nations worked out a $22.6 billion Russian bailout, seemingly demonstrating that there was no financial problem that they couldn't fix. (Much of the bailout money would be stolen by Russian oligarchs and siphoned out of the country.) Then Goldman Sachs induced investors to swap their short-term Russian notes for twenty-year bonds—as if the next twenty weeks in Russia were clear, much less the next twenty years. But investors had stopped analyzing Russia as a credit; they were falling back on a cliché: "Nuclear powers don't default." It seemed an echo of Walter Wriston, the Citibank chairman who had made loans to Latin America in the 1970s and early 1980s, proclaiming that sovereign nations didn't default.

To their credit, Travelers' Weill and Dimon smelled a rat in Russia when others didn't. "Sandy hated Russia," according to one of his London traders. "He said it was lawless." An IMF official met with Salomon in June and urged the bank to back Moscow, whose leadership he praised. The IMF mission chief in Moscow tried a different tack, assuring Salomon that the United States would never let a nuclear power default. But Weill and Dimon were uncomfortable with being exposed to surprises, and they sensed that Russia would bring nothing but. Though fascinated by geopolitics and Russia in particular, Weill thought it was a poor arena for an investment bank to be laying bets in. The order went out to sell.

Once again, Long-Term and Salomon were on opposite sides of a trade. Haghani and Hawkins were taken by the idea that Russia couldn't—and simply *wouldn't*—let its currency fail. (Economists were trooping from hedge fund to hedge fund, including Long-Term, peddling this very notion.) Long-Term knew, of course, that a default was conceivable. But the professors had a model that, they believed, forecast what would occur if Moscow did default.[20] To Haghani, this was altogether reasonable. "What we did is rely on experience," he noted later of the portfolio in general. "If you're not willing to draw any conclusions from experience, you might as well sit on your hands and do nothing."[21] But could a "model" truly anticipate a country— not merely its markets but its politicians, its legislators, its passions, too? Russia was a singularly poor laboratory for Long-Term's type of trading. Less than a decade removed from communism and struggling to become a democratic society, Russia was almost inherently unpredictable. Haghani's knowledge of history should have told him that. (Churchill had declared in 1939, "I cannot forecast to you the action of Russia. It is a riddle wrapped in a mystery inside an enigma.") In 1998, too, Russia was beyond the realm of econometrics, even of the computers in Greenwich.

The Fed was well aware of the danger of banks basing predictions too much on the past. In an open letter to banks, the Fed's top banking supervisor warned, "Banks should resist any tendency to assume . . . that the unusually favorable economic environment of the last few years will continue indefinitely." Though the letter dealt with commercial loans rather than capital markets, it underscored the need to think about "alternative scenarios" such as bankruptcies and defaults, rather than assume that the future would be a seamless extension of the present.[22] In contrast to this well-founded caution, Fed chief Greenspan was still singing the praises of unfettered derivative markets. On July 30, testifying before the Senate Committee on Agriculture, Nutrition, and Forestry, Greenspan declared that derivative traders "have managed credit risks quite effectively through careful evaluation of counterparties." The words can only mean that, in Greenspan's view, a Merrill or a Morgan was carefully scrutinizing clients such as Long-Term—a view that would soon become demonstrably false.[23]

In the second half of July, Long-Term's performance tailed off. It ended the month flat. Stocks in Europe and America swooned. By early August, Russian bonds were sinking again. Rumors swirled of selling by Wall Street banks and hedge funds. And the selling spread to eastern Europe, Latin America, and Asia. Now, Russia was not so contained.

During the second week of August, Russia's markets snapped. On August 13, with dollars fleeing the country, its reserves dwindling, its budget overtapped, and the price of oil, its chief commodity, down 33 percent, the government imposed controls on the ruble. The banking system froze for lack of reliable and solvent banks. The Moscow stock market briefly halted trading. It ended the day down 6 percent—and down 75 percent for the year. Short-term interest rates surged to almost 200 percent. Long-term Russian bonds fell to half their price of only two months earlier, when Goldman had happily floated them.

As the world waited for a ruble devaluation, which the government still insisted would not occur, the Communist-dominated Duma, the lower house of Parliament, rejected reform measures urged on it by the IMF. Then the members went on vacation. When the government begged the Duma to reconvene, the members refused—but by then many government leaders, including President Boris Yeltsin, were also at seaside dachas, leaving the country to sort out its misery. It was a hard thing to model.

In the United States and Europe, markets shuddered from a swelling list of negatives: the crisis in Russia, weakness in Asia, Iraq's refusal to permit full weapons inspections, the possibility of China devaluing *its* currency, and President Clinton's testimony about his relationship with a White House intern, Monica Lewinsky. As global investors bailed out of Russia and Asia, they furiously piled into Treasurys, a bulwark of safety when no one wanted risk. Thirty-year bond yields touched another new low: 5.56 percent.

Naturally, credit spreads kept widening. Since April, the high point for bond arbitrage, A-rated bonds had moved from 60 points over Treasurys to 90 points. U.S. swap spreads were rising, too. At every Wall Street bank, arbitrage desks were cutting back; capital was fleeing from bond arbitrage just as it had fled from Asia. The Fed, at first, had been favorably disposed toward the trend. Spreads had been tight, credit too easy. But now, in the context of Russia's meltdown, the Fed's nerves were on edge.

Long-Term was losing money in August—disturbingly, for the third month in four. The partners could no longer be so standoffish toward Wall Street. Realizing that Salomon, which was continuing to liquidate, was a major headache, Haghani offered to buy the bank's whole position, worth about $2 billion—just to freeze it. Salomon's people thought he was joking—Long-Term no longer had the capital to back such bold talk—but Salomon's traders enjoyed the turnabout in their respective fortunes: Long-Term wasn't calling the shots anymore. Robert Shustak, Long-Term's chief financial officer, was having to field calls every day from a worried Bear Stearns. J. P. Morgan heard rumors that Long-Term was liquidating positions—or at least trying to. Lehman Brothers heard the rumors, too. Though Long-Term had once snubbed the smallish investment bank, now it was making nice with Lehman. "They were coming to us to do more business," Jeffrey Vanderbeek, head of fixed income at Lehman, recalled. "I remember thinking that their liquidity might be drying up. They wanted more financing." As repo loans were rolling over, Wall Street banks, Lehman among them, were finally asking the professors for margin.

Suddenly anxious about their personal well-being, the partners made hurried calls to their advisers and attorneys. Hans Hufschmid, a London partner who was married to a Californian, was about to bid on a house in Malibu. But Hufschmid, who had borrowed heavily to invest in Long-Term, got a case of nerves. On a hunch, he decided not to buy the house. Myron Scholes did buy a four-story home in San Francisco, where his fiancée lived. It was a fantastic home on Russian Hill, with high ceilings and a terrace overlooking Fisherman's Wharf. It cost $6.5 million.[24] But then, Scholes had money outside the fund. And the fund's losses so far had hardly been severe.

Meriwether confidently went ahead with a trip to China in the middle of August. The partners thought they had reason to be optimistic; spreads had widened so much, they felt, that now, surely, they could only narrow. But their optimism had a desperate edge. In mid-August, Long-Term jumped more heavily into Russia, where it already owned hedged Russian bonds as well as some that were unhedged. Now, while the entire world was watching Russia, while its finances were in shambles and its government on hold, Haghani and a researcher named Ayman Hindy, a former professor at Stanford, bought more Russian bonds as though they had the inside scoop on that enigmatic Eastern riddle. Neither the Nobel Prize nor all the degrees mattered now; the professors were rolling the dice. According to one trader at Long-Term, the fund went "outright long in Russia—right at the end." Said another, miserably, "It was so against our way."

8

THE FALL

The question ... is whether the LTCM disaster was merely a unique and isolated event, a bad drawing from nature's urn; or whether such disasters are the inevitable consequence of the Black-Scholes formula itself and the illusion it may give that all market participants can hedge away all their risk at the same time.
—MERTON H. MILLER, NOBEL LAUREATE

THROUGH THE MIDDLE of August, Long-Term Capital had been having a bad year, but only a bad year such as any fund, or any capitalistic enterprise, must sooner or later suffer. Its reputation, like its capital, remained intact. Its overall record sparkled, and its name, among the members of the financial cognoscenti who truly knew the firm, often gave rise to the very term "genius." Long-Term was unknown to the general public, but that is how Meriwether and his boys wanted it, and that, of course, is how they expected the fund to remain. They could hardly have had a glimmer of the large, even historic, events in which they were to play a leading role, nor of how radically their fortunes would change. Much less could they have imagined the stunning swiftness with which such events would unfold. In late summer, as Wall Streeters scurried for the Hamptons, the partners were among America's most prosperous, most successful, and most highly esteemed investors. Their fund had $3.6 billion in capital, of which two fifths was personally theirs. It would take only five weeks for them to lose it all.

On Monday, August 17, Russia declared a debt moratorium. The government simply decided it would rather use its rubles to pay Russian workers than Western bondholders. Nor would it attempt to maintain the value of those rubles in foreign markets. In short, it was a devaluation and, on at least some of its borrowings, a default from a government that had promised that it would do neither. Enigmatic to the end, Russia said its moratorium would apply to $13.5 billion of *local* (ruble) debt—breaking the rule, honored even in the depths of the Latin American debt crisis, that a government honors its own coin.

The reaction in markets was muted, at least at first. Mexican and Brazilian bonds fell, and stocks in Japan and various emerging markets weakened. But the Dow rose nearly 150 points. American banks, honoring a tradition that extended back to 1929, quickly declared that they expected to weather the storm with little ill effect. Robert Strong, chief credit officer at Chase Manhattan, whose stock price was to fall 50 percent within six weeks, confidently proclaimed to Wall Street security analysts, "I do not view Russia as a major issue" for Chase or for other U.S. banks.[1] In terms of its total indebtedness, Russia was no big deal, barely another Venezuela.

Except that Russia was not Venezuela. Supposedly, nuclear powers did not default. And when Russia did, something in the markets died. The comforting notion that the global financial cops would always be there to put matters right was now exposed as a fallacy. This time, there was no rescue by the IMF, no hurried bailout by Robert Rubin or the Group of Seven Western powers. "The fund and the G7 finally managed to say no," remarked Morris Goldstein, a former senior IMF official.[2] The implications of this truth chilled global markets like a Siberian gale. The default shattered the lazy but convenient assumptions of investors that the safety net would always be there. It "punctured a moral hazard bubble"[3] that had been inflating expectations since Rubin had ridden to the rescue of Mexico. Investors, at first singly and then en masse, concluded that no emerging market was safe. In seventy years, Russia's Communists had not succeeded in dealing markets such a telling blow as did its deadbeat capitalists.

On Thursday, three days after the default, markets around the world buckled. Shares in eastern Europe and Turkey were weak. The stock market in Caracas plunged 9.5 percent. Venezuelans panicked and rushed to buy dollars. Brazil's far larger *bolsa* was off 6 percent.

THE FALL • 145

Germany's stock market fell 2 percent, as if the Russian menace could actually tramp across the eastern front.

Investors now were running not just from emerging markets, but from investment risk wherever it lurked. The panic proved that the Asian storm had never truly been forgotten. Swap spreads—those basic thermometers of credit markets—rose like a dangerous fever. The British bank Barclays ordered its traders to unload short positions in U.K. swaps, even though its traders, like those at Long-Term, thought swaps were unreasonably high. Barclays' decision to abandon the trade merely pushed them higher.* Barclays' management didn't care. The bank wanted out. It was done with taking risk.

The next day, Friday, August 21, traders everywhere wanted out. Stock markets in Asia and in Europe plunged. The Dow fell 280 points before noon, then recouped most of its losses. This palpable surge in volatility cost Long-Term several tens of millions of dollars.

The damage to credit markets was far worse. Treasurys rallied, but it was a rally driven by panic, for investors bought Treasurys to get out of inferior credits. A few months before, they had not distinguished one risk from the next. Now it was all they thought of. A rose-colored world had suddenly gone dark, discolored by Russia, Japan, even the Clinton-Lewinsky scandal. In every market, investors wanted only the *safest* bond. In the United States, it had to be the thirty-year Treasury; in Germany, the ten-year Bund. All over the world, people were buying safer (lower-yielding) bonds and selling riskier (higher-yielding) ones, pushing the spreads between such bond pairs ever wider. Minute by minute, Long-Term was losing millions.

In Greenwich, on that golden late-August Friday, Long-Term's office was largely deserted. Most of the senior partners were on vacation; it was a sultry morning, and the staff was moving slowly. Jim McEntee, the colorful "sheik" whose doleful warnings had been ignored, was minding the store. Bill Krasker, the partner who had constructed many of the firm's models, was anxiously monitoring markets, clicking from one phosphorescent page to the next. Krasker clicked from governments to mortgages to foreign debt, the entire atlas of credit.

---

* To exit a short position, a trader must buy back his trade; thus, the effect is bullish.

When he saw the quotation for U.S. swap spreads, he stared at his screen in disbelief. On an active day, Krasker knew, U.S. swap spreads might change by as much as a point. But on this morning, swap spreads were wildly oscillating over a range of 20 points. They ended an astonishing 9 points higher, at 76, up from 48 in April. In Britain it was the same story: swap spreads surged to 62, a dozen points wider than they had been in July.

Krasker couldn't believe it. He sought out Matt Zames, a trader, and Mike Reisman, the firm's repo man, and heatedly broke the news. One of the staffers grimaced and said, "Holy shit." The traders hadn't seen a move like that—ever. True, it *had* happened in 1987 and again in 1992. But Long-Term's models didn't go back that far. As far as Long-Term knew, it was a once-in-a-lifetime occurrence—a practical impossibility[4]—and one for which the fund was totally unprepared. One of the analysts called a trader at home and asked, "Would you like to guess where swap spreads are?" When the analyst told him, the trader snapped, "Fuck you—don't ever call me at home again!"

That Friday, Long-Term lost money wherever it looked. Credit spreads simply exploded. Mortgage spreads surged to 121 points, up from 107 only weeks before. High-yield bonds climbed from 269 to 276. Off-the-run Treasurys vaulted from 8 basis points to 13! Though these moves may seem small in absolute terms, the effect on Long-Term was magnified by the fund's potent level of leverage and its immense position size.

Even in seemingly unrelated markets, Long-Term suffered a drubbing. The riskier Russian and Brazilian bonds that Long-Term owned plunged, and by far more than the safer Russian and Brazilian bonds that it had sold short as the hedges that were supposed to have made its bets so safe. In fact, nothing in any market went right that day. Long-Term had dubiously invested in Ciena Corporation, a telecommunications company that was planning to merge with Tellabs Inc., and had continued to hold the stock even when it had crept to within 25 cents of the acquisition price. On that same Friday, August 21, the merger was postponed and Ciena stock plummeted $25.50, to $31.25 a share. Long-Term lost $150 million. Years earlier, Rosenfeld had been warned that risk arbitrage was like picking up nickels in front of oncoming bulldozers. One had finally nipped him.

The losses came from every corner. They were so swift, so encyclopedic in their breadth, so utterly unexpected that the partners felt abandoned. They had suddenly lost control, as though the gods of science had been dislodged and some unseen diabolical power had taken hold of their fates. In Greenwich, the skeleton crew frantically called around the globe to reach the other partners. Victor Haghani was in Italy; he hurried back to London. Eric Rosenfeld had just arrived in Sun Valley, Idaho, for a two-week vacation with his family. He got a red-eye back to New York. Meriwether was in China. His partners tracked him down at a dinner in Beijing, and the boss took the next flight home. Before he left, J.M. called Jon Corzine, the chief executive of Goldman Sachs, a major Long-Term trading partner, at Corzine's home. "We've had a serious markdown," Meriwether advised him, "but everything is fine with us."[5]

But everything was not fine. Long-Term, which had calculated with such mathematical certainty that it was unlikely to lose more than $35 million on any single day, had just dropped $553 million— 15 percent of its capital—on that one Friday in August. It had started the year with $4.67 billion. Suddenly, it was down to $2.9 *billion*. Since the end of April, it had lost more than a third of its equity.

Worried by such serious losses to a major client, Mike Alix, the Bear Stearns executive who monitored credit risks, hurriedly called Robert Shustak, Long-Term's chief financial officer. Shustak patiently went over the firm's liquidity. Alix was amazed by Shustak's calm, a thought that was to come to Alix often in the weeks ahead about Shustak and about the other partners. They were true poker players, Alix thought.[6]

Two days after the debacle, on Sunday, August 23, the partners assembled in the conference room at 7 A.M. Outside the glass-and-granite headquarters, a fountain spewed jets of water over a sculpture of a copper osprey. As if stricken by a premonition, Meriwether had summoned Jim Rickards, the general counsel, to advise the group and also keep a record of the proceedings. Having been blindsided by the Mozer scandal, J.M. knew from bitter experience that once such matters became public, it was too late to seek advice. From that Sunday on, whenever the partners met, Rickards, a lawyer with degrees from Penn, Johns Hopkins, and New York University, was almost always in attendance.

J.M. had each trader report on his area of expertise: Hilibrand on risk arb, Hawkins on Brazil, Modest on equities, Haghani (by phone from London) on U.K. swaps and Royal Dutch/Shell. Disturbingly, the traders said there was no demand for Long-Term's trades, despite their seeming soundness. The Tokyo partners reported a similar story: there simply weren't any buyers.[7] In such a climate, there was no way Long-Term could get out of its humongous trades without moving the markets even more. The partners had assumed that other arbitrageurs would recognize the values that they saw; their failure to step forward mystified them.[8] Now, like generals who overcommit to a distant war, they found the road out blocked.

Instinctively, Meriwether and the other senior partners gravitated toward the same strategy: they would raise fresh capital to give the firm a cushion and wait until its trades turned around. They were certain that spreads would eventually converge, just as they had when a young J.M. had daringly bailed out Eckstein. His early heroics had been an almost faultless guide to J.M.'s career: *Spreads always come back*.

But owing to its loss of capital, Long-Term's leverage had become dangerously high—dangerous because losses accumulate faster as leverage increases. Therefore, to reduce their risk, the partners would have to sell *something*. But what? Investors wanted only the least risky bonds, and Long-Term didn't own any. One candidate was merger arbitrage. Long-Term's deal portfolio had mushroomed to a stunning $5 billion worth of merger positions,[9] including Citicorp/Travelers and MCI/WorldCom (the latter a successor to MCI's never-consummated union with British Telecommunications). The partners thought most of these marriages would go through (as, indeed, they did). But they were hardly central to the fund's portfolio. And if all of them did collapse, as the Ciena merger had, Long-Term calculated that it could lose more than half a billion dollars—now an intolerable risk.[10]

That same Sunday night, Rosenfeld called Warren Buffett, reaching him at his home in Omaha. Rosenfeld had won Buffett's admiration in 1991 after the Mozer scandal, when he had worked diligently to get Salomon past the crisis, helping also to restore its name. Now Rosenfeld figured there was no one better to offer Long-Term's merger portfolio to than Buffett. The billionaire liked to deal in size. He had done risk arbitrage before. And thanks to widening deal spreads, prices were attractive.

Buffett listened attentively. But he quickly noted that he hadn't been involved in merger arbitrage in a while and wasn't up to speed. No sale. Graciously, he asked if there was anything else he could do.

Rosenfeld couldn't think of anything.[11]

The next day, August 24, the partners started dialing for dollars. With their gilt-edged roster of contacts, their brilliant record, their lustrous reputations, no modern Croesus was beyond their reach. Greg Hawkins tapped a friend in George Soros's fund and set up a breakfast for Meriwether, Soros, and Stanley Druckenmiller, the billionaire's top strategist. Soros, a wily refugee from Communist Hungary, and Meriwether were as different as could be. Soros's Eastern European origins oozed from his every pore. Formal and stiff, he had a tendency to launch into philosophical disquisitions. He looked like a graying owl. Meriwether was informal, unpretentious, midwestern; he could have been the State Farm agent down the street. They represented unlike styles in investing, too. Long-Term envisioned markets as stable systems in which prices moved about a central point of rational equilibrium. "I had a different view," Soros noted.[12] The speculator saw markets as organic and unpredictable. He felt they interacted with, and were reflective of, ongoing events. They were hardly sterile or abstract systems. As he explained it, "The idea that you have a bell-shape curve is false. You have outlying phenomena that you can't anticipate on the basis of previous experience." Russia, where Soros's funds had just lost $2 billion, was an example of just such an "outlying phenomenon" that lay outside the professors' curves.

■

Meriwether argued, calmly but persuasively, that Long-Term's markets would snap back; for those with deep pockets, the opportunities were great. Soros listened impassively, but Druckenmiller peppered J.M. with questions. He smelled a chance to recoup Soros's Russian losses in a hurry. Then, Soros boldly said he would be willing to invest $500 million at the end of August—that is, a week later—provided that Long-Term could restore its capital by raising another $500 million in addition.

Now Rosenfeld called J. P. Morgan, a firm that long had thirsted for closer ties to Greenwich. The bank sent two teams—one versed in bonds, the other in equities—to comb through Long-Term's books. From then on, Morgan people and Long-Term people were talking almost constantly about how to salvage various of Long-Term's positions.[13] Naturally, Long-Term turned for help to Roberto Mendoza, the Morgan vice chairman to whom it had offered a partnership. Though close to the partners, especially Merton, Mullins, and Rosenfeld, Mendoza had had no idea that Long-Term was in serious trouble. Rosenfeld told him, "We need a large amount of money." His bluntness shocked Mendoza. Understandably, the banker wanted to know a *little* something about Long-Term's portfolio. J.M. asked Hilibrand to explain the swap position to Mendoza, but the wary Hilibrand refused. Almost in tears, Hilibrand spluttered that he couldn't say a word about his precious portfolio. He had been so certain—he had borrowed so freely. Now his tightly ordered world was beginning to crack. Personal bankruptcy was not out of the question. The possibility that he had been so wrong was devastating.

But this time, J.M. insisted: Hilibrand would have to disclose a little something. The arbitrageur grudgingly complied. Mendoza, the partners' friend, loyally promised that Morgan (or its clients) would be good for $200 million. Now Long-Term needed $300 million more; it did not seem so much. Rickards, the house lawyer, drafted papers for an imminent closing.

On Tuesday, August 25, Meriwether made two more calls. One was to Herb Allison, the Merrill president. Ordinarily, the two would have been chatting about the upcoming trip to Waterville, but this September there would be no golf weekend. J.M. disclosed that the fund's capital had fallen to *$2.7 billion*. He stressed that Long-Term had plenty of liquidity and, indeed, that liquidity wasn't an issue—an assertion that, even if sincere, was naively at odds with the fund's escalating leverage. J.M. still believed in the models, and the models were still flashing bullish signals.

Nonetheless, J.M. noted, Long-Term would have to report its losses to investors at the end of the month; he would feel better if he could show them that new money was coming in. Smoothly switching gears, he emphasized the splendid opportunity for anyone who invested now. Playing his trump card, he implied that a big investor— Allison guessed he meant Soros—was already in. Perhaps Merrill would like to join him and commit, say, $300 million to $500 million before the end of August? Though fond of Meriwether, Allison thought it was a curious invitation. It was a lot of money to be wanting in a week.

J.M.'s other call that day was to Jamie Dimon at Travelers, the parent of Salomon Smith Barney. Instead of the two firms pecking each other to death by liquidating arbitrage trades, he suggested, why not unite Long-Term's portfolio with what was left of Salomon's Arbitrage Group and manage them together? Going back to the mother firm, in a sense. A couple of J.M.'s partners called Salomon, too, soliciting their old friends for capital. They said that the fund needed $1 billion but was well on the way toward getting it.

But Long-Term was losing ground, not gaining it. Markets were steadily turning on the fund. Mortgage spreads jumped an additional 4 points that Monday, 6 more on Tuesday, and 3 more on Wednesday, August 26. High-yield spreads blew out another 25 points. With each tick, more of Long-Term's once abundant capital drained away—the firm was losing money faster than it could raise it. Stunned by the unceasing losses and helpless to do anything about them, its traders were becoming dazed, like infantry in a slaughter. "It was bizarre," one of them said. "Day after day we had massive losses, and they didn't stop." The firm was hemorrhaging.

Long-Term knew it had to reduce its positions, but it couldn't— not with markets under stress. Despite the ballyhooed growth in derivatives, there was no liquidity in credit markets. There never is when everyone wants out at the same time. This is what the models had missed. When losses mount, leveraged investors such as Long-Term are *forced* to sell, lest their losses overwhelm them. When a firm has to sell in a market without buyers, prices run to the extremes beyond the bell curve. To take just one example, yields on News Corporation bonds, which had recently been trading at 110 points over Treasurys, bizarrely soared to 180 over, even though the company's prospects had not changed one iota. In the long run, such a spread might seem absurd. But long-term thinking is a luxury not always available to the highly leveraged; they may not survive that long.

The end of August is always a slow time in markets, but this August, trading in bond markets all but vanished. The market for new bond issues simply dried up. Scheduled new offerings were abruptly withdrawn, which was just as well, because there was no one to buy them. The lesser investors, the copycats, the fashionable hedge funds, the newcomers to arbitrage, and the smaller, European-based traders were quitting the spread-trading business or withdrawing their capital from it in droves.[14]

Wary of their clients' mounting losses, banks were finally tightening their credit lines to hedge funds. Steve Freidheim, the hedge fund manager at Bankers Trust, was getting margin calls. His loan brokers had changed their tune. Once they had shoveled money at him; now they were demanding more margin. Freidheim watched in horror as the value of his bonds sank beneath the value of the loans against them. Since many of his bonds were unsalable, Freidheim sold other credits—Brazil, Turkey, Thailand, U.S. mortgage securities, high-yield bonds. It didn't matter what he sold; the point was, he had to sell *something*. At such a time, capital naturally flows from riskier assets to less risky ones, irrespective of their underlying value. To a tiny degree, Freidheim's own actions made it do so. Multiplied by a thousand other Freidheims all over Wall Street, the crisis of fear became a self-fulfilling prophecy, just as Merton's father, who had coined the phrase, had theorized. As prices fell, banks backed away from hedge funds. And as banks backed away, hedge funds had to keep selling.

Sandy Weill, far from wanting to partner with Long-Term or anyone else in arbitrage, was telling his troops to lower their exposure to hedge funds. Even as its own traders were liquidating assets, Salomon was reeling from losses in bond arbitrage as well as in Russia. Weill is said to have ordered his minions to reduce the number of hedge funds doing business with Salomon from five hundred to twenty! Weill's buddy Warren Buffett was monitoring *his* people, demanding to hear, in very detailed terms, about Berkshire Hathaway's exposure to hedge funds. Buffett, who instinctively tightened his grip on his company's cash when times got tough, wanted to know if a Berkshire insurance subsidiary was holding adequate collateral on swap trades.[15]

Goldman Sachs was nervous about its exposure to swaps, particularly with Long-Term. When Corzine, who had been jarred by J.M.'s call from China, called Meriwether back, he warned him, "We aren't getting adequate feedback. It could hurt your credit standing." Goldman was trying to pry information loose from the always tight-lipped hedge fund, but Long-Term was still reluctant to share information. It was trying to operate on a business-as-usual basis. But the firm no longer had the capital to dictate terms willy-nilly. Under pressure from Goldman and other banks, knowledge of Long-Term's positions was slowly leaking out.

Now it was Wednesday, August 26, and Merrill's Allison called to say no dice. Still in the dark, Allison added, "John, I'm not sure it's in your interest to raise the money. It might look like you're having a problem!"

Soros's deadline was five days off, and the market news continued to be bad. Equity volatility notched up two more points, to 29 percent. Bonds in Latin America weakened. Ominously, Western banks started admitting to losses of their own in the former Soviet Union. Credit Suisse First Boston and Republic National Bank of New York, both heady champions of the new capitalist Russia, disclosed huge losses there. A trendy investor in ruble debt, the appropriately named High Risk Opportunities Fund, run by III Offshore Advisors of West Palm Beach, Florida, was wiped out. William McDonough, president of the New York Fed, hurriedly canceled his trip to Jackson Hole, Wyoming, where the Fed was holding its annual late-summer retreat. With bears on the prowl, McDonough had no time for moose.

Increasingly desperate, Meriwether and Rosenfeld placed another call to Buffett.[16] Some of the partners had never forgiven Buffett for, in their eyes, riding Meriwether out of Salomon. They resented the folksy billionaire's tendency to preach, particularly since he liked to heap disdain on academic models, which he eschewed in favor of his simple buy-and-hold approach to common stocks.[17] As we have seen, Long-Term's partners had even shorted Berkshire, an arbitrage on which they had lost about $150 million. But Buffett and the partners still respected each other as talented investors, albeit from different schools. And now Long-Term needed money, and no one in America save for Bill Gates had more of it than Buffett.

Buffett agreed to see Hilibrand, who flew out to Omaha on Thursday, August 27. By now, the firm's capital was down to $2.5 *billion*. The morning's *New York Times* intoned, "The market turmoil is being compared to the most painful financial disasters in memory."[18] By the time Hilibrand was airborne, he knew that stocks in Tokyo had fallen 3 percent, to a twelve-year low. "The most basic thing is not to panic," Kiichi Miyazawa, Japan's minister of finance, observed.[19] That day, Russian stock prices would fall 17 percent, leaving them a cool 84 percent below their level at the start of the year. In fact, markets around the world were plunging: London fell 3 percent, Spain 6 percent, Brazil 10 percent.

America's markets fell in sync with the world's. The Dow dropped 357 points, or 4 percent. Commodity prices, shuddering from fear of a world recession, touched a twenty-one-year low. The next day's *Wall Street Journal* would call it a "global margin call."[20] Everyone wanted his money back. Burned by foolish speculation in Russia, investors were rejecting risk in any guise, even reasonable risk. Yields on long-term Treasurys fell to 5.35 percent, the lowest since Lyndon Johnson was president. Yields on single-A credits—issued by the blue-chip Ford Motors of the world—soared to 115 over Treasurys, though Ford was no less safe a credit than in April, when it had traded at a spread of only 60. Investors wanted safety; moreover, they wanted the peace of mind that safer bonds delivered, no matter the price.

Buffett met Hilibrand at the airport that Thursday and escorted him back to his office, a modest suite in a pale high-rise across the street from a pizzeria. Hilibrand was his usual methodical self. He was candid about Long-Term's losses but totally controlled. He did not strike Buffett as desperate. The arbitrageur went over his battered portfolio in detail. Hilibrand stressed that he saw great potential going forward—given his personal debts, he had little choice. But Long-Term was in a hurry to raise money, Hilibrand said, and thus he offered to cut the fund's usual fee in half.

This was hardly enough for Buffett. In his opinion, Long-Term's fees had been too high as they were.[21] In any case, he had little interest, at least for now. Buffett said thanks, but no thanks.

When Hilibrand left and called Greenwich, the news was even worse. The fund had lost $277 million Thursday—its second worst day ever. Its capital was down to *$2.2 billion*. For four years, the brain trust in Greenwich had made money faster than anyone else. Now, like a movie that reveals an unsuspected horror on rewind, they were losing it incomparably faster. And then the unthinkable happened. On the next day, Friday, August 28, Long-Term earned a profit. Credit spreads narrowed, and the fund's capital rose by $128 million—its first substantial up day in months. The partners nourished a tiny hope that the long-awaited turn was at hand.

But the partners had another worry, aside from the fund, that required fast attention: LTCM, their personally owned management company, was facing serious cash flow problems. LTCM owed a total of $165 million to a group of banks—Fleet, Crédit Lyonnais, Chase Manhattan, and Lloyds. By late August, the banks, especially Fleet, were screaming that the fund's poor performance constituted an event of default and that, therefore, the banks were entitled to demand repayment. But the management company didn't have the cash—most of the money had been poured into the fund to heighten the partners' investment. Effectively, the management company was close to being insolvent. If that fact became public, both the firm and the fund could face a debilitating spiral.

Some of the partners, including Hans Hufschmid, who was worried about his personal debt, thought LTCM should simply sell some of its stake in the fund and pay off the banks. But Rickards, the lawyer, properly warned that if insiders took out money now, when the outside investors had no such option, it could look very bad later. Meriwether, who did not want a second censure from the SEC, agreed. Moreover, he realized that he could scarcely ask others for new investment if the partners were cashing out. For better or worse, the partners' money would have to stay in the fund.

And the fund (as distinct from LTCM) had cash flow worries, too. As August trickled away, the partners were feeling pressure from Bear Stearns, the fund's clearing broker, which was nervously eyeing the drop in Long-Term's equity. Thanks to Hilibrand's hardball negotiating tactics, the fund and Bear had never signed an agreement, meaning that Bear was free to stop clearing its trades whenever it pleased. Thus, Hilibrand's tactics had misfired, for Long-Term now was at Bear's mercy.

One strategy for freeing cash was to pair the trades that Long-Term had done with separate banks. Because none of its banks had the whole picture, none saw that most of its trades were hedged and tended to offset one another; therefore, each was demanding more margin than it otherwise would have. Long-Term was trying to move pairs of trades to the same house, but the job was overwhelming: the fund had a mind-boggling sixty thousand individual positions.[22]

Long-Term's earlier diffidence had become a liability (the problem of pairing trades wouldn't have arisen but for Hilibrand's earlier insistence on keeping banks in the dark). Hilibrand and the other traders had gotten away with being secretive and even arrogant when the fund was on top, but now their smug superiority was coming back to haunt them. Long-Term was having to plead for leniency to the very banks that it had offended. And the partners were tortured by the memory of having returned—despite the Sheik's strenuous objections—$2.7 billion to investors. Worse, they had *forced* their investors to take it! That money would have solved their problems, but of course, the investors were no longer enamored of Long-Term, nor were they begging to reinvest. What's more, many of the banks were themselves under stress. This is a timeless irony: when you need money most, the most likely sources of it (in Long-Term's case, other operators such as Soros, as well as investment banks and institutions) are likely to be hurting as well.

The partners began to sense that they might not make it. Their exquisitely wrought experiment in risk management, to say nothing of their fabulous profits, was in danger of unraveling. "We were desperate at the end of August," Rosenfeld admitted. Their tone changed to disbelief and bitterness at having left themselves exposed to such needless humiliation. They were much too rich to have gotten into so much trouble. Modest, the newest partner, lamented that his partnership was virtually worthless.

In another sign of their growing desperation, the partners scrambled to keep their personal assets from being contaminated by Long-Term's troubles. Hilibrand, once worth half a billion dollars, was paying for the work on his extravagant new mansion out of his wife's checking account. Meriwether quietly maneuvered to protect himself from the nauseating specter of creditors. He signed over his only real estate property—a twenty-acre lot in tony Pebble Beach, California—to his wife (his Westchester estate was already in Mimi's name).[23]

Badly in need of a lift, Meriwether called an old friend, Vinny Mattone, who had been the fund's first contact at Bear Stearns. Mattone, who had retired, was everything that J.M.'s elegant professors were not. He wore a gold chain and a pinkie ring, and he showed up at Long-Term in a black silk shirt, open at the chest. He looked as if he weighed three hundred pounds. Unlike J.M.'s strangely wooden partners, Mattone saw markets as exquisitely human institutions— inherently volatile, ever-fallible.

"Where are you?" Mattone asked bluntly.

"We're down by half," Meriwether said.

"You're finished," Mattone replied, as if this conclusion needed no explanation.

For the first time, Meriwether sounded worried. "What are you talking about? We still have two billion. We have half—we have Soros."

Mattone smiled sadly. "When you're down by half, people figure you can go down all the way. They're going to push the market against you. They're not going to roll [refinance] your trades. You're *finished*."

Not long after Mattone's visit, Meriwether and McEntee went for a drink at a local inn favored by J.M. and other transplanted Wall Streeters. Sipping his trademark gin and tonic, Meriwether looked at his pal and said in a voice that was completely flat, "You were right." The Sheik looked at him. "I should have listened to you," J.M. said.

■

Outsiders would later comment on how the group held together, but it was their only palatable choice. The deeper their fix, the less the partners wanted to be with anyone else and the more they closed ranks. They suppressed, for the moment, their resentments and bitter dislikes; they avoided recriminations and blame. Grim and determined, they got to the office at dawn and worked late into night, as if their physical presence alone could stop the hemorrhaging. They stayed on the phone for hours, trying to liquidate trades, stroking old investors, seducing new ones, fending off bankers. Rosenfeld and Leahy tried to keep up morale. They told the staff, "We're going to be fine. We have a lot of liquidity. We're raising new money. We just have to be smaller—we have too much risk." The partners continually retreated to the conference room, always with the curtains drawn to block out prying eyes, to hash out their problems in secret. Their meetings seemed endless. When they exited, a staffer might plead for a bit of news. But the partners barely responded, not even to their own employees. The tightly wound Hilibrand would brush right by as though he didn't hear.

■

By the final weekend in August, Long-Term was further than ever from meeting Soros's terms, and most everybody on Wall Street who had the power to write a check was out of town for the end of summer. Long-Term had lost scores of millions or hundreds of millions of dollars day after day, every single day for weeks—until, finally, it had enjoyed that single up day on Friday. Still hoping against hope, Meriwether made yet another round of calls.

One was to Merrill's Dan Napoli, to ask when Napoli thought the bleeding would stop—as if Napoli or anyone else could know. Then J.M. called Siciliano, reaching the UBS manager in Tokyo.

"Does *anyone* in your bank want to invest?" Meriwether queried. "These trades are mispriced. We think we have a tremendous opportunity." Keeping his composure, J.M. added that Long-Term believed it had up to $1 billion in other new money virtually sewed up.

UBS, though, was already Long-Term's biggest investor. "You must be down twenty-five percent," Siciliano said.

J.M. replied coolly, "More like forty-five percent."

Siciliano was stunned. He wondered who would want to risk putting in the first billion. He knew it wouldn't be he.

On Saturday, August 29, Meriwether called Edson Mitchell, the Merrill Lynch banker who had spearheaded Long-Term's maiden fund-raising effort in 1993. Mitchell had since moved to London to launch a global bond business for Deutsche Bank. Could Mitchell and Deutsche raise capital for Long-Term now?

Mitchell said it was unlikely.

Meriwether was running out of friends. When you need money, Wall Street is a heartless place.

On Monday, August 31, as the month ran out, the Hong Kong Monetary Authority, which had been buying shares of local stocks, suddenly stopped supporting the market. Yet another safety net had been exposed as porous. The local bourse tumbled 7 percent, triggering a run on Wall Street. The Dow crashed 512 points, a 6 percent plunge that took the average down to 7,539. It had fallen 19 percent since mid-July. Secretary Rubin, back from salmon fishing in Alaska, tried to calm markets by declaring that the U.S. economy was "sound." This merely deepened the mystery of the crash, for no one piece of news was responsible. *The Wall Street Journal* cited a "disappointing Chicago purchasing managers index," an almost comically trivial explanation. The paper was closer to the truth when it noted, "On the margin, there is no incremental buyer."[24] The Main Street economy *was* sound, but financial markets were overleveraged and overextended. The entire Street had lost its nerve. The cool, unemotional traders of Merton's models no longer existed, if they ever had. Now they were in full-fledged panic.

The damage in Long-Term's markets was acute. Equity volatility broke above 30 percent. Yields on Treasurys dropped, widening credit spreads ever more. Spreads on investment-grade bonds exploded upward—on that one day—from 133 points to 162! In truth, such spreads had to be inferred, because almost nothing in bond markets traded that day. The bond market had effectively closed; no one could trade out of anything, or not without suffering horrendous losses. It was as if a bomb had hit; traders looked at their screens, and the screens stared blankly back. Buyers were simply nowhere to be found. "August thirty-first was a unique day," said Curtis Shambaugh, the bond strategist at Credit Suisse First Boston. "So few issues traded, you had to guess where they were." For a fund that had to lighten its load, the month had ended with the most nightmarish kind of bond market imaginable: no bond market at all.

■

August was the worst month ever recorded in credit spreads.[25] In the past, such ballooning spreads had presaged an economic collapse. But this time, no depression threatened Main Street; perhaps a slowdown, but nothing more. The bond market collapse was caused by a panic not in the mainstream economy but on Wall Street itself, where too much optimism (and too much leverage) had suddenly come undone.

Three quarters of all hedge funds lost money in August, and Long-Term did the worst of any of them. In one dreadful month, Meriwether's gang lost $1.9 billion, or 45 percent of its capital, leaving it with only $2.28 billion. The Soros opportunity was gone—hopelessly gone. And Long-Term's portfolio still was dangerously bloated. The fund had $125 billion in assets—98 percent of its prior total and an extraordinary fifty-five times its now-shrunken equity—in addition to the massive leverage in its derivative bets, such as equity volatility and swap spreads. This leverage was simply untenable. If its assets continued to fall, its losses would eat through that $2.28 billion sliver of equity in an eye blink. Yet that leverage could not be reduced—not given the size of the trades and the utter loss of liquidity.

The partners were in an unfamiliar place, a territory the modelers hadn't explored. Stavis felt the partners had gotten to "a kind of volatility they didn't understand." Theoretically, the odds against a loss such as August's had been prohibitive; such a debacle was, according to the mathematicians, an event so freakish as to be unlikely to occur even once over the entire life of the Universe and even over numerous repetitions of the Universe.[26] But it had happened to Long-

Term not quite four years after Meriwether had written to the firm's investors, confidently endorsing Merton and Scholes's so finely tuned assumptions about the fund's risks. Alas, in the partners' lingo, the "correlations [among the trades] had gone to one." Every bet was losing simultaneously. The dice were not being thrown at random, or at least they seemed as if tossed by the same malevolent hand.

9

THE HUMAN FACTOR

A T THE BEGINNING OF September, Meriwether had to tell his investors about the fund's horrendous losses, and his letter did not mince words:

> As you are all too aware, events surrounding the collapse in Russia caused large and dramatically increasing volatility in global markets throughout August. . . . Unfortunately, Long-Term Capital Portfolio has also experienced a sharp decline in net asset value . . . it is down 44 percent for the month of August, and 52 percent for the year-to-date. Losses of this magnitude are a shock to us as they surely are to you, especially in light of the historical volatility of the fund.[1]

However, J.M.'s letter was guardedly optimistic about the fund's future. No doubt this rosy view reflected his honest assessment, but by now the partners' view of their prospects had seriously diverged from that of the outside world. According to the letter, the seeds of Long-Term's disaster had been sown earlier in 1998, when credit spreads had widened. Long-Term had bet on spreads to narrow again, but investors had fled from illiquid securities, pushing spreads wider still. Owing to this "flight to liquidity," as J.M. phrased it, "our losses across strategies were correlated after the fact"—a tortured construction intended to mean that Long-Term had done everything it could to avoid such correlations "before the fact."

His analysis was devoid of any suggestion that anyone at Long-Term had made a mistake—for instance, by not trimming the balance sheet at the end of 1997, when opportunities had been so scarce. By implication, J.M. faulted not his traders but the markets that had moved against them.

Meriwether assured the investors that "steps have been taken to reduce risks now, commensurate with our level of capital." But this was a rather misleading comment, given that Long-Term had done little in the way of selling and that its leverage had bolted to 55 to 1—a fact that Meriwether omitted. The kindest explanation is that Meriwether, under the strong influence of Hilibrand and Haghani, did not consider the core trades to be all that risky. "We see great opportunities in a number of our best strategies," he noted. In the meantime, J.M. asserted, the fund was "quite liquid"—a point that was true but that failed to address the serious cash flow problems developing at LTCM, the partners' management company.

Long-Term faxed the confidential letter on September 2, but one of the investors leaked it to Bloomberg, the financial news service, which published it even before the last investor had gotten his copy. This dollop of unwanted publicity hit the partners like a splash of ice water. *The Wall Street Journal* gave top billing to Long-Term's losses in a broader story on financial distress,[2] and James Cramer, an on-line financial columnist, stingingly observed that perhaps the term "genius" should be reserved for Mozart and not for arbitrageurs.[3]

Though embarrassed by the hooting press, the fund was expecting a turnaround now that traders were returning from the Hamptons. August, presumably, had been a quirk. "People were on vacation," the partners told one another. "Now it will come back." But the day after Meriwether's letter, Moody's Investors Service downgraded Brazilian debt. This was a bad sign. The global traders who carried the germ of financial crisis from country to country were now, as if by unspoken accord, focusing on Brazil. Currency speculators were putting the squeeze on São Paulo, which—following the dubious example of Moscow—was denying that it would ever devalue. The last thing Long-Term wanted was another Russia.

Inevitably, the banks tightened credit in Brazil. Herb Allison, Merrill's president, called a meeting for September 4, the Friday before Labor Day, to go over Merrill's repo exposures in emerging markets. Allison, once so supportive of the relationship with Long-Term, demanded to know why Merrill was financing the fund's Brazilian trades. "What do you mean, Herb?" one of Allison's underlings retorted, alluding to his boss's former fondness for Long-Term. "It's because of you!" Allison laughed and told his staff not to let it happen again.

The banks were agitated not just about hedge funds but about their own mounting losses. Goldman, Morgan, Salomon Smith Barney, Merrill, and the rest owned huge portfolios of bonds that, in different configurations, were generally similar to Long-Term's. The banks, too, had hedged their portfolios by shorting U.S. Treasurys, and they were exposed to the same merciless widening of credit spreads. Moreover, the banks' share prices had tumbled. Goldman, which had suffered the biggest losses, was especially nervous lest the bear market ruin its public offering, planned for the following month. Salomon was nervous, too. Sandy Weill was terrified that the losses from Arbitrage might jeopardize his pending merger with Citicorp, also slated for October. Under Weill's steely orders, Salomon continued to liquidate. The mercurial Haghani had been so upset that he wanted to buy what remained of Salomon's portfolio, just to stop its selling. His partners thought Haghani was daft—Long-Term wasn't in a position to *buy* anything. They all but suspected that the nervy Haghani was not doing his all to unload assets, almost as though he secretly enjoyed the thrill of having everything at stake. When in London, he continued to pedal to work, as if nothing was wrong.

But the partners noticed an ominous pattern: *their* trades were falling more than others'. There was a rally in junk bonds, for instance, but the specific issues that Long-Term owned stayed depressed.[4] Similarly, swap spreads were widening in England much more than in Germany—the exact opposite of what Long-Term had bet on—without any apparent economic rationale. In the United Kingdom, swap spreads soared to 82 points, while in Germany they lingered at 45. "It didn't make sense," a Long-Term trader fumed. If England was suffering from a flight to quality, it should logically have struck in Germany, too. But logically or otherwise, Wall Street traders were running from Long-Term's trades like rats from a sinking ship.

This was no longer purely coincidence. As it scavenged for capital, Long-Term had been forced to reveal bits and pieces and even the general outline of its portfolio. Ironically, the secrecy-obsessed hedge fund had become an open book. Markets, as Vinny Mattone might say, conspire against the weak. And thanks to Meriwether's letter, all Wall Street knew about Long-Term's troubles. Rival firms began to sell in advance of what they feared would be an avalanche of liqui- dating by Long-Term. "As people smelled trouble, they started get- ting out," Costas Kaplanis, then a trader at Salomon, remarked. "Not to attack LTCM—to save themselves." As they hammered away at Long-Term's trades, Leahy felt sick, as though the firm's competitors were liquidating Long-Term's own positions for it.[5] Hili- brand had not been wrong: when you bare your secrets, you're left naked.

Meriwether may have felt the fund was liquid, but Bear Stearns was not so sure. Long-Term's assets "in the box"—that is, the cash and securities it kept on call at Bear—were dropping by the day. Bear was increasingly uncomfortable about clearing for the fund. Making mat- ters worse, Robert Shustak, who updated Bear on the fund's results every afternoon, repeatedly underestimated the fund's losses. This wasn't intentional on Shustak's part. Long-Term had to estimate the value of many of its trades, particularly derivatives, which weren't publicly quoted. Long-Term got its "marks"—its prices—from other traders. And now rival banks were either playing it safe or exploiting Long-Term's woes by marking down its trades, forcing Shustak to go back to Bear with more accurate numbers.

Mike Alix, Bear's credit manager, felt it was time to put Long-Term on notice. Alix advised Shustak that if Long-Term's assets in the box went below $500 million, Bear would stop clearing for the fund. Un- derlining Bear's state of *agita*, Alix ordered Long-Term to find new fi- nancing for some futures contracts it had financed with Bear. The prudent Bear wanted no excess exposure to the hedge fund.

The pressure from Bear put Mike Reisman, Long-Term's repo man, in a state of *agita* as well. Reisman was Long-Term's money guy, the one who found the financing, and usually the best possible fi- nancing, for its bonds. He was also the closest that Long-Term had to a genuine character. Only thirty-three, Reisman was a stand-up comic who owned a piece of the Gotham Comedy Club in Manhattan. If anyone kept the office light, it was Reisman. But in early September, the repo guy was in no mood for comedy. Reisman, who more than anyone else had his finger on the fund's pulse, told a colleague that if Long-Term didn't raise new money by the end of the month, the fund would lose its repo lines, without which it couldn't survive.

The staff had a personal reason for feeling anxious. They had their own capital in the fund, yet they remained in the dark about what the partners were doing to save it. The employees were quiet heroes, working long days even as their future became increasingly cloudy. Naturally, they resented the partners, who worked alongside them but never shared their secrets. When the bosses shut the door for meetings, the staffers would wait with clenched teeth. When the partners exited, a staffer would say, "Hey, guys, what's going on?" The typical response: "We're working on it." As a substitute for solid info, employees mockingly developed a "necktie index": the more partners who wore a tie, the employees kidded, the more big meetings and thus the deeper the firm's trouble!

The partners were, in fact, worried that the employees would bolt. The issue could not be ignored, because LTCM, which paid the employees' salaries, was anything *but* liquid. In the first week of September, Fleet Bank called its loans to LTCM. This meant that LTCM was living on a thread; Fleet could put it into bankruptcy at any time. Presumably, if that happened, Long-Term's trading counterparties would then claim a default on their swap agreements and tip the fund itself into bankruptcy.

Facing their worst crisis yet, the partners moved $38 million out of the portfolio and into LTCM (which they personally owned) in the form of a loan. This dubious transaction provided the cash to pay salaries through the end of 1998, buying LTCM some time with the employees. The fund's outside directors approved the loan, reasoning that if LTCM failed, the fund itself could topple. But the loan, even though contractually permissible, was shot through with conflicts of interest. The partners were withdrawing—or, technically, borrowing against—their own investment in the fund without giving the same opportunity to the outside investors for whom they were trusted fiduciaries. It was a sign of rank desperation.

Even this fancy footwork was not enough. Still facing a threat from Fleet, LTCM persuaded David Pflug, the Chase Manhattan banker, to assume Fleet's loans, which totaled roughly $46 million, and to agree not to call the $62 million loan already outstanding from Chase. Rosenfeld was deeply grateful for Chase's "incredible move."[6] But now LTCM was in hock to Chase for $108 million, to Crédit Lyonnais for $50 million, to Lloyds for $7 million—and to its own fund for $38 million.

Seeking capital yet again, Meriwether called a trio of Merrill executives September 6, the Sunday before Labor Day. Duly alarmed, Merrill's Richard Dunn spent the holiday sifting through the bank's exposures to Long-Term. Merrill was now worried about more than its own direct exposure. Dunn was thinking about what would happen to markets if a collapse by Long-Term sparked a run for the exits: Could the entire Street fit through the same door at once? Merrill was so concerned that it deputized Dunleavy, the salesman, and Bob McDonough, the credit manager, to get some facts in Greenwich. Dunleavy, who was on friendly terms with the partners, asked them point-blank, "Are you guys OK?" The partners, putting their usual positive spin on matters, said that the firm, despite its problems, was liquid. Dunleavy later told colleagues that the partners had lied to him.[7]

But J.M. and company truly believed that with spreads so wide, a golden vindication lay around the corner. "We dreamed of the day when we'd have opportunities like this," Rosenfeld said.[8] What they lacked was the means to exploit them. J.M. was now in Eckstein's position, facing the prospect of having to let some new J.M. make the killing. Just to be on the safe side, Meriwether told Bill McDonough, the New York Fed president, that Long-Term was having to look for new money. J.M. and other Salomon executives had once been criticized for not having advised the Fed of a problem early enough; J.M. would not make that mistake again.

■

Throughout the end of August and into September, the partners' mood gyrated with their prospects for fresh investment. They sidestepped the delicate issue of LTCM's cash problems and dwelled on the supposedly bright prospects for anyone who invested now. Morgan's Mendoza was still promising $200 million. He breezily dropped the names of blue-chip investors on his list, including Jack Welch, the chairman of General Electric. However, Mendoza was often distracted from LTCM by other affairs. He was genuinely fond of the firm, but the partners were divided on whether Mendoza was their most effective ally or simply a sympathetic voyeur. In any case, the partners had plenty of tony names in their own Rolodexes. Myron Scholes contacted Michael Dell, the personal-computer magnate, who sent a team to inspect the fund's books. The Basses, the Texas financiers, and a host of others followed. Superficially, the blitz resembled Long-Term's first campaign of 1993.

But though they seemed not to realize it, the partners had lost the aura of invincibility that had opened doors for them before. They had the flashy résumés but not the magic—and without it, they were just another fund. Hoping to land the Ziff brothers, the publishing moguls, Meriwether offered to cut Long-Term's uncommonly high fee for—and only for—the first three years. Perhaps such a teaser might have worked once, but now J.M.'s offer of only a temporary discount struck the Ziffs as arrogant. Such is the ephemeral glitter of Wall Street: investors will knock down the door of a high-priced manager and then abandon him when he cuts his rate.

A group of the partners also visited Julian Robertson, the head of Tiger Management, a big hedge fund operator. Robertson, who was about to disclose a $2 billion loss on a misplaced yen bet, may not have been in a speculating mood. In any case, Robertson, a shrewd southerner, was not impressed; he saw little to convince him that Long-Term had any superior expertise. Once again, the partners came up empty. Rarely had such heady credentials and such a gaudy list met with such dim results.

Even Long-Term's existing investors were beginning to see the fund in a harsher light. Marlon Pease, the director of finance of the University of Pittsburgh, flew to Greenwich to see Merton and Scholes, who had virtual hero status in academia. The professors were close-mouthed about their recent losses but talked up the fund's potential. Scholes, ever the salesman, expressed confidence that Long-Term would raise a billion dollars in September and another billion by year-end. But Pease declined to contribute more.[9]

"We had been lulled into this dreamlike state," said William Sharpe, a Stanford professor who advised one of the fund's investors. But now Sharpe snapped out of it. When Scholes, his former colleague at Stanford, called to raise more money, Sharpe was wary. His client, a wealthy Chinese American, was ready to invest $30 million; the professor said it was too risky. They agreed that the client would invest $10 million now and another $10 million if Long-Term could corral a major investor. They were ready to wire the money to an escrow account, but Scholes delayed the closing. Long-Term knew it would be pointless to collect money in small amounts.

For the big money, Meriwether continued to angle with Herb Allison at Merrill, Edson Mitchell at Deutsche Bank, Donald Layton, a vice chairman of Chase, and Gary Brinson, who ran an asset management unit for UBS. Among them, these Wall Street lions easily had enough resources. But could the lions be roused from their den? The partners' glowing forecasts notwithstanding, the bankers had a nose for trouble. And with Long-Term increasingly desperate, the bankers could afford to be patient. Every day that passed, the "rare opportunity" merely got cheaper.

Improbable as it seemed, Long-Term's markets kept sinking. Risk-arb spreads opened to their widest since the 1987 crash.[10] Public stock offerings ground to a halt, sending a shudder through the bankers at Goldman Sachs.[11] Yields on B-rated bonds climbed to 570 basis points above the yields on blue chips—up from 200 points a year before. The price of short-term stock market insurance (equity volatility) doubled.[12] "It's like a blanket of fear has descended over the market," an options trader told *The Wall Street Journal*.[13] Overseas, prices reflected sheer panic. Interest rates on an index of emerging-market debt soared to 1,700 points above U.S. Treasurys—up from 300 points a year before![14] Alan Greenspan ominously warned that the United States could not expect to be an oasis of prosperity in such a troubled world.[15] It was a bear market in risk no matter what the asset.

And Long-Term had bet on risk all over the world. In every arbitrage, it owned the riskier asset; in every country, the least safe bond. It had made that one same bet hundreds of times, and now that bet was losing.

Thursday, September 10, was a very bad day. Swap spreads jumped another 7 points; other spreads widened, too. In a spot of bad luck—or was it a portent?—a rocket ferrying a dozen Globalstar satellites fell out of the sky and exploded. Long-Term, as it happened, owned Globalstar bonds. The partners almost laughed: even the heavens were against them. In the risk-management meeting, the traders went around the table, each reporting his results. When it be-

THE HUMAN FACTOR · 169

came clear that every trader had lost, Mullins demanded sarcastically, "Can't we *ever* make money—just for one day?" So far in September, they hadn't, not once. Markets were simply on strike. Everyone was selling now—except for Long-Term.

The fund was immobilized by its sheer mass. The smaller fish around it were liquidating every bond in sight, but Long-Term was helpless, a bloated whale surrounded by deadly piranhas. The frightful size of its positions put the partners in a terrible bind. If they sold even a tiny fraction of a big position—say, of swaps—it would send the price plummeting and reduce the value of all the rest. Ever since his Salomon days, Haghani had pushed his colleagues to double and even quadruple their positions. Now he saw that size extracts a price.

By late afternoon on the tenth, the partners knew they had crossed a debilitating psychological barrier: their capital had fallen below $2 billion. It was late that day when Meriwether got the call he had dreaded—from Warren Spector, executive vice president of Bear Stearns. Long-Term's assets in the box had dipped below $500 million, though they were restored by day's end. Apparently, J.M. explained, some of Long-Term's trading partners had started to take their time sending in monies due. No one wants to pay a prospective bankrupt. But Spector was past the point of explanations. He curtly told J.M. that Bear would be sending a team to look at Long-Term's books on Sunday. Otherwise, it wouldn't clear Long-Term's trades on Monday.

The next day, September 11, Meriwether called Corzine. The Goldman chief was en route from Venice, where he had been celebrating his wedding anniversary. J.M. had a simple message: Long-Term needed to raise a lot of money in a hurry. One billion dollars was no longer enough. To have any hope of surviving, the fund would have to raise at least $2 billion. Then J.M. called McDonough again, diligently updating the New York Fed chief on Long-Term's efforts to save itself.

When the team from Bear arrived on Sunday, Long-Term was on its best behavior. Suddenly a model client, it opened its books and set out a spread of sandwiches. Past the point of raising a fuss, Hilibrand patiently took the visitors through every trade. Meriwether and Rosenfeld attended the entire briefing, showing that Long-Term was taking Bear's threat seriously. Alix was impressed by the performance but disturbed by the size of Long-Term's trades. The next day, after Bear's executive committee met, Alix reiterated to Shustak that Bear truly regarded the $500 million threshold as inviolate. If Long-Term pierced it again, the game would be over.

UBS, Long-Term's biggest investor, was feeling even worse than Bear. David Solo, a derivatives whiz from the old Swiss Bank, realized—too late—that the newly merged UBS was in for horrendous losses. As Solo analyzed the warrant package, UBS had taken a huge risk for a potential return of only 8 percent—which now, of course, it would never realize. "All this discussion of option hedging, volatility and premiums is ridiculous," he tapped in an urgent September 14 e-mail to Marcel Ospel, formerly head of Swiss Bank and now CEO of UBS. In a dig at their merger partners, Solo added conspiratorially, "This trade was approved by the UBS group executive board and by many people sitting around your table."

Meanwhile, that Monday, Meriwether, Rosenfeld, and Leahy called on Lehman Brothers. Jeff Vanderbeek, who ran the bond side of Lehman, immediately asked if the rumors he was hearing about the fund's extreme distress were true. "Before we answer, what we'd like to talk about is the possibility of raising money through your private equity group," J.M. began, as though nothing were wrong. "We gave some money back last year. Now we see the best opportunities in twenty years." His hosts were stunned by Long-Term's nonchalant pose. Still, the pressure it was under showed. Meriwether asked Rosenfeld to explain the portfolio but then curtly interrupted him— a rare show of impatience toward the trusty partner whom he treated like a son. The Lehman crew was hardly mollified.

■

Long-Term did have one escape hatch: the revolving credit it had obtained in 1996 from the bank syndicate led by Chase. The $900 million revolver (raised from $500 million initially) was a standby facility that Long-Term could tap when it wanted. Usually, such facilities terminate automatically if the borrower suffers a sharp deterioration, known as a "material adverse change." But in its eagerness to deal with Long-Term, Chase had omitted the material-adverse-change clause. The revolver *was* cancelable if, at the end of any accounting period, Long-Term's equity fell by more than half. And the banks were squawking that the fund's losses had freed them of their obligation to fund. But the last "accounting period" had ended on July 31—at which time Long-Term had still had plenty of equity. So technically, the banks were on the hook. Thanks to Chase's sloppy drafting, the banks would have to lend $900 million to an insolvent.

But the partners were badly split on whether they *should* borrow. Mullins thought they shouldn't. If the fund went down, why take the banks with them? An additional loan would only complicate matters. J.M., Hawkins, Modest, and the Nobelists agreed. Hilibrand, Haghani, Leahy, and Rosenfeld argued strongly for drawing on the revolver. How else, they asked, could they hope to replenish their capital at Bear? Krasker, McEntee, and Shustak were for funding, too. Rickards, the lawyer, pointed out that Long-Term might be liable to its own investors if it didn't pursue every option. "We don't have to decide at this juncture," J.M. finally said, cutting off the debate. They didn't need the money *quite* yet.

The partners still had Goldman Sachs and Corzine, who now, in mid-September, emerged as Long-Term's one best hope. Tall and bearded, Corzine had always seemed an unlikely financier. Born in a farmhouse in southern Illinois, he had played basketball in college and married a girl from his kindergarten class.[16] In 1975, a year after Meriwether had been hired by Salomon, Corzine had joined the bond department at Goldman. He had developed into a talented trader, though less celebrated than Meriwether, whom he frankly admired and whose arbitrage unit he viewed as a model for his own firm. As Corzine climbed the ranks at Goldman, he remained unaffected and easygoing, known for fuzzy patched sweaters in a world of three-piece suits.

Goldman, Wall Street's last private full-service investment bank, shared certain traits with Long-Term. Its partners were secretive and, for many decades, had been unusually close. The Goldman culture was exceptionally discreet (there is no indication of Goldman's presence in the lobby of its headquarters at 85 Broad Street). Until recent times, Goldman had been known for the care that it lavished on blue-chip corporate clients. An apostle of relationship banking, Goldman had disdained hostile takeovers and even eschewed trading for its own account, on the noble premise that trading could put the bank into conflict with its customers.[17] But in the 1980s and early '90s, such drawing room niceties were cast aside. The leadership duo of Stephen Friedman and Robert Rubin, later of Treasury fame, confidently expanded into trading, and as Goldman's bankers removed their white gloves, conflicts with customers became common. When the bond market cracked in 1994, Goldman—which, like Long-Term, had set risk limits according to statistical models of volatility—suffered enormous and destabilizing losses. Goldman discovered that its leveraged positions were well known to other traders, and it could not get out of them without suffering heavy losses.[18] Partners defected en masse, saddling the unpretentious Corzine, who took over in the fall of 1994, with the job of rebuilding the partnership as well as the business. The firm bounced back, but Goldman's partners—again like Long-Term's—realized that they needed more capital, which was the reason for their planned stock offering. Meanwhile, Corzine further emphasized the lucrative business of trading for the bank's account.

Corzine had been intrigued with the idea of joining forces with Meriwether before, and now he could deal with his rival from a position of strength. He agreed to provide capital, but at a price: he demanded half of the partners' management company, full access to Long-Term's strategies, and the right to set a limit on the fund's exposures. The congenial financier was proposing nothing short of a takeover. However, Corzine was offering $1 billion of Goldman's and its clients' money, as well as a promise to help Long-Term raise a second billion. And merely informing the world that Goldman was in Long-Term's corner might stop the bleeding. Meriwether could not say no.

The two firms quickly struck a deal, conditional on Goldman's raising the money and on Long-Term's passing an inspection, a customary process. Goldman had to move fast, before any more of Long-Term's capital was lost. The week of September 14, the fund handed over mountains of files and dispatched Rosenfeld, Merton, and four of the staff to Broad Street. Merton waxed poetic about the supposed strategic value of the two firms' joining. A Goldman team peppered the arbitrageurs with questions. Then a half-dozen lawyers from Sullivan & Cromwell, Goldman's outside law firm, marched in and subjected the emissaries from Long-Term to a torturous grilling.

In Greenwich, Goldman's sleuths, who had the run of the office, left no stone unturned. Long-Term's staff couldn't keep track of who the Goldman people were, so many were rummaging through the hedge fund's files. A key member of the Goldman team was Jacob Goldfield, a lanky and brilliant but abrasive trader. According to witnesses, the headstrong Goldfield appeared to be downloading Long-Term's positions, which the fund had so zealously guarded, from Long-Term's own computers directly into an oversized laptop (a detail that Goldman later denied). Meanwhile, Goldman's traders in New York sold some of the very same positions. At the end of one day, when the fund's positions were worth a good deal less, some Goldman traders in Long-Term's offices sauntered up to the trading desk and offered to buy them.[19] Brazenly playing both sides of the street, Goldman represented investment banking at its mercenary ugliest. To J.M. and his partners, Goldman was raping Long-Term in front of their very eyes.

On Monday, the day the Goldman invasion was launched, equity volatility climbed to an astonishing 32 percent! On Tuesday it hit 33 percent—each point cost the fund $40 million. Throughout the fund's portfolio it was a similar story. Long-Term's trades—its trades *in particular*—were mercilessly battered, from Danish mortgages to Volkswagen shares to junk bonds of Station Casinos and Starwood. Shell Transport, which Long-Term had purchased at an 8 percent discount to Royal Dutch, disastrously widened to a spread of 14 percent. Even the reliable trade in Italian bonds, which had made money during most of 1998, now fell back, too.

In every class of asset and all over the world, the market moved against the hedge fund in Greenwich. Rickards, the house attorney, described it to colleagues as the "LTCM death trade." The correlations had gone to one; every roll was turning up snake eyes. The mathematicians had not foreseen this. Random markets, they had thought, would lead to standard distributions—to a normal pattern of black sheep and white sheep, heads and tails, and jacks and deuces, not to staggering losses in every trade, day after day after day.

The professors had ignored the truism—of which they were well aware—that in markets, the tails are always fat. Stuck in their glass-walled palace far from New York's teeming trading floors, they had forgotten that traders are not random molecules, or even mechanical logicians such as Hilibrand, but people moved by greed and fear, capable of the extreme behavior and swings of mood so often observed in crowds. And in the late summer of 1998, the bond-trading crowd was extremely fearful, especially of risky credits. The professors hadn't modeled this. They had programmed the market for a cold predictability that it had never had; they had forgotten the predatory, acquisitive, and overwhelmingly protective instincts that govern real-life traders. They had forgotten the human factor.

Meriwether bitterly complained to the Fed's Peter Fisher that Goldman, among others, was "front-running," meaning trading against it on the basis of inside knowledge. Goldman, indeed, was an extremely active trader in mid-September, and rumors that Goldman was selling Long-Term's positions in swaps and junk bonds were all over Wall Street. In fact, its high-yield traders were said to be bragging about it.

But Goldman was hardly alone. Knowledge of Long-Term's portfolio was, by now, commonplace. Salomon was, and had been, pounding the fund's positions for months. Deutsche Bank was bailing out of swap trades, and American International Group, which hadn't shown any interest in equity volatility before, was suddenly bidding for it. Why this sudden interest, if not to exploit Long-Term's distress? Morgan and UBS were buying volatility, too. Some of this activity was clearly predatory. The game, as old as Wall Street itself, was simple: if Long-Term could be made to feel enough pain—could be "squeezed"—the fund would cry uncle and buy back its shorts. Then, anyone who owned those positions would make a bundle.

Yet the extent of predatory trading was less than one might suppose, and certainly less than was later asserted in certain paranoid theories in Greenwich. The partners' bunkered view of the world made them highly susceptible to conspiracy theories, particularly since such explanations shifted the blame for their losses to others. Being so self-absorbed, the arbitrageurs naturally assumed that the banks were obsessed with Greenwich, too.

But the simple fact is that by mid-September, the Wall Street banks were not principally worried about Long-Term Capital—they were worried about themselves. Given that every bank had many of the same trades as Long-Term, exiting from their positions was a matter of self-preservation. Goldman in particular was steeped in losing trades and, with its stock offering just weeks away, was desperate to cut its losses.

It made no difference whether the banks were consciously trying to profit at Long-Term's expense or merely protecting themselves from the tidal wave of selling that they anticipated from Greenwich. *Either motivation would have produced the same behavior*—a wholesale flight from Long-Term's trades. One Long-Term trader saw his best friend, a fellow former academic now at Deutsche Bank, dumping Long-Term's positions. The other traders knew that if Long-Term collapsed, the ground would tremble. "If you think a gorilla has to sell, then you sure want to sell first," noted a Goldman trader in London. "We are very clear on where the line is; that's not illegal."

With the exception of stocks in America, which are specifically subject to insider trading laws that are enforced as nowhere else, trading on private information goes on all the time. Investment banks that also operate proprietary bond-trading desks, such as Salomon and Goldman, publicly boasted of exploiting their knowledge of the "customer flow." Translated, this meant that when a Salomon or a Goldman got wind of which way its customers were running, it often ran there too—and fast. This was why Goldman's previous stewards had refused to get involved in proprietary trading; the possibility of conflicts of interest was just too great. But by 1998, Goldman was known as an aggressive, bare-knuckled trader that had long since abandoned any pretense of being a gentleman banker.

Of course, if Goldman or anyone else took advantage of information it obtained while providing investment banking help, it could, theoretically, be liable under fraud statutes, though such a charge would be difficult to prove. Corzine, for his part, did not deny that Goldman traders "did things in markets that might have ended up hurting LTCM. We had to protect our own positions. That part I'm not apologetic for."

Corzine did deny that Goldman traded any differently as a result of its access to Long-Term than it otherwise would have. Given the kind of quarter it was having, he added wryly, it was strange to hear that Goldman was accused of making untoward profits.[20]

■

Long-Term was completely at such rivals' tender mercy because its trades were so arcane and specialized. For instance, only a handful of dealers—Morgan, Salomon, UBS, Société Générale, Bankers Trust, and Morgan Stanley—traded equity volatility. They knew that Long-Term was massively short, and they knew that sooner or later the fund would have to buy its way out of the trade. So, the dealers refused to sell. In desperation, Long-Term called Société Générale, seeking a bid for its position, but the French bank quoted a ridiculously lofty price: 10 percentage points above the market! Absurd as it was, there were no other potential buyers of equity volatility. Inevitably, the price ballooned.

Normally, a free market cures such bubbles on its own. In 1980, for instance, the Hunt brothers had tried to corner the silver market, briefly taking the price to $50 an ounce. But then people began to sift through attics for stowed-away silver, and scrap dealers all over the world started melting it down. When all that metal reached the market, the price went back to $5 an ounce, and the Hunts filed for bankruptcy. But equity volatility was a rare bird. No one had stored volatility in his attic, there was no surplus source of supply. "Equity volatility was the ultimate short squeeze," said a knowledgeable Long-Term employee. "There were only four or five dealers. And they refused to sell."

As the firm's losses mounted, the latent divide between the inner group of partners and the others fermented into sour wine. Inevitably, the lesser partners blamed Hilibrand and Haghani for blowing so much wealth. Hawkins and Hilibrand, never the best of friends, became bitter toward each other, and Scholes and Hilibrand were barely speaking. The unhappy partners resented not just Hilibrand's and Haghani's investment calls but their domineering, insensitive style. Scholes felt that the secretive Hilibrand hadn't really been a partner; Larry hadn't trusted the others. Ironically, it was the same complaint that the banks had been making all along. McEntee, meanwhile, was increasingly absent from the firm. He was immobilized by an aching back, a symbolic expression of the partners' despair, and increasingly bitter that Meriwether hadn't heeded his warnings.

Given their frayed nerves and their enormous losses, it was only human for the partners to show some tension. They were losing not only their fortunes but also their reputations. Meriwether was facing the unbearable indignity of a second disaster in a once shining career. And his traders, no matter what they might accomplish later, would always be known for their role in Long-Term's stupendous rise and fall. Rosenfeld, the most emotional of the group and the most devoted to the firm, was touchingly affected. At least he was not afraid to scream when the anguish overcame him.

Merton, his teacher, was upset, too; he was distraught and not himself. Worrying that Long-Term's collapse would undermine the standing of modern finance—all he had really worked for—Merton repeatedly broke into tears. The professor was wonderfully human, after all. Scholes, too, knew that if the firm failed, many would consider their Nobel Prizes tarnished. Coincidentally, as the fund plummeted, Scholes made a long-scheduled visit to his hometown, Hamilton, Ontario, where he was honored as a local boy turned

Nobel laureate. His audience had no idea of the trouble at Long-Term, and the tension on the guest of honor must have been unbearable. After fondly recalling his youth there, Scholes nearly broke down.[21]

Mullins's prospects had darkened, as well. The natty banker had once imagined that he might be a successor to Alan Greenspan. Now that would never happen.

Yet amid this unceasing agony, the partners mostly kept their feelings in check. Their simmering resentments never, or very rarely, bubbled into the open. They continued working together and refrained from shouting or openly pointing fingers. Indeed, given the circumstances, they functioned remarkably well. It said something about the bonds between them, particularly within the inner circle. They muttered under their breath but didn't shirk their jobs. If any one person was to blame, at least in the eyes of the lesser partners, it was Meriwether—for not having run the firm with a stronger hand. And no one wanted to blame J.M.

Meriwether, typically, kept his emotions under wraps. Although deeply distressed about the losses, he stayed cool—indeed, Rosenfeld had barely seen him angry in fifteen years. Meriwether seemed to unburden himself only in moments of levity, when the tension of working fifteen-hour days, seven days a week, gave way to a sense of the absurd. One night, around 2 A.M., J.M. was sitting with Leahy, Rosenfeld, and Rickards. Exhaustion had made them giddy, and the group started to talk about renaming the company if it managed to survive. J.M. said wryly, "I guess we could call ourselves 'No-Haircut Capital Management.'" That broke up the group; J.M.'s humor always cheered them. Then, as if to make light of their brutal handiwork, Meriwether whistled and added, "Oh, we took the Swiss down big." He meant UBS, the big Swiss investor. J.M. joked, "We'll never be able to set foot in Switzerland again—they'll arrest us the moment we get off the plane!"

As Goldman's bankers looked for money, they discovered a fact that Meriwether hadn't disclosed: the best prospects on Goldman's list, such as Buffett, Soros, Michael Dell, and Saudi Prince Alwaleed bin Talal bin Abdulaziz al-Saud, had already been called by Long-Term—and had already rejected the fund. Corzine was more than a little piqued; with the situation so desperate, it was no time for Long-Term to be playing coy.

Long-Term was still losing scores of millions of dollars each day. It was desperately trying to pair its trades, but its progress was slow. It was juggling positions to stay above its minimum at Bear, but its mounting losses, compounded by unfavorable marks (prices), moved it ever closer to the edge. The firm tried to dump positions on its banks, but the Merrills and the Goldmans had no interest: they were overinvested in the same trades.

■

By mid-September, the partners were praying for three strokes of luck to turn markets: for Congress to approve more aid to the IMF, for the IMF to approve a bailout of Brazil, and for Greenspan to lower interest rates. Of the three, Greenspan was the most crucial and the least predictable.

The Fed was deeply concerned about the widening of credit spreads, and the New York branch had repeatedly been advised of Long-Term's plight. Also, on September 11, Representative Richard Baker, a Louisiana Republican, alerted Greenspan to the fact that hedge funds were aggravating the condition of publicly traded banks. In a perceptive letter, Representative Baker, who was getting inside dope from a Morgan graduate on his staff, warned, "It has come to my attention that unregulated hedge funds which are often highly leveraged may be contributing to very substantial declines in the market value of regulated financial institutions." The crisis was now public. On September 15, George Soros warned the House Banking Committee that Russia's implosion had led to a global credit crunch. He blamed banks for fostering a "daisy chain of derivatives transactions"—language that seemed informed by his secret dealings with Long-Term.

The following day, September 16, Greenspan went before the same panel. He dashed the market's hopes, telling Congress that a rate cut was out of the question. Incredibly, he again downplayed the risks posed by rogue investors such as hedge funds. The chairman's credulity seemed to know no bounds: "Hedge funds are strongly regulated by those who lend the money," Greenspan asserted. Given that Long-Term's lenders had bankrolled the runaway hedge fund, it is hard not to conclude that Greenspan was either woefully out of touch or willfully deaf to what he had heard. Secretary Rubin, at least, acknowledged that the bull market had inevitably dulled many bankers' sense of prudence. "Where you've had five, six, seven years of good results," he told the panel, "people who extend credit tend to get a little less careful."[22]

■

Finance is often poetically just; it punishes the reckless with special fervor. Long-Term's creditors were discovering that their past leniency had made the current crisis worse. Whereas when a typical client defaulted, a reserve would exist in the form of margin money held by lenders, Long-Term could theoretically drop all the way to zero. The banks' willingness to finance Long-Term without any haircuts had enabled the fund to operate right up to the edge. Now, if it defaulted, nothing would be left.

Not surprisingly, the lenders were horrified by what they had wrought. "We had no idea they would have trouble—these people were known for risk management. They had taught it; they *designed* it," reflected Dan Napoli, the Merrill risk manager who had so enjoyed golfing with the partners in Ireland. "God knows, we were dealing with Nobel Prize winners!" Ironically, only a very intelligent gang could have put Wall Street in such peril. Lesser men wouldn't have gotten the financing or attracted the following that resulted in such a bubble.

In a sure sign that the credit net around the fund was tightening, General Re, an insurance company that was in the process of merging with Berkshire Hathaway, was contesting Long-Term's "marks"—that is, arguing about where to price its trades—virtually every day. Tony Iliya, the London-based head of General Re's derivatives subsidiary, which had financed yen swaps with Long-Term, was waking people in Tokyo in the middle of the night to press claims against the fund.

Even J. P. Morgan, which was offering capital to Greenwich with one hand, was sifting through its exposure to Long-Term to prepare for a possible default with the other. "It was going to be really ugly," a Morgan executive confided. Bankruptcy does not prevent derivative parties from seizing collateral. If Long-Term filed, it could expect to find its fax machine humming with claims from each of its fifty or so counterparties. In fact, if Long-Term defaulted on *any* of its seven thousand derivative contracts, it would automatically trigger a default in every one of the others, which covered some $1.4 trillion in notional value. In a bizarre touch, even a *contemplation* of bankruptcy was considered an act of default. Long-Term's lawyers wouldn't even mention the B-word. They cloaked their deliberations in a childlike game. One lawyer would ask another, "What if there was a fund that lost a lot of money; do you think it would file?" Notwithstanding this playacting, Meriwether knew he had less than a week to save his firm.

■

Salomon Smith Barney—Long-Term's progenitor—had stayed aloof from the rescue efforts. But on Wednesday, September 16, Salomon jumped into the action. The bank sent Rob Adrian, Salomon's head of risk management for equities, Andy Constan, who ran derivatives trading for the firm, and Marc Weill—Sandy's son—to Greenwich. They expected to join Goldman and others of the banks in a wide-ranging meeting. However, by the time the Salomon group arrived, just after 4 P.M., the meeting was over. Adrian noticed an eerie quiet; doors were closed, and the trading floor was deserted. Haghani took them to an office and bluntly announced that only one topic remained on the agenda. "We need money," he noted.[23]

Haghani offered to show them the books, which were now an open secret, but Weill, knowing of his dad's antipathy to arbitrage, didn't want to compromise Salomon by seeing too much. So the group drove home.

The next day, Salomon sent a more senior team: Steve Black, Thomas Maheras, and Peter Hirsch. By now Haghani seemed to be in shock. Over the last five trading days, Long-Term had lost $530 million. The losses seemed even worse for having been so relentless. On Thursday, September 10, the firm had lost $145 million; on Friday, $120 million. The next week it hadn't stopped: on Monday, Long-Term dropped $55 million; on Tuesday, $87 million. Wednesday, September 16, was especially bad: $122 million. Like a biblical plague, the losses gave no respite. Haghani went over the losses with a clinical air, as if they had happened to someone else. He couldn't get over the fact that Long-Term's diversification hadn't worked. The August losses he understood, but September's—when the markets should have recovered—baffled him. U.S. swap spreads had climbed to an astonishing 83 points; U.K. swaps, incredibly, were at 88! Long-Term's massive positions in these two trades alone could bankrupt it. Haghani bitterly blamed Wall Street, especially Goldman, for ganging up on the friendless fund.[24]

Though furious at Goldman, the partners were, quixotically, counting on the bank as a savior. Rosenfeld and others were calling Goldman throughout the week, with growing desperation. Despite Goldman's initial optimism, it hadn't yet raised the money, and Long-Term now figured that it needed not two but *four* billion dollars— quite a sum. Meriwether, Hilibrand, Rosenfeld, and Merton went to press their case with Goldman on Thursday morning, September 17. Corzine and John Thain, the narrow-set, angular chief financial officer, ushered them in.

Rosenfeld said, in so many words, "You're our last chance."

Later that Thursday, Meriwether advised Bill McDonough of Long-Term's plight. Ironically, the fund made money that day, its first profit all month. But the profit was a pittance, $6 million—far too little and too late. Long-Term's equity was down to *$1.5 billion*. It was astonishing to think that only a month had passed since Russia's default. In that one month, Long-Term had lost six tenths of its capital, one of Wall Street's epic collapses.

On Friday, Long-Term heard from Goldman. Thain noted that very few people could invest in the amounts that Long-Term needed. Buffett might be good for a chunk, and Soros might, but Long-Term had already called them, as well as virtually everyone else on Goldman's list. Peter Kraus, a Goldman investment banker, had talked to Buffett that very morning. Buffett had reiterated that, as he had told Hilibrand, he wasn't interested. The others had refused, too. Therefore, Thain didn't think it was possible. Thain didn't bother to say what he was thinking privately: to all appearances, Long-Term was going under.

■

But Goldman didn't stop trying. Kraus and Buffett spoke several more times that day. The biggest stumbling block for Buffett was that he didn't like Long-Term's complicated partnership structure. He had no interest in its various feeder funds and certainly none in the tangled details of LTCM. Buffett had folded his own partnership decades ago, partly for such reasons; he had no use for somebody else's. But if it was just a matter of buying Long-Term's portfolio—which now was pretty beaten down—without keeping Meriwether, his staff, or his company, that might work, Buffett told Kraus. Refining this thought, the two began to talk about Berkshire and Goldman jointly bidding for Long-Term's assets, perhaps along with AIG, the insurer. Meanwhile, Kraus reported this slight progress to Corzine. Throughout the day, Goldman kicked around the notion of a Berkshire-Goldman bid as well as other ways of saving the fund.

At Long-Term, the situation was becoming dire. The firm got a letter from Bear flatly stating its intention to stop clearing below $500 million—clearly the final step before cutting it off. Now it was time to talk to Chase. Though Long-Term felt that legally it could draw on its loan facility anytime, the partners wanted to hear Chase say so, too. Mullins, the house banker, called David Pflug. Pflug had already stuck his neck out for Long-Term by assuming Fleet's loan. Would he do it again?

Pflug, a banker's banker, knew that if Chase and the other syndicate members did fund, they might not get the money back. But if Chase didn't fund, it could be liable. Moreover, Pflug was afraid that if Long-Term collapsed, it might reverberate all over Wall Street. And Wall Street was a major client. Calling Walter Shipley, Chase's chairman, Pflug said, "I don't think we have any choice."

Meanwhile, Long-Term's markets were tumbling again. Incredibly, equity volatility jumped to 35 percent. U.S. swaps widened to 84½. And on it went. Mortgage spreads widened by 7 points, junk bonds by 5. The Dow fell 218 points; Japanese stocks fell to levels not seen since 1986.

Friday evening, Rosenfeld called Morgan's Peter Hancock, who lived in Mamaroneck, the same town as Rosenfeld, and whose children attended the same school as Rosenfeld's. The usually collected arbitrageur was highly agitated; he was petrified that Bear would pull the plug and confided that Long-Term might not survive the following week. Long-Term was losing its credit lines, and its woes were being exacerbated by rumors (many of them false or wildly exaggerated) about its positions.

On a whim, Rosenfeld suggested that the Morgan banker call Thain at Goldman. As far as is known, that was the first time anyone had asked the banks to coordinate their efforts. Hancock and Thain spoke that night.

Kraus, the banker spearheading the Goldman effort, had taken his wife and a client tð a Beethoven concert in Newark on Friday. At intermission, Kraus ducked out to a pay phone and dialed Omaha. He and Buffett penciled out some numbers for a deal. Buffett said something about going on a trip, and Kraus went back to Beethoven, saying nothing to his wife or the client. Then Buffett called Joseph Brandon of General Re, Berkshire's soon-to-be insurance acquisition. "There are folks that are in meltdown. They may not make it," the billionaire warned. "Accept no excuses for anyone who doesn't post collateral or make a margin call. *Accept no excuses.*" Then he hopped a plane for Seattle to meet a Bill Gates–led group that was planning a two-week holiday in Alaska and some of the western national parks.[25]

Now the dream was alive that Buffett would rescue Long-Term— as he had, coincidentally, Salomon seven years earlier. Nonetheless, Corzine thought the Fed should be brought into the loop. He called McDonough, who also spoke with the heads of other big banks. To a man, the bankers said that Long-Term's troubles were depressing markets. Moreover, they were worried that if Long-Term failed it could have a seriously destabilizing effect.

With such fears in mind, Corzine offered to have Goldman brief the Fed on Long-Term's portfolio. Meriwether agreed that the Fed should be briefed but naturally preferred to have Long-Term do it directly. Thus, on Saturday, Mullins, a former central banker, called McDonough and invited the Fed to Greenwich.

McDonough, of course, had been thinking about Long-Term for a while. He had known that eventually he might have to step in; he also knew that doing so would expose the Fed to criticism. A regulator is part protector, part godfather. He dislikes a public spectacle; he is most effective when he can wield his power discreetly, by merely threatening to act or by cajoling others to do his bidding. Most ideal, in McDonough's mind, would be for some private Wall Street leader to orchestrate a solution. He and John Whitehead, the chairman of the New York Fed, talked about who could do it. Once, Walter Wriston of Citibank or Gus Levy of Goldman could have rallied Wall Street. A century ago, of course, J. P. Morgan, Sr., had played the part to perfection. But who could play the part today? McDonough and Whitehead agreed on the answer: no one. Wall Street had many bankers but no J. P. Morgan.[26] Therefore, although the Fed was agreeing only to be briefed, not to play an active role, McDonough was ready to take the first step.

The meeting was scheduled for Sunday. But McDonough was planning to fly to London the night before. He decided not to cancel—it would upset markets—and to send Peter Fisher, his deputy, to Long-Term instead. Before McDonough left, he briefed both Greenspan and Rubin and told them that Long-Term's attempt to raise capital had failed.[27]

But Goldman was still on the case. By chance, David Solo, the Swiss-based derivatives maven at UBS, was in New York for the wedding of a friend. Corzine tracked him down and asked if UBS would want to join a fund-raising effort for Long-Term. Solo said, "Fine, but do you realize we're their biggest equity investor? I don't think our interests are exactly aligned." Corzine, who hadn't known, rang off, obviously irritated. He was getting tired of trying to rescue a firm about which, apparently, he was still in the dark.

Corzine also talked to Buffett on Saturday, though only when Buffett could get a connection via cell phone from the depths of an Alaskan fjord. "He was doing this float-around," Corzine recalled, his exasperation showing. "You'd lose contact and couldn't speak for two or three hours."[28] According to Buffett, who had never had much use for nature and had been arm wrestled into the trip by Bill Gates, "The guy in the boat wanted to go over and look at the moose, and I wanted to get in line with the satellite connection. It was just a horrible connection."[29]

But he got his point across all the same. Buffett was willing to let Goldman handle the details, but under no circumstances did he want his investment to be managed by LTCM or to have anything to do with John Meriwether. Then the connection blacked out.

AT THE FED

Markets would . . . possibly cease to function.
—WILLIAM J. MCDONOUGH, PRESIDENT,
FEDERAL RESERVE BANK OF NEW YORK

THE FEDERAL RESERVE SYSTEM was created, in 1913, for many reasons, but the underlying one was that people no longer trusted private bankers to shepherd the financial markets. Prior to the Fed's founding, the government had had no effective weapon to temper the country's economic cycles, nor was there much it could do to ease the periodic crises that afflicted Wall Street. Too often, the government had had to go hat in hand to a private banker for help. By the Progressive Era, with its suspicion of trusts and its faith in regulation, people wanted a bank that would represent the public interest. Ever since, the Fed has been a public servant but one that works in close proximity to private banks and to Wall Street. It is a delicate role, for the Fed is supposed to regulate banking but not to shelter bankers. It must protect the functioning of markets without appearing to be too close—too protective—of the banks it watches over.

The side of the Fed most often seen in public is its governing board, in Washington, which has the high-profile job of adjusting short-term interest rates. The chairman of this body is the country's chief inflation fighter and, in a larger sense, the steward of its economy. Alan Greenspan, who has been chairman since 1987, is probably the most respected of all those who have held the job, thanks to the economy's stellar performance during his tenure. If Greenspan has perfected a convoluted, often impenetrable style of public utterances, this has only heightened his image as the nation's economic oracle.

More than is commonly realized, Greenspan relies on the Fed's individual branches, particularly on the New York Fed, which, among its other roles, functions as Washington's periscope into markets. William McDonough, the beefy president of the New York Fed, kept in close touch with private bankers and reported on what he heard to Greenspan. His associate was Peter Fisher, in 1998 a forty-two-year-old bureaucrat who had joined the Fed straight out of Harvard Law School. Fisher ran the Fed's trading desk and oversaw a $450 billion portfolio of government securities. When Greenspan wanted to tighten or loosen monetary conditions, Fisher and his staff actually carried out the directive by either buying more securities or selling some.[1]

Fisher, who is six feet, three inches tall with graying curly hair, had been paying attention to hedge funds well before the Long-Term crisis. In his view, hedge funds were merely one more sign of the economy's increasing tendency to parcel out to specialists the jobs (such as lending and investing) that had previously been handled by commercial banks. For instance, in the 1980s, when Latin American governments couldn't pay their loans, the damage had been borne entirely by a few big banks. But in the 1990s, when Mexico defaulted, the pain was felt by dozens of hedge funds and mutual funds, and by their investors—who had assumed the banks' traditional role of providing capital to emerging markets. Fisher's overall view of hedge funds was not dissimilar to Merton's notion that Long-Term was essentially a bank.

However, Long-Term was not a bank, and the Fed does not have authority over hedge funds. Had Fisher demanded to see Long-Term's books—or any hedge fund's—it could in theory have refused. But in practice, Fisher routinely talked to traders at hedge funds, some of whom freely shared their opinions on the market and all of whom tacitly recognized the Fed's authority. And for Sunday, Fisher had an invitation.

Canceling plans to watch his eight-year-old son and six-year-old daughter play soccer, Fisher, who lived in Maplewood, New Jersey, a middle-class suburb light-years from Greenwich, hitched a ride with Dino Kos, one of his assistants, in Kos's Jeep. At Long-Term's offices, they rendezvoused with Gary Gensler, an assistant secretary of the Treasury and former partner of Rubin's at Goldman Sachs, and with another official from the Fed.

Long-Term's offices were quiet. The Sun workstations were mostly unattended. Mullins ushered the visitors into the conference room with the other partners, passing by a room where, Fisher noticed, Jacob Goldfield and his Goldman team were poring over Long-Term's files.

After some brief cordialities, Hilibrand showed the bureaucrats a document so secret that even most of Long-Term's employees had never seen it. The document was known as the "risk aggregator." Long-Term was hard for outsiders to understand because many of its positions consisted of multiple trades. What's more, its derivatives book was a monstrosity of contracts each of which was offset by other contracts. The risk aggregator simplified the portfolio by summarizing Long-Term's exposure to each individual market.

Fisher studied the report like a pathologist scanning an X ray. As he listened to the presentation, he realized that the patient was in critical condition. Each exposure in the risk aggregator was listed in a separate row, and the rows were grouped into separate boxes by category. For instance, the first box was Account "LT003," which dealt with "USD (FI/US)," or U.S. dollar fixed income. The first entry in the first box said:

USD_Y-shift . . . 2s-10s @ 45 . . . -2.80 . . . 5 y-sh . . . 14.00

This line gave Long-Term's exposure to a flattening of the yield curve between two-year and ten-year Treasury bonds, for which the spread was then 45 basis points. For each movement of five basis points, Long-Term could make (or lose) $2.8 million. The expected volatility of the trade over one year was five such jumps, meaning that, according to its models, Long-Term's yearly exposure was no more than $14 million.

The next entry, "USD_Z+D-shift," showed Long-Term's exposure to a change in short-term interest rates. It wasn't until the fifth line that Fisher saw a truly alarming number. Under "USD_Swap Spread," Long-Term showed an exposure of $240 million—but that was assuming that swap spreads stuck to their historic volatility of only 15 points a year. And given that swaps had already moved in a 40-point range in 1998, that assumption had become laughable. There were twenty-five entries in all—on just the first page. And the risk aggregator went to fifteen pages. The sheer mass of it was numbing.

Turning to the international trades, Hilibrand showed Fisher rows of entries for bonds and swaps in Great Britain, mortgages in Denmark, swap spreads in New Zealand, bonds in Hong Kong, and various exposures in Sweden and Switzerland as well as in Germany, France, and Belgium. Fisher saw bonds in Italy, Spain, and the Netherlands, too.

And then Fisher saw more entries, now pertaining to the fund's positions in stocks. He was shocked by the massive entries for stock market volatility. Then came Long-Term's exposures in emerging markets: Brazil, Argentina, Mexico, Venezuela, Korea, Poland, China, Taiwan, Thailand, Malaysia, and the Philippines. There were three entries for Russia, including "Russia Hard Currency Direction"—meaning that the fund had gone directional, or speculated outright.

At first it seemed astonishing that so many trades should have collapsed simultaneously. But gazing over the portfolio, Fisher had an epiphany: Long-Term's trades were linked—they had been correlated before the fact. "They had the same spread trade everywhere in the world," Fisher thought. Gensler had a related thought: During a crisis, *the correlations always go to one.* When a quake hits, all markets tremble. Why was Long-Term so surprised by that?

When the partners finished with the risk aggregator, they went through another document, breaking down Long-Term's exposure according to counterparty. In theory, its counterparties were protected by their collateral. But in fact, if the fund suddenly failed, each of its counterparties would attempt to sell—in unison—and the value of the collateral would necessarily plunge. Moreover, each of Long-Term's swap counterparties would be "naked," or holding on to only one side of a contract for which the other side no longer existed. Each counterparty would rush to neutralize its one-sided swaps, overwhelming markets as in a bank run. If that happened, according to Long-Term, its seventeen biggest counterparties—banks such as Merrill, Goldman, Morgan, and Salomon—would stand to lose a total of $2.8 billion.

Fisher eyeballed the number and thought, "That might be plausible in a normal market." But markets were already sorely frayed; now they could go totally haywire. Mentally, Fisher adjusted the potential losses to $3 billion to $5 billion, and even that was a guess. It wasn't just Long-Term that was on the hook—it was all of Wall Street. Who knew when the losses would start to strain the system? Who knew if the system had a breaking point? The more Fisher heard, the worse he felt. "I'm not worried about markets trading down," he confided. "I'm worried that they won't trade at all."

Once the visitors had an overview, the group began to explore some solutions. In 1990, Gensler noted, a bankruptcy filing by Drexel Burnham Lambert, the junk-bond king, had actually eased the panic in junk bonds.

But in this case, Rickards explained, bankruptcy would not stop anything; it would merely ring the bell for counterparties to start going after their collateral. And the Drexel crisis had involved only bonds, not derivatives. Long-Term's case was far more complex. It would be hopeless to try to unravel all those overlapping swaps, Fisher knew. Furthermore, finding a buyer for the firm was out of the question. Nobody would touch positions such as equity volatility. "So this is a new paradigm," Gensler said unhappily.

The partners were particularly agitated about the pressure from Bear Stearns. What Long-Term needed, Fisher concluded, was breathing space. After some give-and-take, the arbitrageurs and officials came up with a plan. Suppose the banks were to visit four days hence, on Thursday, on the understanding that they would be shown the portfolio in the strictest confidence? After a quick study, the banks could bid for the assets at an auction the following Sunday. When markets reopened Monday, Long-Term would effectively have disappeared.

But there was one problem with the plan: Long-Term had only $1.5 billion of equity left, Rickards reminded them. Deducting the cash locked up at Bear Stearns and the monies tied up in margin accounts and the like left free cash of exactly $470 million. The company had been losing hundreds of millions of dollars a day. In all probability, Long-Term wouldn't make it until Thursday.

And now it was 4 P.M. on Sunday, only hours from the opening of the Tokyo markets. They had spent six hours working on the problem and solved nothing. The officials went to a side room, and Gensler called the Treasury. Midterm elections were six weeks off;

thus far, the economy had been the government's one bright spot. The last thing it wanted was a financial meltdown. Rejoining the partners, Fisher told them, "You're composed and we're composed, but Washington is going crazy." Then he held out his hand to Meriwether. J.M. said that, come what may, he wanted to handle the problem right. "Thanks," Fisher said. "You're the first one to tell us in advance."

Sunday afternoon, Corzine talked to Buffett, who was still on a tour of the Alaskan fjords and still seemed uncertain about a rescue of Long-Term. That night, the Goldman chief called Fisher and told him not to count on a private rescue. Fisher had one thought: "How do we get to another weekend?" For the first time, he broached the idea of getting a group of banks together. Corzine, who was feeling pessimistic about the Buffett bid, encouraged him.[2]

J. P. Morgan was having similar thoughts. Morgan analysts in Tokyo and London had spent the past twenty-four hours downloading files similar to those that had been seen by Goldman and by the Fed. Interestingly, the Morgan analysts were surprised that Long-Term's trades hadn't been more exotic. They were big but not unusual. Still, since Long-Term was known as a bond house, Morgan *was* surprised by the size of its equity book.

Morgan saw two options. One was to let the fund fail. Then every bank would seize collateral for itself; Morgan figured that would cost the bigger banks $500 million to $700 million apiece. Or, Morgan could buy big chunks of the portfolio itself. But that would pose another problem. Morgan knew that other banks had seen the portfolio. If any *one* bank acquired it, it would be in the same spot as Long-Term—the whole Street would be shooting at it. So all the banks would have to be in.

Corzine, who had been having thoughts similar to Morgan's, called Komansky, the Merrill Lynch chairman, Sunday afternoon. Komansky, who is half Russian Orthodox Jewish, half Irish Catholic, and 100 percent The Bronx, was preparing for Rosh Hashanah at sundown. "LTCM has some real problems. It looks like they're going bankrupt in a day or two," Corzine told him. He mentioned that Goldman's people had been in Greenwich—but not that Goldman had gotten an exclusive peek at Long-Term's books. Nor did he mention that Goldman and Buffett were, at the moment, mulling over a takeover bid.

Komansky, citing the holiday, rang off and had Herb Allison, his trusted lieutenant and Merrill's president, pick up the ball. Corzine was playing golf, but at 10:30 that night, he and Allison connected. Bit by bit, Wall Street's top bankers were starting to talk to one another. Through their carelessness, their reckless financing, their vain attempts to ingratiate themselves with a self-important client, the Wall Street banks had created this fiasco together. Their instinct had been to savage as much of the carcass of Long-Term as possible, but now they had begun to see that doing so would risk bringing themselves down as well. One by one, they were concluding that they might have to do the very thing that was most antithetical to their nature: they might have to work together.

Monday, September 21, was yet another bad day. U.S. swap spreads climbed to 87; U.K. swaps soared to 95. The spread between on-the-run and off-the-run Treasurys—both of them perfectly safe U.S. government credits—jumped, incredibly, to 19 points. (Just a month before, the spread had been the customary 6 points.) Prices had an air of unreality, as though traders were selling *anything* connected, even by the faintest rumor, to Long-Term. Banks were "bending the marks" against the fund, grabbing all the collateral they could while there still was something to grab. Steve Black, the Salomon Smith Barney executive, heard from his troops in Tokyo that Goldman was "banging the s——" out of Long-Term's trades, especially swaps. Goldman said Salomon was doing the same in Europe.[3]

Around midday, equity volatility jerked up 3 percentage points on one rather small trade—to 38 percent! The options market was now implying a catastrophic level of volatility, maybe a crash every month. To Rosenfeld, it was simply nonsensical; it felt as though volatility was rising only because traders knew that Long-Term was vulnerable—which at that point was probably true.[4] The obvious manipulation cost the fund $120 million. As Vinny Mattone had prophesied, hungry traders were finishing the job of killing Long-Term that the crisis in Russia had begun.

Long-Term's total loss on Monday was $553 million, coincidentally equal to its loss of a month before. In percentage terms, this Monday's loss was far worse: it ate through a third of Long-Term's equity, leaving it with just under a billion dollars. And the fund still had more than $100 billion in assets. Thus, even omitting derivatives, *its leverage was greater than 100 to 1*—a fantastic figure in the annals of investment. Now, if Long-Term lost even a mere 1 percent more, it would be wiped out.

Though the magnitude of the loss wouldn't be known until after the markets closed, the partners knew early in the day that Monday was high noon. Jim Rickards, the attorney, called Warren Spector, Bear's executive vice president, and threatened to sue if Bear stopped clearing. The fund had nothing to lose, and Rickards knew it. Then Rickards called Chase and demanded an immediate dispersal of $500 million from the revolver.

Minutes later, the syndicate banks, twenty-four in all, began to squawk. Rickards and Bruce Wilson, the fund's controller, insisted that the banks had no choice but to lend the money. But would they own up to it before the client expired? The stalwart Pflug said that Chase would fund. What's more, he telexed the other banks and told them that, in his opinion, they would have to fund as well. Long-Term got $475 million, most within that day (only Crédit Agricole held out). The loan did nothing for Long-Term's equity, but it was money in the box at Bear. It bought, perhaps, a few days' time.

At the Fed, Fisher was in touch by phone with Goldman's Corzine and Thain, Merrill's Allison, and J. P. Morgan's chairman, Douglas Warner. The calls convinced Fisher that the private efforts to raise capital were failing—and, what's more, that markets were on the brink of a disaster. He had a growing sense that the three big banks should take *some* collective action. Allison and Corzine spoke throughout the day. Allison, not as competitive as some of the traders, naturally gravitated toward a joint approach. Corzine, still concealing the Buffett card, did so as well, but only as a backstop. That Monday, Corzine contacted Maurice Greenberg, the chairman of AIG, the insurer, and convinced him to join the Buffett-Goldman bid. AIG had the necessary derivatives expertise, and with a third member, the group would be stronger. Buffett, who was traveling, was again unreachable, but he had made his strategy clear: buy the portfolio, let the world see that it was now in strong hands, let prices recover—and then sell.

At Morgan, a group involving Mendoza; Peter Hancock, Morgan's global bond chief; and Clayton Rose, its head of equities, was thinking about going it alone, too. Curiously, Merrill, which had brought Long-Term into being, was the least well informed of the big three banks. Allison spent Monday trying to get up to speed. He dispatched a team to Greenwich via helicopter in the afternoon to find out just how desperate his client was. Hilibrand and Rosenfeld, who were working through the Rosh Hashanah holiday, took the visitors through the portfolio—was there *anyone* left who had not seen the books? Meriwether remained remarkably calm, even graceful. "We misjudged the markets," he admitted.

But J.M. still felt that Long-Term's trades were sound—if it could just get past the temporary crisis, the momentary implosion of liquidity. J.M. so much wanted the fund to live. He was like a man about to embrace his lover, if only he can land his plane in a storm. But the margin calls, the traders shooting at them, the rumormongers, the mercenaries at Goldman . . .

The Merrill team was stunned by the huge dimensions of Long-Term's trades, especially in equities and European swaps (which were far less liquid than U.S. swaps). "Do you realize these are fairly *substantial* positions?" Merrill's Richard Dunn inquired.[5] The arbitrageurs seemed not to get it. The Merrill people were puzzled by the mysterious presence of Goldfield, the ubiquitous Goldman·trader; he was bent over his laptop and didn't look the Merrill people in the eye.

■

Monday night in London—still afternoon in Greenwich—Andy Siciliano, the UBS manager, decided he had to see the hedge fund firsthand. He hopped the Concorde and bumped into Victor Haghani on the flight. Though both were jet-lagged by the time they arrived, neither man had any intention of sleeping. They shared a limousine to Greenwich, where J.M., Rosenfeld, and the laureates were holding court in the conference room. Goldman was still in the building, like an invading army that had established a beachhead. In the conference room, a bunker mentality prevailed. The partners couldn't stop talking about how the Goldman traders were calling New York on their cell phones—though of course they couldn't know what the traders were saying. But the notion that a conspiracy had done them in had become an obsession for the partners. When they finished with Goldman, they heaped their fury on Bear Stearns, disingenuously implying that Bear had sprung its letter out of the blue. Conveniently forgetting how disdainful they had been before, the partners abjectly wondered why their friends had abandoned them.[6]

Rosenfeld went over the portfolio for what seemed the hundredth time, sizing up the prospects trade by trade. Siciliano, the only out-sider, realized with a start that no one objected to his presence. Long-Term had no secrets now. In fact, Siciliano was strangely welcome. He was a bridge to the outside world the firm had shunned but now so desperately needed. The partners implored Siciliano to help, to spread the word of their positions' inherent logic—anything for cap-ital. They were still selling. But a faint odor of self-delusion colored their confabulations. The theme of revenge bubbled beneath the sur-face like the curd of sour milk: if only Long-Term could throw fresh capital into the breach, prices would snap back and those nasty op-portunists who had traded against them would be begging for mercy.

By Monday, market gossips were attributing every slight dip in prices to selling from Greenwich. But the general press had been stun-ningly silent. Since the day after Meriwether's September 2 letter, the press hadn't breathed a word on the runaway hedge fund. Wall Street pundits were preoccupied with the expected release of a videotape of President Clinton's testimony in the Monica Lewinsky sex scandal, which was said to be depressing markets. Fisher was of the opinion that sex had nothing to do with what was depressing Wall Street. In his opinion, Long-Term was weighing on markets like a corpse.

After talking with the banks, Fisher concluded that Wall Street would be willing to participate in a rescue, but given the bankers' mutual distrust and competitive predispositions, none would take the risk of initiating one. That would leave it to the Fed. Corzine, still hedging his bets, had the same thought. Should Goldman's exclusive bid fall through, he wanted to avoid a competitive free-for-all. He would much prefer to join hands under the Fed's protective banner. And Herb Allison was pushing Fisher to bring some banks together on neutral ground.[7] Sensing that time was running out, Fisher invited the big three banks to breakfast at the Fed.

Fisher maintained that neither he nor McDonough was worried about the loss to Long-Term, nor even about the potential loss to other firms. If the estimate of $3 billion to $5 billion over seventeen banks were correct, losses of up to $300 million per firm were cer-tainly tolerable. Even if they were *not* tolerable, these private Wall Street banks had put their own shareholders' money at risk; they had no call for help from the Federal Reserve.

Fisher's concern was the broader notion of "systemic risk": if Long-Term failed, and if its creditors forced a hasty and disorderly liquidation, he feared that it would harm the entire financial system, not just some of its big participants. Greenspan later used the phrase "a seizing up of markets," conjuring up the image of markets in such disarray that they might cease to function—meaning that traders would cease to trade.[8] McDonough evoked a parallel fear—that losses in so many markets and to so many players would spark a vicious circle of liquidations, extreme fluctuations in interest rates, and then still further losses: "Markets would . . . possibly cease to function for a period of one or more days and maybe longer."[9]

Since the Great Depression, the United States has not experienced anything like a real meltdown, though at times markets have seemed to be spinning toward one. But the fear of a financial Armageddon has inspired an imaginative literature that at the extreme has its parallel in natural-disaster plots, mass-computer-failure sagas, and the like. In the abstract, no one can say whether systemic risk presents a real threat—the very phrase is vague and ill defined—but regulators naturally err toward caution. As Fisher readied to meet his guests, Asia was already in the throes of a recession if not a depression; Russia was most certainly falling into one; and South America was on the brink. In the United States, the vast widening in credit spreads suggested that lenders were refusing to lend—a classic sign of a contraction. The previous day, September 21, Treasury yields had touched a low of 5.05 percent. According to an economist quoted in *The Wall Street Journal*, "Treasurys are purely a measure of fear now"—fear of holding any bond that was not a Treasury.[10] Stocks had plunged everywhere from Switzerland to Brazil to Singapore. Stepping back from Wall Street, Fisher would have noticed that America's economy was still quite vibrant (unlike in the fall of 1929, when, by the time of the Great Crash on Wall Street, it was already in recession). Indeed, most Americans were unaware that the financial crisis—which Secretary Rubin said was the worst in half a century—even existed.[11] But it certainly existed in the mind of the Fed.

■

Fisher's guests—Komansky and Allison from Merrill, Corzine and Thain from Goldman, and Mendoza from J. P. Morgan—arrived at 7:30 that morning. If an executive's mood may be surmised from the price of his stock, Fisher's visitors must have been dour indeed. Merrill's stock was at $54; in July, it had traded at $108—twice as high.

Morgan's was off by more than 40 percent. Goldman had not yet gone public—which meant that Corzine's mood was probably the worst of anyone's. In such a market, Goldman could have no hope of selling stock.

Fisher said he had spent Sunday at Long-Term and was worried about systemic risk. The bankers were sympathetic. Merrill Lynch was in something close to shock—not over Long-Term but over its own spiraling losses in bonds. Merrill, which had purposely shied away from arbitrage-type operations, had never dreamt that it could be so vulnerable. Morgan, though in better shape, had been having a terrible quarter. Goldman was on its way to a stunning (except in comparison with Long-Term) trading loss for August and September of $1.5 billion. Thus, when Fisher suggested that the system was in danger, his guests, without necessarily pondering the fine points of global capitalism, were, at least for their own reasons, more than ready to believe him.

Each bank floated a different possible solution. Corzine revealed that Goldman knew of a prospective bidder—a "Mr. Big"—who was waiting in the wings. Mendoza of Morgan proposed an intricate scheme whereby the banks with debt exposure to Long-Term could "lift" (that is, acquire) its bond trades and those with equity exposure could divvy up its equity trades. Komansky, who owned a slug of Long-Term himself, thought this was far too convoluted and time-consuming. He and Allison favored a simple consortium that would make an investment.

But no solution could work if Long-Term's equity continued to melt away. The banks had to stop their traders from shooting at the fund, one of the bankers admitted. Komansky said gruffly, "Well, just tell the yuppies to sit down and shut up." The comment may have been directed to Corzine. Komansky said later that while he didn't specifically recall the remark, he had heard that Goldman's traders had downloaded "all of Long-Term's positions" into their own computers, which Goldman of course denied. In any case, the speculation about Goldman's trading had surfaced among the top executives. "I don't know anybody who knew it as a fact," Komansky said. "But the issue was there."[12]

The bankers adjourned around 9:30, agreeing to send two groups to Long-Term to investigate the Morgan approach. One would explore lifting Long-Term's bond positions; the other, its equities. A third group, led by Allison, would retreat to Merrill Lynch to study the consortium idea. Also, they agreed to invite UBS, Long-Term's biggest investor, to join them.

Meriwether greeted the bankers with aplomb, but Hilibrand looked haggard and nervous; the losses had taken a toll on the master trader, who was also so personally leveraged. By now, meetings between Long-Term and inquiring bankers had a staged, too-familiar air. The partners were weary of reluctant suitors; what's more, markets were moving so fast that the bankers had no way of knowing what the portfolio was worth. Conservatively valuing the portfolio at a discount, the bankers arrived at bids for the various pieces that added to little more than zero. Haghani seemed wounded by their minimal valuations. "Thank you for coming," he told a Merrill banker with an air of rebuke, "but we don't think you're right. You ought to be investing *with* us." He was like a drowning man trying to dictate terms to a rescuer on shore; in his heart of hearts, he was unsinkable.

But Long-Term had sustained another loss Tuesday of $152 million, taking its equity down to *$773 million.* Jimmy Cayne, chief executive of Bear Stearns, advised Fisher that Long-Term had enough cash to get through Tuesday—but Wednesday could be a problem.[13] What could it possibly do in twenty-four hours? The Morgan option was dead. Corzine doubted that "Mr. Big" would surface, either. That left it to Allison.

Allison, a fifty-five-year-old investment banker, was a rarity among top executives at Merrill, most of whom had been plucked from the firm's legion of stockbrokers. The prototypical Merrill man was Komansky, a personable, heavyset former broker who had never gotten a college diploma but had starred in sales. Allison, a philosophy major at Yale with an M.B.A. from Stanford, was far more bookish. Wispy, balding, and bespectacled, he was more a detail man than a rainmaker and—despite his ambition—a consummate number two. Undeniably smart, he had a talent for deconstructing a deal and fitting the parts into working order. Tuesday afternoon, holed up in a conference room overlooking the Statue of Liberty, Allison and a small cadre of bankers hammered away at a plan. By 4 P.M., when the four banks and Fisher hooked up in a conference call, Allison had worked up a succinct outline, on three quarters of a page, for a consortium.

For Allison's plan to have any chance, it would need the support of most of the banks on Wall Street. Moreover, he explained to Fisher, the only way to get the banks together was for the Fed to call them and offer to hold a meeting.[14] Fisher agreed. While insisting that the Fed was not backing any particular approach, the regulator swung into action behind the Merrill plan. Around 6 P.M., Fisher and some aides called the dozen banks that—along with Merrill, Morgan, Goldman, and UBS—were Long-Term's biggest counterparties and announced an emergency meeting at the Fed at eight that evening. McDonough, who had been speaking to international regulators in London about the dangers of derivatives, was in touch by phone. By nightfall in London, McDonough was jetting back to New York.

Bankers from the Big Four banks met with Fisher at seven. Allison's plan called for the sixteen banks to invest $250 million each. Thain had insisted on the $4 billion total—anything less, and the portfolio would come under attack. But the bankers disagreed on everything else. Should the package be equity or—as the more gun-shy bankers proposed—a temporary loan? Should the Long-Term partners be allowed to stay, or should they be fired? If they did stay, who would control the fund? Corzine strongly argued that the Long-Term partners should forfeit control. At 8:20, the four lead banks were still debating. Meanwhile, the chief executives of the other big banks had begun to arrive and were cooling their heels outside the boardroom.

Fisher called a halt, opened the massive wooden doors, and invited the others in. It was an awesome gathering, the cream of Wall Street. Fisher spied Deryck Maughan, co–chief executive of Salomon Smith Barney; Thomas Labrecque, president of Chase; Jimmy Cayne, the CEO of Bear Stearns; Allen Wheat, chief executive of Credit Suisse First Boston; Philip Purcell, chairman of Morgan Stanley Dean Witter; and senior executives from Lehman Brothers and Barclays of Britain. From the Big Four, Fisher saw Komansky, Allison, Corzine, Thain, Warner, Mendoza, Rose, and David Solo. Twelve banks had sent twenty-five bankers—all men, all middle-aged. Even these thick-necked bankers, though familiar to one another, were unaccustomed to seeing so many of their brethren on such short notice and in such a place, squeezed into soft, leather-backed chairs under the quiet gaze of the gold-framed oil portraits that rimmed the boardroom. Morgan's Sandy Warner broke the ice, jovially declaring, "Boys, we're going to a picnic, and the tickets cost $250 million."

Fisher, though a bureaucrat who earned a pittance of what his guests did, commanded their attention because he alone could represent the "public interest" that now seemed so imperiled. Fisher spoke for just a few minutes. He said the Fed was interested in seeing whether the private sector could find a solution that would avoid a chaotic liquidation—one that would spare the system. Otherwise he adopted a neutral stance, intentionally staying aloof from the particulars. Allison said, "It was like he had rented out a hall." Of course, Fisher had done more than that. The Fed does not invite the heads of Wall Street to its boardroom every day, and the executives knew it.

Gazing about the room, Thomas Russo's first thought was awe— a fleeting satisfaction at being part of such a group. As the debate got under way, Russo, the chief legal officer for Lehman, became conscious of an irony. "When you get to a high level, how much do you really understand about the details under you?" he wondered. They had all been trained to exercise due diligence, but none had been trained for an emergency like this.

Allison summarized his plan, and each of the lead banks spoke in favor. Komansky said, "It's not my first choice of what to do with the money, but I think it's the right thing." Komansky didn't bother to add that he was scared that if Long-Term collapsed, Merrill's astonishing trading losses would spiral out of control. The other bankers were worried, too. But Lehman objected that it shouldn't be asked for the same contribution as the bigger banks—why shouldn't each bank invest according to its exposure? Thain retorted that that was too complicated—there wasn't time. Each bank now began to jockey for its particular interest. Chase's Labrecque fired a shot at Bear for precipitating the crisis. Bear still held the trigger, he knew. Cayne, whose firm had earned $30 million a year clearing for Long-Term, and who was personally an investor in the fund, was notably silent.

Then the bankers vented their ire at Long-Term. They had taken all they wanted to from the gang in Greenwich. For four years, the partners had held themselves aloof, picking off the best trades from each of the banks and not even trying to hide their smug superiority. Now the partners had the look of false prophets. The bankers felt taken—they had been so credulous. Several said the partners should be fired. Why give *them* the money? Allison and Corzine repeatedly broke away from the talks to give Meriwether updates (at least two banks were in on every phone call, to avoid the possibility of secret dealing). Meriwether sounded mortified to hear of the anger directed at him. "Look, I'll help however I can," he murmured.

Goldman's Thain, who had the most intimate knowledge of Long-

Term, described the portfolio risks. The group agreed that any investment should be in the form of equity, but no one beyond the four lead firms was ready to commit. Most of the banks thought they would lose less than $250 million if Long-Term failed; why throw good money after bad? Allison said that the fallout could be truly scary, even worse than after Russia. Long-Term had $100 billion of assets and $1 *trillion* in notional derivative exposure, he reminded the group.

Moreover, its equity positions were spooky. Some investors would not be in stocks were it not for the insurance policy provided by options, and Long-Term was easily the biggest supplier. Without Long-Term, it was possible that investors would back away from stocks. None of the bankers wanted to see the stock market tumble further. Pflug felt a pervasive fear in the room. Then he had the depressing thought that it was his birthday and he was spending it locked in a conference room.

Around 11 P.M., Fisher suggested they break until ten the next morning. Allison and a Merrill colleague, Tom Davis, returned to the office to redraft the terms. Now and then, to resolve a fine point, they called Meriwether, who was keeping vigil in Greenwich. Around 1 A.M., Allison updated Corzine and Mendoza; Allison wanted no surprises on Wednesday. At 3 A.M., when the business day in Paris began, Allison faxed the new terms to Long-Term's French counterparties. Then he went home. The next day, he would need each of the banks to commit. He wondered if it could be done.[15] No one had ever raised $4 billion in a day before.

Merrill had realized it would also need some lawyers in a hurry. Philip Harris, a partner at Skadden, Arps, Slate, Meagher & Flom, Merrill's outside law firm, had worked on Long-Term during its initial fund-raising, but Harris, who specialized in investment funds, wanted a workout specialist, too. At 2:30 A.M., Harris called a Skadden partner named J. Gregory Milmoe, waking him at his home in Scarsdale. Milmoe, a fifty-year-old soft-spoken attorney with white hair and gold-rimmed glasses, specialized in bankruptcy. A former piano player, Milmoe had gotten a job in Skadden's mail room and later gone to law school. "Something has come up," Harris said. "We need you."

Milmoe promised he'd be in first thing in the morning.

"No," Harris explained. "We need you to come in *now*."

Milmoe showered, dressed, and hopped into his Volvo. He cruised into Manhattan at the city's quietest hour. By 3:30, he reached the gleaming black skyscraper where Skadden had its headquarters and went to work.

■

McDonough, who had just arrived from London, got to the Fed early Wednesday. Pushcarts were jostling for street space with stretch limousines, which moved at a ponderous pace through the narrow alleyways. The Federal Reserve building loomed above, its high outer wall rising to a vacant balcony, as if the architect had wanted to convey both the ceremony of a palace and the implacability of a fortress. McDonough called his peers at European central banks, notifying them of the crisis. Fisher, his colleague, took a call from Jimmy Cayne at Bear Stearns. Cayne, whose firm had little exposure, said Bear would *not* contribute to any rescue. Fisher pleaded with Cayne to keep an open mind. Cayne said darkly, "Don't go alphabetically if you want this to work."

At 10 A.M., the bankers returned. Wednesday's gathering was larger, about forty-five in all. The group was a who's who of Wall Street power brokers: Sandy Weill, Komansky, Corzine, Chase's Labrecque, Morgan's Warner, Credit Suisse First Boston's Wheat, and Richard Fuld, chairman of Lehman Brothers. Rounding out the spectacular assembly were executives from five Swiss, British, and French banks as well as Richard Grasso, chairman of the New York Stock Exchange, who had been summoned due to Long-Term's monster trade in equity volatility. Edson Mitchell of Deutsche Bank was connected by phone. As they filed into the boardroom, the bankers noticed the portrait of George Washington above an antique clock on the mantel, alongside those of McDonough's predecessors. The curtains were drawn. The elegant, black-trimmed mahogany table was too small to accommodate such a crowd; a larger cover had been hastily slung over it.[16]

The boardroom itself was an add-on, the Fed having acquired it in 1935, when an adjacent property owner who had held out in boom times had agreed to sell. The joke was that the Fed had engineered the stock market crash to get hold of the space. The joke carried a sting, since the Fed's failure to curb stock speculation on margin debt early in 1929 has ever since been viewed as a singular missed opportunity—one that might have averted the crash and, perhaps, the ensuing Great Depression. It was this sort of debacle—albeit on a lesser scale—that McDonough was seeking to prevent with Long-Term Capital.

However, McDonough was not in the boardroom. The Fed president was closeted in an anteroom with the executives of the four lead banks, who had become a sort of roving Security Council to the other banks' General Assembly. It was a warm morning, and the other CEOs, not accustomed to being kept waiting, were becoming impatient.

At 10:25, McDonough, a burly, sixty-four-year-old Chicagoan with thinning silver hair and thick arching eyebrows, suddenly appeared and said he was suspending the meeting until 1 P.M. He added cryptically, "Not all avenues have been exhausted," but refused to elaborate. The CEOs were dumbfounded and absolutely at a loss. As they learned later, about ten minutes into the meeting of the Big Four, Corzine and Thain had pulled McDonough aside, pleading a sudden new development: Buffett was ready to bid. "I thought we were in this together!" Solo snapped angrily. But McDonough could not pass up this seeming godsend; he much preferred a solution that did not involve the Fed. Just to make sure it was real, he called Buffett, who was now at a Montana ranch. Buffett confirmed that an offer was on the way. In the main room, the CEOs rose with a look of disgust. They were furious at Goldman for dealing behind their backs. Even Komansky felt that Corzine had played it too close to the vest.

While Kraus, Goldman's investment banker, prepared a written offer, Buffett placed a call to Meriwether. "John," he said in his unmistakable twang, "you're going to get a bid for the portfolio with my name on it. I just want you to know that it's me." Meriwether was noncommittal.

There was a hiatus while Goldman dotted the *i*'s and crossed the *t*'s. Finally, at 11:40, Meriwether pulled a one-page fax from the machine. It said that Berkshire Hathaway, AIG, and Goldman Sachs would be willing to buy the fund for $250 million. If accepted, they would immediately invest $3.75 billion more to stabilize the operation, with $3 billion of the total coming from Berkshire.

Buffett was proposing to pay *$250 million* for a fund that had been worth *$4.7 billion* at the start of the year. By day's end, Long-Term, which was suffering yet another down day in markets, would be worth only $555 million. But even next to this startlingly reduced net worth, Buffett's offer was decidedly cheap. The partners—worth hundreds of millions apiece only weeks earlier—would be wiped out. What's more, they would be fired. Also, just to make sure that Meriwether would not shop his offer around, Buffett issued a deadline of 12:30 P.M., not quite an hour away. Meriwether handed the fax to Rickards. "What do we do with it?" J.M. asked.

To Meriwether, the proposal must have been an especially bitter pill. J.M. was furious at Goldman and AIG for trading against the fund—indeed, for helping to knock it down before trying to buy it on the cheap. Moreover, the proposal would reenact the central trauma of J.M.'s career: losing his company, and his job, to Warren Buffett. Nonetheless, the partners studied it with care. UBS's Siciliano, who was with the partners again that day, was impressed by their mood of earnestness. Their first concern, Siciliano believed, was to fashion a clean solution that would avoid a generalized catastrophe. Buffett's bid, at least, could provide one.

Unfortunately, Rickards saw problems with the bid. It was mistakenly worded as an offer to buy the assets of LTCM—the management company—which Buffett did *not* want.[17] John Mead, Goldman's counsel at Sullivan & Cromwell, explained to Rickards that Buffett was really after the fund's portfolio. The *portfolio's* assets—the stocks, bonds, and so forth—could of course be sold at any time. Not so its derivative contracts, because the parties on the other side would have to approve. Moreover, one of Buffett's conditions was that the portfolio's financing remain in place. As Rickards read it, Buffett would have to buy the portfolio *company*—that is, Long-Term Capital Portfolio, the Cayman Islands partnership. But LTCP was merely the hub in the original, complicated feeder structure. The hub was owned by eight separate spokes and by its general partner and, according to Rickards, was absolutely unsalable without a change in the partnership agreement, which would need the consent of the investors in each of the spokes. In short, Rickards said, the bid was a nonstarter.

However, he thought it would work in a different form—if the Berkshire group simply invested in the fund as it was currently structured. And Buffett, as the biggest investor, would still be free to fire the partners.

But Mead did not have authority to change the bid, and Buffett was bizarrely unreachable. Indeed, one wonders how badly he wanted Long-Term. In the past, Buffett's ability to do complex deals on a single sheet of paper had been one of his charms, and this proposal—all of five paragraphs—certainly bore his trademark. But perhaps his bid for Long-Term was *too* simple or too arbitrary, for it could not accommodate the fund's more subtle particulars. Moreover, Kraus, the investment banker, who might have set Buffett straight, had himself been inexplicably unfamiliar with Long-Term's structure and had sorely mishandled the bid.

Mead, Goldman's outside lawyer, was left with little choice. At 12:20, Mead told Rickards the bid was withdrawn, and Rickards walked back to J.M.'s office and said, "The Buffett bid is off the table." Meriwether immediately called McDonough—truly his last hope. "OK," McDonough said, "I'll call the banks, but I don't know if they're coming back or not."

J.M. was later said to have deliberately scotched the Buffett bid, figuring that he could do better with McDonough. This version, though, credits J.M. with a rather full understanding of a confused and quickly moving drama. It is true that Meriwether did not attempt to resolve the legal problems, and such complications are often worked out later on, after an agreement in principle has been signed. But Buffett was not exactly being flexible either. At noon Wednesday, J.M. could not assume that Buffett would agree to *anything* outside the terms of his letter. Perhaps the harshness of its terms or some faint element of personal mistrust deterred J.M. from pursuing Buffett further, but what J.M. did know was that for the consortium effort to have any chance, it had to return to the Fed—and quickly.

The bankers came back at one, in a sullen mood. Goldman's minuet had reminded them of how little they trusted one another. They didn't want to be there; they had no stake in Long-Term. Purcell, chairman of Morgan Stanley, saw little risk to *his* bank if the fund collapsed. Sandy Weill had just shut down his own arbitrage unit— why save someone else's? Weill hadn't even returned (he was represented by Deryck Maughan and Jamie Dimon). Credit Suisse First Boston was skeptical, too. Labrecque of Chase said he would go in only if the bank syndicate's loan were repaid. Allison and Komansky were still in favor of a deal, but now they doubted it was possible.[18]

The bankers debated the likelihood of systemic collapse but got nowhere. It was a parlor topic, not something the bankers wanted to spend $250 million on. Lehman Brothers simply couldn't afford it.

Lehman's own stability was the subject of whispers in the Street, and its funding costs had been soaring. Dick Fuld, Lehman's chairman, bluntly asked Corzine if Goldman's buyer had backed away on account of price—and if so, why should the consortium offer more? Corzine said there had been legal issues. The CEOs listened sourly; who knew what to believe? McDonough was mostly silent.

It was Allison's meeting now. The numbers man decided to take a poll. Bankers Trust said it was in. . . . Barclays was in.

All eyes darted to the hulking Cayne, slouching next to Spector, his colleague. The Bear CEO said, "We called this morning to tell people we wouldn't be in." There was a deathly silence. Then, in unison, the CEOs demanded an explanation. This only made Cayne more resolute. Bear had enough exposure as a clearing agent, Cayne said. He wouldn't say more. The others thought it ludicrous. Bear was holding $500 million—it was the *least* exposed. "They had a different view of the world," one participant said acidly. "They're completely self-interested." Suddenly these paragons of individual enterprise seethed with communitarian fervor. Purcell of Morgan Stanley turned beet red. He fumed, "It's not *acceptable* that a major Wall Street firm isn't participating!"[19] It was as if Bear were breaking a silent code; it would pay a price in the future, Allison vowed.

McDonough asked the Bear team to come into McDonough's office. "You have to say *something*," McDonough noted. "Komansky is really upset." A moment later Komansky came in, and he was crimson. Turning to Cayne, the Merrill chief exploded: "What the *fuck* are you doing?" Cayne wondered, "When did we become partners?" Komansky put a sort of Lyndon Johnson arm around him, and Spector tried to get in the middle so Cayne wouldn't have to deal with all of Komansky's 250 pounds himself.

Something grated on Cayne—the faint suggestion that he was being viewed with dishonor. He said to Komansky, "If you go back in that room and say you've known Bear Stearns for years and that we're an honorable firm, we will say that, as clearing agent, we don't have any special knowledge that makes us uncomfortable. We just choose not to participate." And they went back and said their pieces.

Then, the focus shifted to Long-Term. Corzine said the partners were expendable. "We don't need these guys; they created this mess," Corzine said. No one exactly *sympathized* with Meriwether, but Allen Wheat of Credit Suisse First Boston said it would be a mistake to fire him. If the Street invested all this money in the fund, they would need someone to run it. And the guys in Greenwich obviously knew it better than anyone.

Corzine, though, insisted that the consortium at least had to get full control, including the right to fire J.M. and the other partners. It would need contracts locking the partners in and strict supervision over trading limits. Corzine went from one extreme to the other—now wanting J.M. as his partner, now wanting him in shackles. But he understood the flaws in Long-Term better than anyone else. The firm had no controls, no one above the level of trader. Insisting that Goldman would never invest without accountability, Corzine called Meriwether to make sure he would swallow the terms; otherwise, Goldman was out.

The others could sense that Corzine was under a special strain. Thain, his lieutenant, was getting calls on his cell phone right in the Fed room. No one could hear what Thain was saying, but they could see anguish written on his face. Goldman's losses were big; its IPO was on the rocks, its partners were unhappy. Corzine had the look of a man caught between two armies.

Aside from Corzine, others of the bankers continually left the room. The Europeans called home; the Americans checked their offices. Perhaps, some of the bankers called their traders. Details of the meeting leaked.

At Long-Term there was radio silence. Its markets were tumbling, especially its equity volatility trade. The latest quote was 41 percent! It almost didn't matter now. The firm had come to a halt. Trading had ceased, the phones were finally quiet. There was no one to call; the people the partners had been talking to all these weeks were in the Fed room.

The partners waited together in the glass-walled conference room. Every so often, Allison or Corzine would call J.M. with a question, and the partners would infer a bit of progress. Outside, a group of the nonpartners stood by a television monitor, hoping for a glimpse of the story that had been unfolding for weeks on the other side of the glass. Around 3 P.M., CNBC revealed what was going on at the Fed, in surprising detail. Haghani came out, and Reisman, the repo man, said, "They're going to bail you out." Haghani thanked him and walked off.

In the Fed room, the issue came down to money. Allison had figured on sixteen banks at $250 million apiece. But the French banks wouldn't go above $125 million each. Lehman was stuck on $100 million. Bear was a zero. Allison had counted Salomon Smith Barney and Citicorp as *two* banks, but Citi, reckoning that it was about to merge with Salomon, hadn't shown. Pflug said Citi should be there, but Deryck Maughan told him to mind his own business.

By 4 P.M., the chance was slipping away. They weren't even close to $4 billion. Allison, seeing no other option, hiked the ante to $300 million. This was embarrassing for Corzine, who had to call his Goldman partners for consent. Peter Karches of Morgan Stanley sneered, "What do you mean? You're the boss!" The bankers suspected Corzine of looking for an out, but Corzine fully accepted that Wall Street's leaders should do their bit. His partners, who had a lesser sense of history, did not. They were loath to invest when Goldman itself was seeking capital, and they were distracted by the factional rivalries tearing at Goldman's fabric. To Allison, Corzine cut a tortured figure—angry at LTCM for its irresponsibility, which had put him into this difficult spot, and under intense pressure from his partners but still trying to do the right thing. He and Thain were eyeing each other warily. At one point, Thain got off the phone and whispered into his ear. Corzine plaintively turned to the group and said, "My partners *really* don't want to do this."

Despite his shaky support, Corzine went ahead. Now, with eleven banks at $300 million, plus the French and Lehman, $3.65 billion had been raised. Counting Long-Term's still remaining sliver of equity, it would have $4 billion of capital in total. How much of that should be apportioned to Long-Term's original investors? Some said zero, but Allison said the Long-Term partners would have to be given an incentive. After all, they would be managing the banks' money.

The other issue was how long to invest for. The bankers wanted their money back quickly, but if the consortium were perceived as transitory, other traders would start shooting at it. To be credible, the consortium needed staying power. The bankers agreed on a three-part agenda: reduce the fund's risk level, return capital to the new investors, and—last—try to realize a profit. To a man, the bankers would be happy just to get out whole.

At 5:15 P.M., Allison called Meriwether with the terms. Long-Term would be getting $3.65 billion from a new "spoke" representing fourteen banks. In exchange, the banks would receive 90 percent of the equity of the fund. Long-Term's existing investors would retain a 10 percent interest, worth about $400 million. But the partners' share of the latter would be totally subsumed by the debts against themselves and LTCM. In short, their investment in Long-Term—once worth $1.9 billion—was totally gone, most of it lost in a mere five weeks. The details of the new arrangement had yet to be ironed out, though it was clear that, at least for the next three years (the consortium's expected life), the partners' fees would be cut and their management and operating freedom would be severely curtailed.

Komansky thought the rival banks had done noble work, though of course they had saved their own hides and not just Meriwether's. What the bankers had done was choose a *certain* risk of $300 million over the mere possibility of a loss whose magnitude was unknowable. It signified that the bankers had—finally—lost their appetite for gambling.

Shortly after seven, they handed a press release to a mob of reporters. The release would affect events in an unexpected way, for it communicated to the world a level of finality that this complex deal did not yet possess.

The press naturally focused on the role of the Federal Reserve System in orchestrating the bailout.[20] According to the next day's *New York Times,* the Fed had stretched the doctrine of "too big to fail" to apply to a high-risk, speculative hedge fund. The *Times* story, which buried the fact that no public money was involved, immediately put the Fed on the defensive. The implication that the Fed was even tacitly assuming responsibility for private, unregulated funds was highly disturbing. As a former Treasury official noted elsewhere, "What if George Soros has a problem?"[21] *The Wall Street Journal* editorialized that the rescue continued a decade-long pattern of shielding private investors from the effects of their mistakes—each instance of which emboldened investors to make still further mistakes.[22]

By the day after the rescue, there was already a clamor for a government investigation, both into Long-Term and into hedge funds in general.[23] As if to underscore the damage that hedge funds could cause, UBS humbly announced that it was writing off its entire investment in Long-Term. The "strategic relationship" that Mathis Cabiallavetta had hoped would revitalize UBS had ended up costing the bank $700 million.

Commentators took wicked delight in the fall of the high and mighty Long-Term, with its superrich traders, its esoteric mathematics, and its acclaimed laureates. The *Financial Times* of London observed, "If [David] Mullins enjoyed fixing crises so much, he must be a very happy man."[24] The general, and understandable, reaction was one of horror that the Fed was coming to the rescue of the hero of *Liar's Poker.*

For Meriwether, it was a horror of a different sort. Everything he had done since the scandal at Salomon had been, at least in his mind, aimed at restoring his reputation and career. Now it had all come crashing down. The most inward of men, Meriwether had become a public figure identified with the arrogance, greed, and speculative folly of Wall Street taken to staggering excess. He and his devoted arbitrageurs were the authors of a historic collapse, one that had threatened the entire system. Camera crews descended on Greenwich, and television helicopters buzzed the firm's formerly tranquil offices. Meriwether was at least spared the suggestion of personal dishonor, but otherwise late September was for him the worst kind of nightmare. He retained his uncanny calm, though one wondered if it masked a certain detachment from his tragedy. His only public utterance was a one-sentence remark, released through his press agent, in which he blandly expressed appreciation for the consortium's capital.

In fact, the consortium deal was anything but assured, as the banks first had to resolve a host of sticky issues. One set related to J.M. and his partners and how tightly the banks could control them. Another revolved around the fund's shaky finances: the consortium conditioned the deal on getting waivers from every one of Long-Term's numerous lenders. The banks were petrified that even after the infusion of new capital, a single default would trigger a chain reaction and topple the fund.

Also, each of the banks had to examine—and come to understand—the fund well enough to persuade its own board to go ahead with the deal. When this was done, they would need a contract. And it all had to happen by Monday, September 28, the scheduled closing date—only five days away. Normally, the process takes months, but Long-Term was still hanging by a thread. "It was a mad rush," said Tom Bell, the outside counsel from Simpson Thacher & Bartlett, "to see whether we would close the deal or run out of money first."

Skadden, Arps, Merrill's law firm, was naturally hired to represent the consortium. Merrill offered to make Sullivan & Cromwell, Goldman's law firm, co-counsel, but the cagey Goldman didn't want its attorneys working for anyone else. Nonetheless, Goldman insisted that Sullivan's John Mead be present for the negotiations. This set up an interesting dynamic. While Milmoe, the pleasant-mannered Skadden partner, had to mediate for the entire consortium, Mead negotiated strictly for Goldman. A graying, forty-six-year-old litigator, Mead had a soft oval face and double chin that masked a brutally tough style. Right from the start he took a hard line, pushing Milmoe to make sure that the contract restricted the Long-Term partners as much as possible and otherwise protected the consortium's interests. This was fortunate for the banks, because the partners were hoping to win back through negotiations what they had lost in the marketplace. Incredibly, Meriwether and his cohorts were already plotting a new hedge fund—the partners' only chance of resurrection—as if Long-Term could be put behind them like a bad trade.

Meanwhile, a tempest was brewing on the fund's trading floor. Staffers, who had been wiped out too, were fast becoming embittered. Now that the fund had collapsed, they were demanding explanations; the partners' continued unwillingness to discuss the future seemed like so much vanity. Matt Zames, a young trader who was about to get married and had lost his investment, burst into one of the partner's offices. "No one's giving me answers!" he ranted. Another employee was furious when he realized from a newspaper account how much the partners had been holding back. Cornering David Modest, the employee fumed, "Don't you tell us *anything*?"

Skadden started the negotiations Friday, three days before the deadline. Seventy lawyers from the various banks piled into Merrill's boardroom. The lawyers discovered that the agreement they had come to negotiate actually didn't exist; too many issues divided them. As the lawyers talked, the markets tumbled again, knocking Long-Term's capital down to $400 million—91 percent below its level of January 1.

Mead's notes of the meeting show that the banks were highly concerned that the partners' (and LTCM's) debts would capsize the bailout: "Long-Term needs cash of approximately $122 million to enable certain Principals to repay personal loans and to enable the Management Company to repay, among other things, a $38 million loan to Partnership." Also, Mead noted, the banks remained extremely nervous about investing. J. P. Morgan wanted a guarantee that the banks could redeem their investment after three years. Chase insisted that the $500 million revolver be repaid the day after the closing. Bankers Trust and Deutsche Bank demanded seats on the "Oversight Committee" that would run the fund. Morgan Stanley and Goldman Sachs wanted joint indemnification if any one of the banks were sued, and so on. This was a tall order by Monday.

What Mead's notes didn't say was that Mead was raising more issues than all the other lawyers combined. The Goldman lawyer demanded that J.M. and his partners be stripped of day-to-day control; that they lose their indemnity from investor lawsuits; that they be stuck with full liability. Moreover, he insisted that the rescuers be shielded from liability even for acts that the banks might commit *in the future*. Sacking the ancien régime was not enough; Mead wanted to trundle out the guillotine.

By Friday evening, the cooler Milmoe, who had barely slept over the past two nights, had managed to piece together some basic terms. The consortium, to be dubbed "Oversight Partner I," would invest its money for three years. The partners' fees would be cut, and half of the management company would be transferred to the consortium for a $1 fee.

Meriwether and his partners would still run the fund day to day, but they would report to the Oversight Committee, made up of bankers who would work full-time in Greenwich and sever their ties to their home banks. Ultimate authority would rest with a board of directors from the banks.

The partners got copies of the contract early Saturday. They immediately exploded. It was indentured servitude, they hollered—it denied them bonuses, incentives, liability protection, and freedom to start anew. Accustomed to the extraordinary lives of the superrich, the partners could not conceive of working for a salary, and one of merely $250,000 at that. They had lived in a bubble so long they had forgotten the recent event—their own impending bankruptcy—that had brought them to this pass. On Wednesday, J.M. had been "appreciative"; by Saturday, the gang was refusing to sign. There was nothing in it for them.

This show of petulance carried a serious threat. The consortium could not invest without the partners' signatures. And the consortium was now publicly committed to doing the deal. By contrast, the partners had little left to lose. They could always, they intimated, let the fund blow up, seek cover in personal bankruptcy, and go get seven-figure jobs on Wall Street. Rickards managed to cool the partners off, promising that the final version of the contract would be better. Then a group of them left for Skadden, Arps.

The prestigious Midtown law firm had set out two big conference rooms and a series of private suites on the thirty-third floor to accommodate an expected onslaught of lawyers and bankers. By Saturday morning, 140 lawyers were scurrying back and forth in near pandemonium, trying to get a handle on the hedge fund's numbingly complex assets, its debts, its structure, its management company.

The Skadden attorneys took questions from the bank lawyers in the first conference room, a cavernous space with twenty-foot-high ceilings that was quickly dubbed "the lawyers' room." Milmoe, who ran the meeting, said, "Throw your issues at me," and the lawyers let him have it.

Milmoe was in a terrible bind. Merrill—the consortium's de facto leader—felt it *had* to close, a poor position from which to negotiate. Trying to craft a contract that would be acceptable to fourteen banks *and* each of the partners all within seventy-two hours, Milmoe naturally had to fashion compromises. As the day wore on, the bank lawyers began to feel that Milmoe was conceding too much to Greenwich. At one point, striving for a consensus, the congenial attorney said, "I'd like to represent LTCM's demands."

Mead snapped, "How can *they* have demands? They're going bankrupt on Monday!" Though the irritating Mead made Milmoe's work more difficult, he worked to the consortium's advantage by strengthening Milmoe's negotiating hand.

Meriwether, Haghani, Rosenfeld, Leahy, Shustak, and Rickards showed up at Skadden at noon. The partners, who had to walk past a gauntlet of incensed bankers in the hallway, were respectful and contrite, murmuring expressions of gratitude. In a telling reversal, the formerly nonchalant arbitrageurs had donned spiffy suits while the bankers and lawyers were wearing chinos. The humbled partners were escorted to the second conference room—the due diligence room—where the bankers peppered them with questions. It was mostly fact-finding: the banks wouldn't commit until they understood the fund better. The once-so-secretive partners were unusually helpful, as if eager to dig up treasure they had long ago buried. They left in late afternoon.

By now time was *really* running short, and most of the big issues had yet to be resolved. Mead was demanding that the Long-Term partners personally guarantee their representations, and he wanted the new money (the banks' money) shielded from lawsuits. Also, Mead did not like the look of the partners' intercompany loan; he wanted them to repay it.

The partners had issues, too. They insisted that the little bit of old money that remained should be available to satisfy lawsuits. They didn't want the bankers monitoring them on the premises in Greenwich. And the partners were balking at the bankers' demand that each partner commit to staying for three years—upon pain of forfeiting his equity.

Also, the bankers would have to do *something* about LTCM, the management company, which remained insolvent. Goldman, still eager to stick it to the partners, suggested that LTCM simply be folded. But LTCM also owed money to Chase—lots of money—so Goldman's clever idea would leave Chase high and dry as well. Pflug was furious at Goldman. "We're out," Pflug said suddenly. Tom Davis, the Merrill banker, hurriedly called Allison and told him the deal was falling apart.[25] Things would soon get worse.

Sensing that there were too many issues and not enough time, Merrill made contingency plans. The bank signed default notices on its repo contracts with Long-Term and rushed them to the Cayman Islands, ready for quick delivery to Long-Term's local agent. Later in the weekend, Merrill managers around the world were briefed on the procedures for liquidation. Their assumption was that if Long-Term went under, other hedge funds would fail, too. What would happen then Merrill could only guess, but it knew that in a panic, access to funding disappears, and no brokerage can long survive without funding. Powerful as it was, Merrill was frightened.

Late Saturday, Joseph Flom, Skadden's name partner, called Milmoe to see how things were going. Flom was distressed by what he heard. "This is the first time that one case could fuck up our relations with three quarters of our clients," Flom noted. "So don't screw it up."

The lawyers, including twenty-five assigned to the case by Skadden, gradually drifted to nearby hotels, leaving behind the half-eaten sandwiches, paper cups, and stale coffee that ever adorn these legal Woodstocks. Milmoe kept drafting. He penciled in revisions as a dwindling band of lawyers stood at his shoulder, mumbling suggested changes, and the printer hummed like a sleepless cat. Sometime after 4 A.M., his mind still ringing with Flom's admonition not to let the deal fall through, Milmoe tumbled onto the gray fabric couch in his office and slept.

■

Sunday morning, Allison hustled over to Skadden. He set up shop in the small room between the two big conference rooms—this became "the bankers' room." By midmorning, bankers stood shoulder to shoulder around the cluttered square table where Allison was hoping to save the rescue yet again.

The partners came back, too. Meriwether and some of the others were sitting together in one of the conference rooms. But Hilibrand was off to the side with his personal lawyer. Hilibrand, who was hopelessly in debt, was wondering if he should quit the rescue, file for bankruptcy, and put his debts behind him. Of course, that would take the fund down, too. *Après moi . . .*

Hilibrand's antics reminded the bankers of how little they wanted to be there. They were loath to help the partners personally. Only fear kept them in the deal. Allison thought it would be worse for the markets—much worse—if Long-Term failed now, after a deal had been announced. Moreover, Merrill's reputation was on the line. And Long-Term's lawyers *knew* how badly Allison wanted the deal; they played the game of chicken masterfully. "The consortium said, 'You have no alternative but us,'" recounted Bell, the Long-Term lawyer. "And we said, '*You* have no alternative but *us*.'" Though it is seldom realized, a creditor is also beholden to his debtor.

■

For much of Sunday, the bankers—led by William Harrison, a vice chairman of Chase, who had driven down from Connecticut with Pflug—tried to line up necessary waivers. The stickiest problems related to Nomura, Republic Bank, and the foreign exchange office of Italy, each of which had loans to Long-Term. The bankers insisted they wouldn't go ahead until each of the three agreed to waive their rights to immediate repayment.

Then there was Crédit Lyonnais, which was calling its $50 million loan to LTCM. Merrill's Richard Dunn called a senior executive of the bank in Paris, where it was already nighttime Sunday, and made an extraordinary plea for cooperation. Still no dice. The Western world could hang, but the French wanted their money. Once again Chase had to swallow its pride for the good of saving the management company. LTCM did have $104 million in deferred fees coming its way, and Chase agreed that the money could be used to pay off all of LTCM's other debts, including Crédit Lyonnais and the intercompany debt. Chase would have to carry a $108 million loan to the worthless LTCM into the future.

This patently unselfish act might have saved the day, but Goldman was not quite through. Early Sunday evening, Goldman dropped a bomb. Robert Katz, Goldman's in-house counsel, announced that Goldman would quit the consortium unless Chase agreed to waive its right to repayment of the $500 million bank syndicate. Goldman couldn't see putting fresh money into the portfolio so that Chase could take it out. The point was to rescue Long-Term, not to rescue Chase. This issue had been festering all weekend with many of the bankers—who, typically, were happy to let Goldman play the heavy.

Once again, Pflug was dumbfounded—and tired of always being the noble one. Even the other bankers, though sympathetic to Goldman's purpose, were stunned that it would risk the entire deal over such a point. Russo, the Lehman lawyer, turned to Katz and said, "You're bluffing." Katz merely smiled. The Chase team made it clear that they *would* walk. At that point, Katz reflected later, "There was no deal." It was 7 P.M.

Corzine, who was returning from a weekend at his majestic beachfront home in the Hamptons, called the meeting room from his cell phone. When Corzine reiterated that Goldman would not invest unless Chase left its money in, Pflug, who had steadily been losing patience, exploded. "Jon," he said, "there is no polite way to say this—Goldman can go fuck themselves!" Corzine, who was stuck in traffic on the Long Island Expressway, let it pass; he was used to getting heat from his bickering partners, who were backing away from the consortium again.

After talking to Corzine, Katz said resignedly, "We can't get an answer tonight." So Goldman was out, too. Katz said Goldman's executive committee would meet Monday morning at 6:30 and decide then. Now it was the turn of Steve Black, the Salomon Smith Barney executive, to erupt. All Goldman *really* wanted, he fumed, was twelve hours' time to trade in Japan before it made up its mind. "No way!"

Ironically, the consortium's most intractable problems lay not with Long-Term but among themselves. Frank Newman, chairman of Bankers Trust, had abandoned the meeting, furious that Goldman, Merrill, and Chase were excluding him from their various sidebar chats. And the ugly issue of front-running, which had never gone away, reared its head at the worst moment. Sandy Weill called Allison; the Travelers chairman was seething over reports that Goldman's traders were at it again. Allison pulled Katz aside and then spoke privately to Corzine on the telephone. Both of the Goldman executives denied the reports. Allison told Katz, "If one of us leaves, it all falls apart. Do you really want the deal to fall apart over this?"

Allison did not think Corzine was bluffing; Corzine's partners were just obstinate enough to walk. But with *two* banks holding out, Allison intuitively sensed the basis of a deal: Goldman would reenter the ring if only Chase would agree to its condition, Allison suggested. One always had to indulge the bad boys at Goldman. Harrison and Pflug saw no way out, and Chase consented; the fund could hang on to the $500 million. Corzine polled a few of his partners and decided—perhaps too quickly—that he had their support. Around 9 P.M., Goldman rejoined the consortium.

The bankers *still* needed waivers from Chase's twenty-three syndicate partners, in addition to Nomura, Republic, and the Italians. Otherwise they wouldn't proceed. Also, the French bank Paribas, an investor in the consortium, hadn't given a final assent. Allison went around the room, polling the bankers to see who had contacts at which banks. Then they began to call whatever time zone people were awake in. Allison left a little before midnight.

In Greenwich, Rickards was frenetically negotiating by phone with Skadden. At one point, Haghani darted out of the conference room and blurted out, as if under a delusion, "Remember one thing—we gotta buy this baby back!" *Buy it back with what?* Rickards may well have wondered. Sometime after midnight, the attorney got the consortium to agree to bonuses for the partners. At three, he left for home. Despite all the loose ends, the lawyers expected to close the deal at 10 A.M. Monday.

But Fleet, Republic, and Bank Nova Scotia had refused to sign the waivers. William Rhodes, vice chairman of Citibank, who was friendly with some of the holdouts, and Harrison spent Monday morning polling the banks. Harrison was vehement: they *had* to close on Monday.

At Skadden, the bankers had staked out one conference room and the partners were camped in the other, where a guard stood vigil at the door. Allison shuttled between the two, periodically going off with Meriwether to check on the status of his partners. Haghani bumped into Black of Salomon Smith Barney in the hallway, and said, "I can't believe this has happened." Haghani felt their trades would soar—and now it would all belong to the banks, not to the partners. Black felt sorry for him.[26]

Around eleven, J.M. sent an emissary to convey to Allison that the partners wanted to apologize for the trouble they had caused and wanted to help the consortium. But they were still divided.[27] A majority wanted to sign; they were drained and wanted the trauma over. Hilibrand was holding out.

And the fund was losing money again. The bankers kept watching Bear, wondering if Long-Term would make it through Monday. Amid this nerve-racking vigil, Goldman Sachs bowed to the inevitable and canceled its planned public offering. This was doubly ominous for Corzine, who had pledged to invest $300 million in Long-Term and yet had failed to raise capital for his own firm.

Then Frank Newman, the chairman of Bankers Trust, who had been pouting over his exclusion from the inner circle of bankers, bolted. Incredibly, the insecure banker declared that he was quitting the consortium. It was 3 P.M. on Monday.

Allison now got on the horn with Newman. He was running out of concessions but offered one more: a seat for Bankers Trust on the Oversight Committee. Newman swallowed hard and rejoined the deal.

At 5 P.M., the consortium agreed that the partners could call on "old money" to satisfy potential lawsuits. At 5:30, the consortium agreed that any partners who were fired wouldn't lose their equity, as would those who quit. Meriwether, not quite satisfied, said, "Our guys still won't sign until it says we can go out and do a new fund." That was their goal now—to get free of Long-Term.

Allison, who knew the banks would never invest $3.65 billion if the partners were plotting to desert, pulled J.M. aside and explained that he couldn't put it into writing. The partners would *have* to commit to three years each; markets would have little faith in the new consortium unless it was seen as truly "long term." But in time, Allison ventured, the partners might be free to leave. J.M. heard this as a promise; he had gotten all he could.

The waivers were in, and the Federal Reserve had been alerted to keep its electronic payments wire open past its usual 6:30 closing time. The Fed was expecting wires from fourteen banks totaling $3.65 billion.

The partners were ready to sign. They stood in a knot at the far end of the room, a cathedral-sized space that seemed to dwarf the small band of diminished arbitrageurs. Hilibrand was reading the contract, which was hopelessly illegible to all but the lawyers. The margins were jammed with penciled revisions and crossed-out sentences and arrows up and down, as though the contract were a visual representation of the confusion of the last three days. Rickards and a couple of other attorneys were trying to tell Hilibrand what it meant, but he didn't want to listen, he wanted to read it himself, and he could barely see it through the tears that were streaming down his face. He didn't want to sign, he wailed; there was nothing in it for him, better to file for bankruptcy than be someone else's indentured servant with no hope of ever earning his way out. Meriwether took Hilibrand aside and talked to him about the group, and how the others were in it and needed him to be in it, and still, Hilibrand, who had never needed anyone and who had once rebelled at paying for his share of the company cafeteria but now couldn't pay his debts, refused. Then Allison talked to him and said they were trying to restore the public's faith in the system and not to destroy anybody, and J.M. said, "Larry, you better listen to Herb." And Hilibrand signed, and the fund was taken over by fourteen banks.

Epilogue

The result was a downward spiral which fed upon itself driving market positions to unanticipated extremes well beyond the levels incorporated in risk management and stress loss discipline.
—LTCM Confidential Memorandum, January 1999

Long-Term's debacle was a tragedy for its partners. Motivated by insatiable greed, they had forcibly cashed out their outside investors only months before, leaving themselves to withstand, virtually alone, the brunt of the collapse. The wizards of Wall Street personally lost $1.9 billion. Larry Hilibrand, the most cocksure of traders, who had previously been worth close to half a billion dollars, awoke to discover that he was broke. Forced to live off the assets of his wife, Deborah, he had to plead with Crédit Lyonnais to spare him the ignominy of personal bankruptcy while he tried to work off a crushing $24 million debt. Most of the other partners lost 90 percent or more of their wealth—that is, everything they had invested in the fund. Thanks to the smooth takeover encouraged by the Federal Reserve and managed by Herb Allison, most of the partners remained far richer than ordinary Americans; high finance rewards success, but in the twilight years of the twentieth century, it strangely protected failure as well. The partners (including Hilibrand) kept their elegant homes, even though their days among the superrich were over. Never conspicuous spenders, they suffered more for the way their epochal loss branded them as socially irresponsible speculators in the public eye and for the way it ruined their reputations among Wall Street colleagues. But no moral scandal ensued. The money was lost, but honestly lost.

Eric Rosenfeld, Long-Term's manager, auctioned off caseloads of the wine collection he had once so lovingly assembled—some of it to Merrill Lynch's Conrad Voldstad, who, as a member of the Oversight Committee, had thus inherited Rosenfeld's portfolio as well. Worse yet, Rosenfeld had to endure the knowledge that relatives of his wife, who were by no means rich, had suffered losses at his behest. But he seemed to take these setbacks in stride. When Bill McIntosh, a former colleague at Salomon Brothers, called to see if there was anything he could do, Rosenfeld responded wryly, "Just send money."

Others of the partners became morose or desperate for vindication. Haghani, the master trader, was haunted by the fund's brief, brutal devastation, so much of it caused by his repeated insistence on betting the house. "This is a personal tragedy," a friend of the mercurial Haghani noted. "It's with him every day, and it's not going away."

The fund's collapse got wide coverage around the country, virtually none of it sympathetic to the partners. *Time* dubbed them "The Brightest and the Brokest" and noted that "outrage was mingled with shock." Headline writers had a field day with the failed geniuses. "We're So Rich, We Can Be Dumb," jeered the *San Francisco Chronicle.* Merton's hometown paper, *The Boston Globe,* chimed in with "Fast (and Suspect) Fix for a 'Long-Term' Problem." The press naturally seized on the bald unfairness of the Fed's helping to bail out Wall Street moguls. In Philadelphia, the *Inquirer* pointedly demanded, "When a Hedge Fund Fails, All Investors Suffer—Is That Fair?" while *The Miami Herald*'s "The Bolder They Are, the Softer They Fall" ripped the arbitrageurs as pampered rich kids.[1]

Merton was more distraught over the stain that Long-Term's failure cast on modern finance and on his own prodigious academic oeuvre. Though tacitly conceding that the models had failed, he insisted that the solution was to design ever-more elaborate and sophisticated models.[2] The notion that relying on *any* formulaic model posed inescapable risks eluded him.

Merton's fellow laureate, Myron Scholes, was remarried, to a San Francisco lawyer, at the elegant Pierre Hotel in New York, a week after the bailout. Scholes could not escape signs of the catastrophe even at his wedding. Meriwether and Rosenfeld kept darting off to make telephone calls, and Merton Miller gave the groom a gentle roasting, observing that Scholes had now found out for himself just how dangerous it was to try to beat the market.[3] At least the dashing Scholes maintained his wit. Refusing to duck, the Nobel laureate dryly informed the revelers that rather than his wife, Jan, taking his name, he would take hers.

As for J.M., he never spoke publicly about his feelings and didn't speak much about the "extreme event," as the fund referred to its collapse. Eager to flee the limelight and horrified by the reporters who banged at his door,[4] the retiring trader reacted to his personal tragedy like very few others in this overly public era: with utter silence. Surely, as he had said to Allison, he regretted it all. Perhaps he brooded over how, after a lifetime of carefully playing the odds and avoiding the limelight, he had become a notorious symbol of speculative excess. But it would have been more like J.M. to banish the disaster from mind. Long-Term had been a bad trade; there would be others.

■

The Federal Reserve reduced interest rates on Tuesday, September 29, the very day after the bailout. However, the Fed's action did not bring any relief to Long-Term or its new owners. In the wake of the rescue, U.S. swap spreads widened to 96½ points and Britain's soared to 120. The spread on Royal Dutch/Shell—8 percent when Long-Term had entered the trade—ballooned to 22 percent. The two classes of Volkswagen shares—Long-Term had invested at a 40 percent differential—widened to more than 60 percent. And on it went.

Recapitalized with a fresh $3.65 billion, Long-Term continued to plummet, like a parachutist who yanks the rip cord but keeps falling anyway. In its first two weeks, the consortium lost $750 million. It was happening again—for the consortium, the scariest of all possible epilogues.

By mid-October, all of Wall Street seemed to have caught Long-Term's disease. One by one, Merrill Lynch, Bankers Trust, UBS, Credit Suisse First Boston, Goldman Sachs, and Salomon Smith Barney—the linchpins of the new consortium—divulged large losses that in sum matched those of Greenwich. The banks' stocks plummeted, signaling a pervasive loss of confidence in the very institutions that had come to Long-Term's rescue. In the wake of the bailout, investors became obsessed with Wall Street's careless sponsorship of hedge funds. One after another, the banks dutifully reduced their exposure to this noxious class—a category that so recently had been the envy of all Wall Street and now had become a pariah.

In fact, the exposures, while big, were not as threatening as alarmists maintained; there was no "second Long-Term" waiting in the wings. But Long-Term (and other hedge funds) did have a corrosive effect on Wall Street all the same. The banks had not been able to resist the lure of the funds' fabulous—if fleeting—profits. Flush with capital, they had rushed to set up their own, similar, trading desks and had mimicked the hedge funds' diverse strategies. In the aftermath of Long-Term's collapse, the banks, too, had losses in bond arbitrage, in Russia, and in equity derivatives. Familiarity had bred the desire to imitate; that was the true price of the banks' "exposure."

Merrill Lynch's stock price plummeted by two thirds in a mere three months—not as severe, and certainly not as enduring, as the 92 percent loss from top to bottom in Long-Term's equity, but astonishing nonetheless. Komansky and Allison had taken such pride in shielding Merrill from proprietary trading, but Merrill's bond traders lost close to a billion dollars all the same. Suddenly anxious that Merrill's own credit rating would come under pressure, Merrill, led by Allison, aggressively cut costs and fired 3,500 people, largely in the bond department. By mid-October, not only was Long-Term imploding again, but its new owners, the leading banks on Wall Street, were in deepening trouble.

And now Alan Greenspan decided he had seen enough. On October 15, the Fed chief cut rates for a second time—a signal that he would cut and keep cutting until liquidity to the system was restored. Wall Street rallied, and bond spreads narrowed. For the first time in months, bond arbitrageurs made a sustained profit. In Greenwich, the portfolio turned around. After six months that had been by turns painful, then surprising, then agonizing, and then utterly devastating, Long-Term Capital, which since April had lost the fabulous total of $5 billion, finally stopped losing. The storm had passed.*

■

The fallout from the bust fell broadly but—as is usually the case— unevenly on various of Long-Term's investors, employees, counter-

---

*In 2000, in an echo of the hedge fund's debacle, Soros and Tiger Management suffered debilitating losses, and Tiger was forced to liquidate.

parties, and Wall Street friends. Herb Allison, who had done more than anyone to save the fund, was soon resented within Merrill Lynch for his role in Merrill's zealous cost cutting. When the crisis passed and memories of the panic faded, Allison was blamed for overreacting. Informed that he was not in line to succeed Komansky, Allison resigned and went to work for Senator John McCain's presidential campaign. Daniel Napoli, Merrill's risk manager, took the fall for Merrill's losses. Replaced, he went on long-term leave.

Goldman's Jon Corzine continued his hot-and-cold romance with Long-Term Capital for just a bit longer. Goldman let it be known that—at the right price—Warren Buffett would still be an eager suitor for Long-Term. Corzine also called Prince Alwaleed to gauge the Saudi's interest in joining yet another buyout bid. But by the end of October, the fund had stabilized and the consortium had no need of Goldman's peripatetic bankers.

Goldman resurrected its IPO and went public in May 1999. But Corzine, who had staked his career on the earlier IPO attempt and had then staked it again on Meriwether, fell before the battle was won. In January, in a rare boardroom coup, his partners sacked him.

Corzine made one final pass with Meriwether, the man he had wanted as his partner for so long. In the spring, the two teamed up to raise money to acquire Long-Term from its Wall Street owners, with the idea that Corzine and Meriwether would run it together. But the effort fizzled. Then Corzine, who had reaped $230 million in Goldman's IPO, quit Wall Street and began a vigorous campaign for the Democratic senatorial nomination in New Jersey. A bundle of contradictions, Corzine was a decent man at the helm of a cutthroat firm, a banker with a sense of his place in the larger world in a society that honored only profits, and a competitor who fell on his sword for Meriwether, a rival who disappointed him but enchanted him all the same.

UBS was left in tatters, devastated by losses not only from its investment in Long-Term but also from Ramy Goldstein's equity derivatives unit. Mathis Cabiallavetta, the former prince of Swiss banking and the architect of UBS's dubious strategy, resigned. Marcel Ospel, the chief executive formerly with the more prudent Swiss Bank, quickly cleaned house. An unlucky victim was Andrew Siciliano, the partners' friend and the manager at UBS who had first expressed doubts about the dubious Long-Term warrant. For failing to take his concerns to the very top, Siciliano was fired.

Bankers Trust suffered catastrophic losses in Russia, where it had been an aggressive buyer of ruble securities, as well as in Brazil and other emerging markets. Making a mockery of the self-important pretensions of its chairman, Frank Newman, the bank was forced to sell out to a German rival, Deutsche Bank. Though judged a failure, Newman, whose fit of pique had nearly scotched the Long-Term rescue, secured a golden parachute for himself estimated at $100 million, an enormous undeserved bounty.[5]

Sandy Weill came out on top, as he always seemed to. Citicorp and Travelers/Salomon merged on schedule. Lehman Brothers, which had been plagued by rumors, quickly recovered. Chase Manhattan—without whose repeated help Long-Term would have surely failed—had its loans repaid and came out whole. Indeed, thanks to the rescue, Long-Term met every margin call. All of its debts to creditors were repaid in full.

■

Most of Long-Term's outside investors came out ahead—saved, ironically, by the forced repatriation of their capital at the end of 1997. Some thirty-eight investors who had been lucky enough to invest at the inception and to have been mostly cashed out in 1997 finished with an average return of 18 percent a year—not quite as high as the major stock averages over the same span but very good all the same. About an equal number of investors who had *fully* cashed out before the catastrophic losses of 1998 did even better.

Investors who had been granted the special dispensation of being allowed to keep more of their capital invested ultimately lost money. Ironically, Bear's Jimmy Cayne, who nearly brought the fund down, was one such "favored" loser. Komansky, chairman of Merrill, who invested at the top, was a loser, too. About a dozen big banks made only single-digit annual returns, and a dozen others—including, notably, UBS, Credit Suisse First Boston, and Dresdner—lost money.

The mixed results of the outside investors in no way diminished the magnitude of Long-Term's failure. Even with the headwind of its first four highly successful years, Long-Term's final, cumulative loss was staggering. Through April 1998, the value of a dollar invested in Long-Term quadrupled to $4.11. By the time of the bailout, only five months later, precisely 33 cents of that total remained. After deducting the partners' fees, the results were even sorrier: each invested dollar, having grown to $2.85, shrank to a meager 23 cents. In net terms, the greatest fund ever—surely the one with the highest IQs—had lost 77 percent of its capital while the ordinary stock market investor had been more than doubling his money.

■

The fund's employees, like those at most Wall Street firms, had gotten most of their pay in the form of year-end bonus money. Most of those bonuses had been invested in the fund and went down the drain. "We all lost our money," said a staffer who worked as an analyst. "We ended up working for nothing," said another, a bond trader.

In October, employees staged a minirevolt, demanding that future bonus money be placed in a trust where it could not be squandered. The staff also craved a measure of recognition, some admission that their bosses had been wrong to keep them in the dark. But the partners' habit of secrecy was deeply ingrained. At one meeting of partners and staff, an employee demanded, "Explain to us why we should be sitting here and not looking for jobs." Replied a partner, "That's a valid question. We'll get back to you." The talented, dedicated workers never did win their bosses' trust.

A month after the rescue, Long-Term laid off thirty-three employees, almost a fifth of the staff.[6] After that, there was a steady stream of defections. The fund offered a small severance package, but even this was a carrot for which J.M. & Co. exacted a price. Departing staff members were cajoled into signing termination agreements in which they repeated a pledge never to say a word about the fund— as if the partners feared the revelation of some secret shame.

■

Once the fund stabilized, the partners found themselves in an unhappy limbo. Though they still presided over a huge fund, their hands were tied by their new Wall Street masters, who monitored the fund's every position like anxious schoolmarms. Investing in new trades was out of the question; the consortium's only interest was to get its money back. The partners, who had fantasized that they might be able to run the fund much as before, were bitterly disappointed. At the consortium's directive, they steadily downsized, trimming positions and reducing exposures. Haghani took his sweet time in unloading trades; the Oversight Committee, which suspected Haghani of foot-dragging, had to dispatch some of its members to London to make sure the unyielding arbitrageur fell into line.

The partners' steely eleventh-hour negotiations had guaranteed them a generous bonus—on average, $500,000—in return for staying the year. Otherwise, they were treated like the hired hands they were, forced to swallow a bitter helping of their own gruel. Disagreements between them and the banks were resolved in favor of the consortium, which now held all the power. The consortium, wanting no more embarrassment from the free-swinging arbitrageurs, monitored the fund's image, too. In a humiliating reversal of roles, they ordered the partners to clear public statements with their new bosses, implying that now it was the partners that couldn't be trusted.

More distressing still, especially to a firm that had prided itself on its clever avoidance of taxes, the Internal Revenue Service launched a global audit of LTCM and its various affiliates. The audit, which focuses on the years 1996 and 1997, and which remained unresolved eighteen months after the fund's collapse, exposed the partners to the possibility, one day down the road, of being billed for massive back taxes owed.

After the crisis, the group's extraordinary unity broke down. Several of the partners came to believe that for the good of the firm, Hilibrand and Haghani should go, not only for their part in losing the money but for their controlling dispositions, too. Neither was suited to teamwork. Meriwether heard complaints about the two from Hawkins, McEntee, Modest, and Mullins. But he was singularly unprepared to deal with them. J.M. held a few meetings and tried to placate the mutineers, but he was too deliberate, and too loyal to his longtime cohorts, to confront his two top traders. Hawkins finally searched out the boss and declared, in effect, that it was either Hilibrand or him. J.M., always spare with words, said, "Good luck to you." Then he left the room.

In the year following the bailout, unhappy partners gradually (and with the consortium's permission) left the firm. Most were able to tap past connections and resume a normal working life. No stigma was attached; second acts on Wall Street are as common as they are in politics. Perhaps one cycle, be it an election cycle or an economic cycle, is the extent of the public's memory.

Scholes, who was bitter about the entire experience, returned with

Jan to the Bay Area, where he took up writing and occasional lecturing at Stanford. He and Chi-fu Huang, the former head of Long-Term's Tokyo office, were hired to manage money for the Basses, the Texas tycoons. Merton continued to teach at Harvard. A year after the rescue, with the benefit of his hard-won firsthand knowledge, Merton was hired as a consultant in risk management by J. P. Morgan.

Modest, the intellectual modeler, became a managing director in equities at Morgan Stanley. Mullins, the central banker, decided on yet a third career change and became an adviser to several start-up companies that provided financial services over the Internet. Hawkins and McEntee drew up plans for an investment fund. With the exception of the outspoken Scholes, who was never shy about offering his thoughts—including on Long-Term, on which he had kept detailed notes—the departed partners contentedly disappeared from public view.

Meriwether never doubted that he and his core group from Salomon would try to raise money and do it again. Almost as soon as the ink on the bailout agreement was dry, J.M. and his loyalists began to chafe under the consortium's restrictions. They continually pestered their overseers to let them raise new money, and J.M. began to mutter that Allison—who insisted that the group should wait a bit—wasn't living up to his promise, as if the group's rescuer was in debt to *them*.

The partners went on the road in late 1998 and early 1999 to visit their investors—ostensibly to explain the disaster but really to seed the ground for future fund-raising. Allison was stunned to learn that J.M. was circulating a brief on the disaster to investors in Europe—a prelude to marketing his next venture—and the consortium ordered him to stop.

"Do these guys *possibly* think they can redeem themselves?" one of the consortium bankers wondered. Clearly, they did. In their one public interview before they were gagged, the partners put forth a redeeming and idealized view of themselves as a band of brilliant ultrarationalists who, most unluckily, had been done in by an unreasoning and venal world.[7]

The partners *appeared* to accept responsibility; they said they did and apologized on various occasions; but they never made clear just what it was they were apologizing for. J.M. & Co. generally denied that either the leverage or the size of their portfolio had been a significant contributing factor; they denied, even, that their basic strategy had been flawed.[8] Rather, in meeting after meeting, the partners blamed the irrationality and venality of *other* traders. They portrayed Long-Term as the victim of outside events, specifically, of a liquidity shortage in August followed by hostile front-running in September.

On the first anniversary of the historic meeting at the Fed, Myron Scholes cogently argued in a talk at New York's Windows on the World restaurant that spreads on lower-rated bonds had widened to greater levels than could have been explained by mere default risk. Therefore, Scholes concluded, the spreads must have been "liquidity spreads," representing the premium that investors were willing to pay for more liquid paper. There is a circular nature to such arguments: when prices fall, one may always blame the absence of buyers and hence of "liquidity." As Scholes himself pointed out, there were very real, underlying events that had scared the buyers away; to wit, investors had been counting on the IMF to bail out developing regions, but the IMF had been incapable of protecting everyone at once:

> The example I like to give is that of a father with several sons. Each son thinks that the father will support him in his time of need. But, if one of his brothers needs support, the father then has fewer resources to support his activities and also those of his other brothers. The value of the support option is diminished in value. This, in part, is the cause of the flight to liquidity in August. Figuratively, another son, Russia, could not be sufficiently supported, and as a result, all of the other sons, the underdeveloped countries, looked less credit worthy.[9]

Scholes lamented that academics and practitioners hadn't modeled this "stress-loss liquidity component" and its implications for prices. But obviously, illiquidity was merely the *expression* of the problem, not its cause. What was missing from these self-serving sound bites was any suggestion that Long-Term had been at fault for exposing itself to such perils. A man driving a car at thirty miles an hour may blame the road if he skids on a patch of ice; a man driving at a hundred miles an hour may not.

Scholes averted the question of *why* "academics and practitioners" had ignored the long-established and basically self-evident liquidity risks. Even after their historic loss, the Long-Term partners admitted no essential mistake. They had been done in, they argued, by an unforeseeable event—a perfect storm such as strikes once in a hundred years. "I believe that," Rosenfeld explained after the crash. "I do think it was something that never happened before."[10] Of course, it had happened, not once in a hundred years but many times—in Mexico, on Wall Street, in stocks, in bonds, in silver, in Thailand, in Russia, in Brazil. People caught in such financial cataclysms typically feel singularly unlucky, but financial history is replete with examples of "fat tails"—unusual and extreme price swings that, based on a reading of previous prices, would have seemed implausible.

Whatever they had learned from the trauma, the partners continued to insist, just as they had before the bailout, that spreads were too wide, that now was the time to invest, that opportunities had never looked better. The models said so! On this they were proven wrong—or at least, a year after the bailout, they had yet to be proven right. Though Wall Street recovered, Long-Term's brand of arbitrage did not. Under its new owners, the fund enjoyed a good last quarter in 1998 and a good start to the new year; then it went into a tailspin. In the summer of 1999, U.S. swap spreads once again ballooned, to 112 points—wider, even, than at the astronomical height of the previous year's panic. The once-in-a-century flood had struck twice in two years.

On September 28, 1999, exactly a year after the bailout, swap spreads remained at 93 points and equity volatility was at 30 percent—each far higher than when Long-Term had entered the respective trade. In the first year after the bailout, the fund earned 10 percent—hardly a dramatic recovery. Then, in addition to this modest profit, the fund redeemed the consortium's $3.65 billion in capital. For practical purposes, the fund had liquidated by early 2000.

So Long-Term's problem had not been just illiquidity. Perhaps the fund's entire strategy had been wrong, and the world's (and Long-Term's) perception of credit in 1998 had been a little too rosy. The evidence suggests that both factors were at work: Long-Term misjudged the markets, and the effect of that misjudgment was sorely compounded in September, when—to protect themselves against Long-Term's imminent collapse—other traders went on strike and "liquidity" disappeared.

■

Alan Greenspan freely admitted that by orchestrating a rescue of Long-Term, the Fed had encouraged future risk takers and perhaps increased the odds of a future disaster. "To be sure, some moral hazard, however slight, may have been created by the Federal Reserve's involvement,"[11] the Fed chief declared. However, he judged that such negatives were outweighed by the risk of "serious distortions to market prices had Long-Term been pushed suddenly into bankruptcy."

If one looks at the Long-Term episode in isolation, one would tend to agree that the Fed was right to intervene, just as, if confronted with a suddenly mentally unstable patient, most doctors would willingly prescribe a tranquilizer. The risks of a breakdown are immediate; those of addiction are long term. But the Long-Term Capital case must be seen for what it is: not an isolated instance but the latest in a series in which an agency of the government (or the IMF) has come to the rescue of private speculators. In one decade, this unfortunate roster has grown to include the savings and loans, big commercial banks that had overlent to real estate, investors in Mexico, Thailand, South Korea, and Russia (where a bailout was attempted), and now the various parties affiliated with Long-Term Capital. It is true that the Fed's involvement was limited and that no government money was used. But the banks would not have come together without the enormous power and influence of the Fed behind them, and without a joint effort, Long-Term surely would have collapsed. Presumably, the banks and others would have suffered more severe losses—though not, one thinks, as great as some suggested. Long-Term's exposure was huge, but, spread over all of Wall Street, it was hardly of apocalyptic proportions. At some point the selling would have stopped. At some point buyers would have returned and markets would have stabilized. Other banks could have failed, though that was an outside chance at best.

Permitting such losses to occur is what deters most other people and institutions from taking imprudent risks. Now especially, after a decade of prosperity and buoyant financial markets, a reminder that foolishness carries a price would be no bad thing. Will investors in the next problem-child-to-be, having been lulled by the soft landing engineered for Long-Term, be counting on the Fed, too? On balance, the Fed's decision to get involved—though understandable given the panicky conditions of September 1998—regrettably squandered a choice opportunity to send the markets a needed dose of discipline.

McDonough always defended his actions, though he seemed displeased and perhaps embarrassed by the fund's survival. A year after the bailout, in an impolitic burst of candor, the Fed president declared, "LTCM is close to being out of business. I can assure you that is a result that pleases me considerably."[12]

Greenspan's more serious and longer-running error has been to consistently shrug off the need for regulation and better disclosure with regard to derivative products. Deluded as to the banks' ability to police themselves before the crisis, Greenspan called for a *less burdensome* regulatory regime barely six months after it.[13] His Neolithic opposition to enhanced disclosure—which, because it allows investors to be their own watchdogs, is ever the best friend of free capital markets—served to remind one of the early Greenspan who (in thrall to Ayn Rand) once wrote, "The basis of regulation is armed force."[14] In fact, it is in countries that lack transparency (such as Russia) that markets need to be defended by soldiers.

If the Long-Term episode proved anything, it is that the system of disclosure that has worked so well with regard to traditional securities has *not* been able to do the job with respect to derivative contracts. To put it plainly, investors have a pretty good idea about balance-sheet risks; they are completely befuddled with regard to derivative risks. Some of the reporting standards are being changed (over the opposition of both Greenspan and the banks), but gaping holes remain. As the use of derivatives grows, this deficiency will return to haunt us.

Moreover, aside from improving reporting on derivatives, there is a strong argument to be made for restricting actual exposure. Regulators limit the amount that Chase Manhattan and Citibank can lend, so that their loans do not exceed a certain ratio of capital. The regulators do this for good reason: banks have repeatedly shown that they will exceed the limits of prudence if they can. Why, then, does Greenspan endorse a system in which banks can rack up any amount of exposure that they choose—as long as that exposure is in the form of derivatives?

The Fed's two-headed policy—head in the sand before a crisis, intervention after the fact—is more misguided when viewed as one single policy. *The government's emphasis should always be on prevention, not on active intervention.* It is altogether proper that the government set rules in advance for regulated bodies such as banks; crisis intervention on behalf of unregulated hedge funds is another matter.

The White House formed a blue-ribbon panel, the President's Working Group on Financial Markets, a multiagency group (including the Fed) to study the Long-Term debacle. Its report concluded, "The central public policy issue raised by the LTCM episode is how to constrain excessive leverage more effectively." Moreover, it recognized the growing role of derivatives, noting, "Balance-sheet leverage by itself is not an adequate measure of risk."[15] However, the report was weaker when it came to proposing solutions. It did call for enhanced disclosure by hedge funds, better risk and credit management policies by banks, and tougher regulatory standards. But the cautiously worded report, which was issued in April 1999, did not have the fire to provoke action from Congress, which in any case was rapidly losing interest in Long-Term. "Last September and October, it was a hot issue," David Runkel, a spokesman for the House Banking Committee, noted the summer after the crisis. "But not now."[16]

The furor over hedge funds also died down—and appropriately so. The Long-Term crisis happened to involve a hedge fund, but the fathers of the crisis were the big Wall Street banks, which let their standards grow lax as their pocketbooks grew flush. At the time of the bailout, the banks were depicted as victims that had been kept in the dark by Long-Term's patented secrecy. Such a view was enhanced by various bankers' assertions of innocence. (Komansky, for one, called a friend upon leaving the Federal Reserve and declared, "When I saw their position, my fucking knees were shaking.") With time, such claims rang increasingly hollow. Each bank had known its own exposure to Long-Term trade by trade; it did not take genius for them to infer that the fund was doing similar business elsewhere.

Patrick Parkinson, a Fed official assigned to the President's Working Group, told a Senate committee a couple of months after the rescue:

> LTCM appears to have received very generous credit terms, even though it took an exceptional degree of risk. . . . Counterparties obtained information from LTCM that indicated that it had securities and derivatives positions that were very large relative to its capital. However, few, if any, seem to have really understood LTCM's risk profile.[17]

So the question becomes, why did the bankers lend? In a public symposium early in 1999, Walter Weiner, the former chairman of Republic, maintained that the banks had had no choice—or at least, no choice other than the rare, courageous one of rejecting business: "To enter the club, you had to play by LTCM's rules. The terms were non-negotiable—take it or leave it."[18] The banks took it. They, too, were greedy, and they were awed by Long-Term's performance and dazzled by the partners' reputations, degrees, and celebrity. "We may have been mesmerized by these supermen," Weiner acknowledged. Unique in Wall Street history, the fund had blazed across the financial skies like a luminous rocket, a half-man, half-machine that seemingly reduced an uncertain world to rigorous, cold-blooded odds. Like visitors from a remote future, the professors seemed to have superseded the random luck and ill fate that had ever lurked in the shadows of markets.

■

Long-Term's saga of riches to rags was replete with lessons for investors. Its astonishing profits looked less impressive in the light of the losses that followed. As with an insurer who collects heady premiums but gives them back when a big storm hits, Long-Term's profits were not, in a sense, all "earned"; in part, they were borrowed against the day when the cycle would turn. No investment—Internet wunderkinds included—can be judged on the basis of half a cycle alone.

Indeed, Long-Term saw that the cycle was turning but inexplicably refused to prune its exposures. As spreads narrowed, inevitably raising the risks in the business, Long-Term *increased* its leverage, as if borrowing could turn an unattractive business into a better one rather than just a riskier one. Long-Term wouldn't have made this mistake but for a major managerial weakness: the absence of any independent check on the traders. In the end, every partner had sat through the risk-management meetings, and every one, ultimately, had acquiesced in the trades. In that sense, every partner was to blame.

Long-Term put supreme trust in diversification—one of the shibboleths of modern investing, but an overrated one. As Keynes noted, one bet soundly considered is preferable to many poorly understood. The Long-Term episode proved that eggs in separate baskets *can* break simultaneously. Moreover, Long-Term fooled itself into thinking it had diversified in substance when, in fact, it had done so only in form. Basically, the fund made the same bet on lower-rated bonds in every imaginable permutation. It is hardly a surprise that when the cycle turned and credit tightened—as, throughout recorded time, it periodically has—Long-Term's trades fell in lockstep.

It is interesting to compare Long-Term's losses from various categories of trades from January 1, 1998, to the bailout:[19]

> Russia and other emerging markets: $430 million
> Directional trades in developed countries (such as shorting Japanese bonds): $371 million
> Equity pairs (such as Volkswagen and Shell): $286 million
> Yield-curve arbitrage: $215 million
> Standard & Poor's 500 stocks: $203 million
> High-yield (junk bond) arbitrage: $100 million
> Merger arbitrage: Roughly even

These seven categories accounted for $1.6 billion in losses—a catastrophic result. However, Long-Term could have survived them. Now consider the losses in its two biggest trades:

> Swaps: $1.6 billion
> Equity volatility: $1.3 billion

It was these two trades that broke the firm. Long-Term got far too big in these markets—a cautionary error. It got so big that it distorted the very markets on whose efficiency the firm relied. This wouldn't have mattered but for the fact that Long-Term also leveraged its capital 30 to 1—again, in addition to the huge leverage implicit in its derivatives book. One can be big (and therefore illiquid); one can (within prudent limits) be leveraged. But the investor who is highly leveraged *and* illiquid is playing Russian roulette, for he must be right about the market not merely at the end, but every single day. (One wrong day, and he is out of business.) Long-Term was so self-certain as to believe that the markets would *never*—not even for a wild swing some August and September—stray so far from its predictions.

Reared on Merton's and Scholes's teachings of efficient markets, the professors actually believed that prices would go and go directly where the models said they should. The professors' conceit was to think that models could forecast the limits of behavior. In fact, the models could tell them what was reasonable or what was predictable based on the past. The professors overlooked the fact that people, traders included, are not always reasonable. This is the true lesson of Long-Term's demise. No matter what the models say, traders are not machines guided by silicon chips; they are impressionable and imitative; they run in flocks and retreat in hordes.

Even when traders get things "right," markets can hardly be expected to oscillate with the precision of sine waves. Prices and spreads vary with the uncertain progress of companies, governments, and even civilizations. They are no more certain than the societies whose economic activity they reflect. Dice are predictable down to the decimal point; Russia is not; how traders will respond to Russia is less predictable still. Unlike dice, markets are subject not merely to risk, an arithmetic concept, but also to the broader uncertainty that shadows the future generally. Unfortunately, uncertainty, as opposed to risk, is an indefinite condition, one that does not conform to numerical straitjackets.

The professors blurred this crucial distinction; they sent their mathematical Frankenstein gamely into the world as if it could tame the element of chance in life itself. No self-doubt tempered them; no sense of perspective checked them as they wagered such staggering sums.

The supreme irony is that the professors were trying to deconstruct and ultimately to minimize risk, not—they believed—to speculate on overcoming it. In this, the fund was not unique. Long-Term was in fact the quintessential fund of the late twentieth century—an experiment in harnessing the markets to the twin new disciplines of financial economics and computer programming. The belief that tomorrow's risks can be inferred from yesterday's prices and volatilities prevails at virtually every investment bank and trading desk. This was Long-Term's basic mistake, and its stunning losses betrayed the flaw at the very heart—the very brain—of modern finance.

None other than Merrill Lynch observed in its annual report for 1998, "Merrill Lynch uses mathematical risk models to help estimate its exposure to market risk." In a phrase that suggested some slight dawning awareness of the dangers in such models, the bank added that they "may provide a greater sense of security than warranted; therefore, reliance on these models should be limited."[20] If Wall Street is to learn just one lesson from the Long-Term debacle, it should be that. The next time a Merton proposes an elegant model to manage risks and foretell odds, the next time a computer with a perfect memory of the past is said to quantify risks in the future, investors should run—and quickly—the other way.

On Wall Street, though, few lessons remain learned. In November

1999, JWM Partners—the principals were Meriwether, Haghani, Hilibrand, Leahy, Rosenfeld, and Arjun Krishnamachar—circulated an offering document for "Relative Value Opportunity Fund II." According to the circular, leverage in their new fund would be held to a relatively modest 15 to 1, discipline would be tighter, and the firm would make use of a "risk control system" that had been designed "to help ensure to the extent practicable that the Portfolio Company can withstand extreme events of the type experienced in 1998." Whether *any* mathematical system designed with a previous crisis in mind can ensure against future debacles is doubtful, but for Meriwether, the successful launch of JWM was yet another astonishing comeback, the sort for which Wall Street is justly famous. In December, fifteen months after he lost $4.5 billion in an epic bust that seemed about to take down all of Wall Street and more with him, Meriwether raised $250 million, much of it from former investors in the ill-fated Long-Term Capital, and he was off and running again.

Notes

Epigraph: Henry T. C. Hu, "Misunderstood Derivatives: The Causes of Informational Failure and the Promise of Regulatory Incremental-ism," *The Yale Law Journal*, 102, no. 6 (April 1993), 1477.

1 ▪ Meriwether

1. Author interview with Thomas E. Creevy.
2. Gretchen Morgenson, "The Man Behind the Curtain," *The New York Times*, October 2, 1998.
3. Ibid.
4. Michael Lewis, *Liar's Poker* (New York: Penguin, 1989), 15.
5. Roger Lowenstein, *Buffett: The Making of an American Capitalist* (New York: Random House, 1995), 371, note. Lewis himself backed away from the tale in a subsequent *New York Times Magazine* piece, saying only that Meriwether had "supposedly" issued the challenge; see Michael Lewis, "How the Eggheads Cracked," *The New York Times Magazine*, January 24, 1999.
6. Morgenson, "The Man Behind the Curtain."
7. Author interviews with Mitchell Kapor and William Sahlman.

8. Michael Siconolfi, Anita Raghavan, and Mitchell Pacelle, "All Bets Are Off: How the Salesmanship and Brainpower Failed at Long-Term Capital," *The Wall Street Journal,* November 16, 1998.

9. The second part of the quotation is from Kevin Muehring, "John Meriwether by the Numbers," *Institutional Investor*, November 1996.

10. Lewis, "How the Eggheads Cracked."

11. Douglas Frantz and Peter Truell, "Long-Term Capital: A Case of Markets over Minds," *The New York Times,* October 11, 1998.

12. Lewis, "How the Eggheads Cracked."

13. Randall Smith and Michael Siconolfi, "Roaring '90s? Here Comes Salomon's $23 Million Man," *The Wall Street Journal,* January 7, 1991; Martin Mayer, *Nightmare on Wall Street: Salomon Brothers and the Corruption of the Marketplace* (New York: Simon & Schuster, 1993), 36.

14. See Lowenstein, *Buffett,* 374–85, for a detailed account of the Mozer scandal.

15. Leah Nathans Spiro, "Dream Team," *Business Week,* August 29, 1994.

16. Author interview with Charlie Munger.

2 ▪ Hedge Fund

Epigraph: Fielding quote: *Oxford English Dictionary,* 2d ed., vol. 7 (Oxford: Clarendon Press, 1989), 94; Holmes quote: Ibid., 96, quoting Holmes's *Pages fr. Old Vol. Life, Bread & Newsp* (1891), 12.

1. Franklin R. Edwards, "Hedge Funds and the Collapse of Long-Term Capital Management," *Journal of Economic Perspectives,* 13, no. 2 (Spring 1999), 193.

2. Gary Weiss, "Fall Guys?" *Business Week,* April 25, 1994.

3. *King John,* 2.1.26, 1595, cited in *O.E.D.,* vol. 7, 96.

4. Edwards, "Hedge Funds and the Collapse of Long-Term Capital Management," 189–90; Ted Caldwell, "Introduction: The Model for Superior Performance," in *Hedge Funds: Investment and Portfolio Strategies for the Institutional Investor,* ed. Jess Lederman and Robert A. Klein (New York: Irwin Professional Publishing, 1995), 5–10.

5. Caldwell, ibid.

6. "Hedge Funds, Leverage, and the Lessons of Long-Term Capital Management," Report of the President's Working Group on Financial Markets, April 1999, 1.

7. Robert K. Merton, "The Self-Fulfilling Prophecy," *Antioch Review,* 8, no. 2 (June 1948), 194–95.

8. Robert C. Merton, unpublished autobiography, May 1998.

9. Gretchen Morgenson and Michael M. Weinstein, "Teachings of Two Nobelists Also Proved Their Undoing," *The New York Times*, November 14, 1998.

10. Peter L. Bernstein, *Against the Gods: The Remarkable Story of Risk* (New York: John Wiley & Sons, 1996), 310–16. See also Bernstein's account of the Black-Scholes model in *Capital Ideas: The Improbable Origins of Modern Wall Street* (New York: Free Press, 1992), 207–16.

11. Author interview with Maxwell Bublitz.

12. Author interview with Eugene F. Fama; see also Bernstein, *Capital Ideas*, 212.

13. Mike Shahin, "The Making of a Nobel Prize Winner: Myron Samuel Scholes Never Felt the Need to Be Conventional," *Ottawa Citizen*, October 25, 1997; Bernstein, *Capital Ideas*, 212.

14. Shahin, ibid.

15. Author interview with William F. Sharpe.

16. Kenneth H. Bacon, "Fed Says Clinton Bank-Regulation Plan Would Limit Its Ability to Handle Crises," *The Wall Street Journal*, December 3, 1993.

17. James Blitz, "Bank of Italy Put $250m into LTCM," *Financial Times*, October 2, 1998.

18. Author interview with Walter Weiner.

19. Author interview with Terence Sullivan; Michael Siconolfi, Anita Raghavan, and Mitchell Pacelle, "All Bets Are Off: How the Salesmanship and Brainpower Failed at Long-Term Capital," *The Wall Street Journal*, November 16, 1998.

20. Peter Truell, "An Alchemist Who Turned Gold into Lead," *The New York Times*, September 25, 1998.

3 ▪ On the Run

Epigraph: Douglas Breeden, in John Muehring, "John Meriwether by the Numbers," *Institutional Investor*, November 1996.

1. Keith Bradsher, "No. 2 Official Is Resigning from the Fed," *The New York Times*, February 2, 1994.

2. This chapter draws extensively from *The Wall Street Journal*'s splendid account of the bond market turmoil: David Wessel, Laura Jereski, and Randall Smith, "Stormy Spring: Three-Month Tumult in Bonds Lays Bare New Financial Forces," May 20, 1994.

3. LTCM, letter to investors, July 12, 1994.

4. Wessel, Jereski, and Smith, "Stormy Spring."

5. Ibid.

6. John M. Keynes, *The General Theory of Employment, Interest and Money* (New York: Cambridge University Press, 1973; first published 1936), 155.

7. André F. Perold, "Long-Term Capital Management, L.P. (A)," Harvard Business School, case N9-200-007, October 27, 1999, 3.

8. Author interview with Eric Rosenfeld.

9. Perold, "LTCM (A)," 6.

10. Ibid., 14.

11. Leah Nathans Spiro, "Dream Team," *Business Week,* August 29, 1994.

12. Perold, "LTCM (A)," 3.

13. Author interview with Michael How.

14. Michael Lewis, "How the Eggheads Cracked," *The New York Times Magazine,* January 24, 1999.

15. Author interview with Michael Friedlander; Gary Weiss, "Meriwether's Curious Deed," *Business Week,* October 19, 1998.

16. Perold, "LTCM (A)," 3.

17. Author interview with Eric Rosenfeld.

18. LTCM, letter to investors, October 11, 1994.

19. Muehring, "Meriwether by the Numbers."

20. Author interview with Eric Rosenfeld.

21. LTCM, letter to investors, July 12, 1994.

22. Seth A. Klarman, Baupost 1993 Partnership Letter, January 26, 1994.

4 ▪ Dear Investors

Epigraph: Author interview with Merton H. Miller.

1. LTCM, letter to investors, "Addendum #1, Volatility and Risk Characteristics of Investments in Long-Term Capital Portfolio L.P.," October 10, 1994.

2. Leah Nathans Spiro, "Dream Team," *Business Week,* August 29, 1994.

3. Peter L. Bernstein, *Against the Gods: The Remarkable Story of Risk* (New York: John Wiley & Sons, 1996), 141–2.

4. Fischer Black and Myron Scholes, "The Pricing of Options and Corporate Liabilities," *Journal of Political Economy,* May–June 1973,

637–54. Many writers have commented on the formula's link to physics; see, e.g., Todd E. Petzel, "Fischer Black and the Derivatives Revolution," *Journal of Portfolio Management,* December 1996, 87–91: "The Black-Scholes formula is a basic heat exchange equation from physics."

5. Quoted in Bernstein, *Against the Gods,* 331.

6. Peter L. Bernstein, *Capital Ideas: The Improbable Origins of Modern Wall Street* (New York: Free Press, 1992), 216.

7. Author interview with William Sahlman.

8. Author interview with Paul Samuelson.

9. Eugene F. Fama, "The Behavior of Stock-Market Prices," Reprint Series, No. 39, Center for Mathematical Studies in Business and Economics, Graduate School of Business, University of Chicago, reprinted from *The Journal of Business of the University of Chicago,* 38, no. 1 (January 1965).

10. Ibid., 94.

11. The first person to notice the phenomenon, Benoit Mandelbrot, documented fat tails in cotton prices. Mandelbrot, a Polish-born mathematician, worked at IBM and Yale and advised Fama on his thesis.

12. Author interview with Eugene F. Fama.

13. Jens Carsten Jackwerth and Mark Rubinstein, "Recovering Probability Distributions from Option Prices," *The Journal of Finance,* 51, no. 5 (December 1996), 1612.

14. Lawrence Summers, quoted in Bruce I. Jacobs, *Capital Ideas and Market Realities: Option Replication, Investor Behavior, and Stock Market Crashes* (Malden, Mass.: Blackwell, 1999), 88.

15. Robert C. Merton, unpublished autobiography, May 1998.

16. Terry A. Marsh and Robert C. Merton, "Dividend Variability and Variance Bounds Tests for the Rationality of Stock Market Prices," *American Economic Review,* 76, no. 3 (June 1986), 483–4.

17. Quoted in Christopher May, *Nonlinear Pricing: Theory and Applications* (New York: John Wiley & Sons, 1999), 29. May's book, a witty and detailed treatise on market disorder, is the best account for anyone who wants to understand more about why markets are not like the cream in your coffee.

18. Till M. Guldimann, J. P. Morgan & Co., Global Research, "RiskMetrics™—Technical Document," October 1994; see especially 1–28.

19. André F. Perold, "Long-Term Capital Management, L.P. (A)," Harvard Business School, case N9-200-007, October 27, 1999, 10.

20. Author interview with Eric Rosenfeld.

21. The numbers in this section are from two sources: Long-Term Capital Portfolio's financial statement, which is on file with the Com-

modity Futures Trading Commission, and Long-Term Capital Management's internal memorandum of January 13, 1999, explaining its losses in 1998.

22. LTCM, letter to investors, July 15, 1995.

23. Figure computed by author, based on monthly asset total disclosed in LTCM internal memorandum, January 13, 1999.

24. Author interview with Eric Rosenfeld.

5 ▪ Tug-of-War

Epigraph: Robert C. Merton, unpublished autobiography, May 1998.

1. "Hedge Funds, Leverage, and the Lessons of Long-Term Capital Management," Report of the President's Working Group on Financial Markets, April 1999, 14.

2. Merrill Lynch, "Q&A on *Financial Times* Story," October 29, 1998.

3. Tracy Corrigan, "Komansky Condemns Lack of Transparency," *Financial Times*, October 14, 1998.

4. Long-Term Capital Portfolio financial statements filed with CFTC.

5. Nikki Tait, "Leverage of LTCM Was Well Known," *Financial Times*, November 19, 1998.

6. Robert Clow and Riva Atlas, "Wall Street and the Hedge Funds: What Went Wrong," *Institutional Investor*, December 1998.

7. André F. Perold, "Long-Term Capital Management, L.P. (A)," Harvard Business School, case N9-200-007, October 27, 1999, 18.

8. Author interview with Simon Bowden.

9. Author interview with Daniel Tully.

10. Author interview with Herbert Allison.

11. Leah Nathans Spiro, "Dream Team," *Business Week*, August 29, 1994.

12. Douglas Frantz and Peter Truell, "Long-Term Capital: A Case of Markets over Minds," *The New York Times*, October 11, 1998.

13. Christopher Rhoads, "A Prince Undone: UBS CEO's Fall from Grace Tells a Tale of Euroland," *The Wall Street Journal Europe*, January 25, 1999.

14. Clay Harris and William Hall, "UBS Suffers Share Fall over LTCM Inquiry," *Financial Times*, October 1, 1998.

15. LTCP financial statements filed with CFTC.

16. LTCM, internal memorandum, January 13, 1999.

17. Peter Truell, "Losses Are Said to Continue at Troubled Hedge Fund," *The New York Times,* October 10, 1998.

18. LTCM, letter to investors, November 1, 1996.

6 ▪ A Nobel Prize

Epigraph: Robert Kuttner, "What Do You Call an Economist with a Prediction? Wrong," *Business Week,* September 6, 1999.

1. Michael Lewis, "How the Eggheads Cracked," *The New York Times Magazine,* January 24, 1999.

2. Burton Malkiel, *A Random Walk down Wall Street,* 5th ed. (New York: W. W. Norton, 1990; first published 1973), 98.

3. Author interview with Eric Rosenfeld.

4. Lewis, "How the Eggheads Cracked."

5. International Swaps and Derivatives Association, New York.

6. Author interview with Nicholas Brady.

7. Chester B. Feldberg, executive vice president, Federal Reserve Bank of New York, letter to chief executive officers of all member banks, branches and agencies of foreign banks, and bank holding companies in the Second Federal Reserve District, April 28, 1994. (Italics added.)

8. Alan Greenspan, "Private-sector refinancing of the large hedge fund, Long-Term Capital Management," testimony before Committee on Banking and Financial Services, U.S. House of Representatives, October 1, 1998.

9. Alan Greenspan, letter to Senator Alfonse M. D'Amato, October 20, 1998.

10. Alan Greenspan, testimony before Subcommittee on Telecommunications and Finance, Committee on Commerce, U.S. House of Representatives, November 30, 1995.

11. The phraseology is so close to that of an earlier writer that I must add an (end)note of gratitude to Louis Lowenstein, my father, for *What's Wrong with Wall Street: Short-Term Gain and the Absentee Shareholder* (New York: Addison-Wesley, 1988), 67.

12. Patrick McGeehan and Gregory Zuckerman, "High Leverage Isn't Unusual on Wall Street," *The Wall Street Journal,* October 13, 1998. The figure is as of June 30, 1998.

13. Robert Clow and Riva Atlas, "Wall Street and the Hedge Funds: What Went Wrong," *Institutional Investor,* December 1998.

14. "Another Fine Mess at UBS," *Euromoney,* November 1998; Michael Siconolfi, Anita Raghavan, and Mitchell Pacelle, "All Bets Are

Off: How the Salesmanship and Brainpower Failed at Long-Term Capital," *The Wall Street Journal*, November 16, 1998.

15. Author interview with Nicholas Brady.

16. Author interview with Eric Rosenfeld; investor notes from February 1999 meeting with LTCM; Anita Raghavan and Michael R. Sesit, "Fund Partners Got Outside Financing—Move to Boost Investments in Long-Term Capital Adds to Financial Woes," *The Wall Street Journal*, September 28, 1998.

17. Anita Raghavan, "Long-Term Capital's Partners Got Big Loans to Invest in Fund," *The Wall Street Journal*, October 6, 1998.

18. Andrei Shleifer and Robert W. Vishny, "The Limits of Arbitrage," *Journal of Finance*, 52, no. 1 (March 1997), 35–54, especially 45.

19. Author interview with John Campbell.

20. Gregory Zuckerman, "Credit Markets: Foreign Bonds Hit by Turmoil in Asia Markets," *The Wall Street Journal*, July 16, 1997.

21. The quotation is from, and this section leans heavily on, Nicholas D. Kristof with David E. Sanger, "How U.S. Wooed Asia to Let Cash Flow In," *The New York Times*, February 16, 1999.

22. Laura Jereski, "Hedge Fund to Shrink Capital of $6 Billion by Nearly Half," *The Wall Street Journal*, September 22, 1997.

23. Author interview with William F. Sharpe.

24. André F. Perold, "Long-Term Capital Management, L.P. (A)," Harvard Business School, case N9-200-007, October 27, 1999, 16.

25. Steven Lipin, "Travelers to Buy Salomon for $9 Billion: Deal to Create Securities Firm of Global Power," *The Wall Street Journal*, September 25, 1997.

26. "Black-Scholes Pair Win Nobel: Derivative Work Paid Off for Professors Who Made Fortune from Investment in Wall Street Hedge Fund," *Daily Telegraph*, October 15, 1997.

27. Mike Shahin, "The Making of a Nobel Prize Winner: Myron Samuel Scholes Never Felt the Need to Be Conventional," *Ottawa Citizen*, October 25, 1997.

28. Michael Phillips, "Two U.S. Economists Win Nobel Prize—Merton and Scholes Share Award for Breakthrough in Pricing Stock Options," *The Wall Street Journal*, October 15, 1997.

29. "The Right Option: The Nobel Prize for Economics," *The Economist*, October 18, 1997.

30. David R. Henderson, "Message from Stockholm: Markets Work," *The Wall Street Journal*, October 15, 1997.

31. Roger Lowenstein, "Intrinsic Value: Why Stock Options Are Really Dynamite," *The Wall Street Journal*, November 6, 1997.

32. Sara Webb, Bill Spindle, Pui-Wing Tam, and Silvia Ascarelli, "Hong Kong Plunge Triggers Global Rout," *The Wall Street Journal,* October 28, 1997.

33. Nicholas Brady, unpublished "Talking Points," Brookings-Wharton Papers on Financial Services, October 29, 1997.

34. Author interview with Eric Rosenfeld.

35. Dirk Schutz, "Excerpts from the Fall of UBS," *Derivatives Strategy,* October 1998, excerpt from Schutz's book *Der Fall der UBS* (Zurich: Bilanz, 1998), Sigrid Stangl, translator.

36. Robert C. Merton, "Applications of Option-Pricing Theory: Twenty-five Years Later," speech at Nobel Prize ceremony, Stockholm, December 9, 1997, reprinted in *American Economic Review,* June 1998.

37. Douglas Frantz and Peter Truell, "Long-Term Capital: A Case of Markets over Minds," *The New York Times,* October 11, 1998.

38. Author interview with David Mullins.

7 ▪ Bank of Volatility

Epigraph: attributed to Keynes.

1. Author interview with Eric Rosenfeld.

2. André F. Perold, "Long-Term Capital Management, L.P. (A)," Harvard Business School, case N9-200-007, October 27, 1999, 12; Perold, "Long-Term Capital Management, L.P. (C)," case N9-200-009, October 27, 1999; Joe Kolman, "LTCM Speaks," *Derivatives Strategy,* April 1999.

3. Kolman, "LTCM Speaks."

4. Michael Siconolfi, Anita Raghavan, and Mitchell Pacelle, "All Bets Are Off: How the Salesmanship and Brainpower Failed at Long-Term Capital," *The Wall Street Journal,* November 16, 1998.

5. Author interview with Eric Rosenfeld.

6. Perold, "LTCM (A)," 17.

7. Riva Atlas and Hal Lux, "Meriwether Falls to Earth," *Institutional Investor,* July 1998.

8. Franklin R. Edwards, "Hedge Funds and the Collapse of Long-Term Capital Management," *Journal of Economic Perspectives,* 13, no. 2 (Spring 1999), 199.

9. Author interview with Steven Black.

10. Kolman, "LTCM Speaks."

11. Betsy McKay and Robert Bonte-Friedheim, "Russian Markets Stabilize as Rates Ease After Rise," *The Wall Street Journal,* May 20, 1998.

12. Gregory Zuckerman, "As Yields Drop to Historic Levels, Future of Rates Depends on Asia," *The Wall Street Journal,* June 15, 1998.

13. Figures are from the end of April 1998 through the end of June, courtesy of Merrill Lynch.

14. This paragraph draws heavily from the splendid account of Goldman's involvement in Russia by Joseph Kahn and Timothy L. O'Brien, "For Russia and Its U.S. Bankers, Match Wasn't Made in Heaven," *The New York Times,* October 18, 1998.

15. Anita Raghavan, "Salomon Shuts Down a Bond Unit," *The Wall Street Journal,* July 7, 1998.

16. Kolman, "LTCM Speaks."

17. Perold, "LTCM (C)," 1.

18. Kolman, "LTCM Speaks."

19. Michael R. Sesit and Robert Bonte-Friedheim, "Investors' Confidence in Russia Fades Further—Bond Yields Jump to 120% and Stocks Fall Sharply amid Rush for IMF Aid," *The Wall Street Journal,* July 8, 1998.

20. Author interview with Eric Rosenfeld.

21. Michael Lewis, "How the Eggheads Cracked," *The New York Times Magazine,* January 24, 1999.

22. Richard Spillenkothen, "Lending Standards for Commercial Loans," June 23, 1998.

23. Alan Greenspan, testimony before Committee on Agriculture, Nutrition, and Forestry, U.S. Senate, July 30, 1998.

24. Gary Weiss with Barbara Silverbush and Karen Stevens, "Meriwether's Curious Deed," *Business Week,* October 19, 1998.

8 ▪ The Fall

Epigraph: Merton H. Miller, "A Tribute to Myron Scholes," speech at Nobel Memorial Prize luncheon of the American Economic Association, New York, January 4, 1999.

1. Robert O'Brien, "Citicorp, J. P. Morgan and Chase Fall on Woes in Russia," *The Wall Street Journal,* August 21, 1998.

2. Mark Whitehouse, Betsy McKay, Bob Davis, and Steve Liesman, "Bear Tracks: In a Financial Gamble, Russia Lets Ruble Fall, Stalls Debt Repayment—Other Markets Face Pressure from Move, but So Far Their Reaction Is Modest—Blow to a Weary Citizenry," *The Wall Street Journal,* August 18, 1998.

3. Franklin R. Edwards, "Hedge Funds and the Collapse of Long-

Term Capital Management," *Journal of Economic Perspectives,* 13, no. 2 (Spring 1999), 203.

4. Myron S. Scholes, "Risk-Reduction Methodology: Balancing Risk and Rate of Return Targets," talk at the *Economist* investment conference, New York, September 22–23, 1999.

5. Author interview with Jon Corzine.

6. Author interview with Michael Alix.

7. Michael Siconolfi, Anita Raghavan, and Mitchell Pacelle, "All Bets Are Off: How the Salesmanship and Brainpower Failed at Long-Term Capital," *The Wall Street Journal,* November 16, 1998.

8. André F. Perold, "Long-Term Capital Management, L.P. (C)," Harvard Business School, case N9-200-009, October 27, 1999, 3.

9. André F. Perold, "Long-Term Capital Management, L.P. (A)," Harvard Business School, case N9-200-007, October 27, 1999, 12.

10. Author interview with Eric Rosenfeld.

11. Ibid.

12. Author interview with George Soros.

13. Author interview with Clayton Rose; Tracy Corrigan and William Lewis, "Merrill Lynch Details Contacts with LTCM," *Financial Times,* October 31, 1998.

14. Author interview with Eric Rosenfeld.

15. Author interview with Joseph Brandon.

16. Carol J. Loomis, "A House Built on Sand," *Fortune,* October 26, 1998.

17. In "How the Eggheads Cracked," Michael Lewis quoted one of the partners as saying "Buffett cares about one thing. His reputation."

18. Sam Dillon, "Economic Turmoil in Russia Takes Toll in Latin America," *The New York Times,* August 27, 1998.

19. Sheryl WuDunn, "Japan Stocks Fall 2% but Rebound from a 12-Year Low," *The New York Times,* August 28, 1998.

20. "Russian to the Exits: 'A Global Margin Call' Rocks Markets, Banks—and Boris Yeltsin—Stocks Drop World-Wide; There's Sober News, Too, About the U.S. Economy," *The Wall Street Journal,* August 28, 1998.

21. Author interview with Warren Buffett.

22. Author interview with Eric Rosenfeld; "Hedge Funds, Leverage, and the Lessons of Long-Term Capital Management," Report of the President's Working Group on Financial Markets, April 1999, 11.

23. Gary Weiss with Barbara Silverbush and Karen Stevens, "Meriwether's Curious Deed," *Business Week,* October 19, 1998.

24. Greg Ip and E. S. Browning, "The Bear Stirs: Stocks Plunge Again,

Battering Stalwarts and Internet Stars—Dow Industrials' 6.37% Drop Wipes Out 1998's Gains; on Nasdaq, It's Worse—Some Say Bottom Is in Sight," *The Wall Street Journal*, September 1, 1998.

25. Author interview with Jack Malvey.

26. Kolman, "LTCM Speaks," *Derivatives Strategy*, April 1999.

9 ▪ The Human Factor

1. John W. Meriwether, letter to investors, Bloomberg, September 2, 1998.

2. Anita Raghavan and Matt Murray, "Financial Firms Lose $8 Billion So Far—Global Fallout from Russia Hits Big Banks, Others; Meriwether Fund Hurt," *The Wall Street Journal*, September 3, 1998.

3. James J. Cramer, "Wrong! Rear Echelon Revelations; Einstein Has Left the Building," thestreet.com, September 3, 1998.

4. Author interview with Eric Rosenfeld.

5. Michael Lewis, "How the Eggheads Cracked," *The New York Times Magazine*, January 24, 1999.

6. Author interview with Eric Rosenfeld.

7. The author asked Dunleavy if Long-Term had been straight with him. He replied, "I won't answer that question. Anything between myself and a client is Merrill Lynch information."

8. Lewis, "How the Eggheads Cracked."

9. Author interview with Marlon Pease; Michael Siconolfi, Anita Raghavan, and Mitchell Pacelle, "All Bets Are Off: How the Salesmanship and Brainpower Failed at Long-Term Capital," *The Wall Street Journal*, November 16, 1998.

10. Shawn Young, "Risk Arbitragers [*sic*] Have Been Feeling the Pressure as Gyrating Stock Prices Affect Value of Mergers," *The Wall Street Journal*, September 14, 1998.

11. Steven M. Sears, "IPO Outlook: Market's Well Is Running Dry," *The Wall Street Journal*, September 8, 1998.

12. Suzanne McGee, "Did the High Cost of Derivatives Spark Monday's Stock Sell-Off?" *The Wall Street Journal*, September 2, 1998.

13. Steven M. Sears, "Options Market Reflects Fear and Uncertainty Despite Yesterday's Sharp Rebound in Stocks," *The Wall Street Journal*, September 2, 1998.

14. Franklin R. Edwards, "Hedge Funds and the Collapse of Long-Term Capital Management," *Journal of Economic Perspectives*, 13, no. 2 (Spring 1999), 199.

15. David Wessel, "Credit Record: How the Fed Fumbled, and Then Recovered, in Making Policy Shift," *The Wall Street Journal,* November 17, 1998.

16. Brett D. Fromson, "Farm Boy to Financier," *The Washington Post,* November 6, 1994.

17. Lisa Endlich, *Goldman Sachs: The Culture of Success* (New York: Alfred A. Knopf, 1999); see especially 126–8.

18. Ibid., 195–207.

19. Author interview with Steven Black.

20. Author interview with Jon Corzine.

21. Gretchen Morgenson and Michael Weinstein, "Teachings of Two Nobelists Also Proved Their Undoing," *The New York Times,* November 14, 1998.

22. Steven Lipin, Matt Murray, and Jacob M. Schlesinger, "Bailout Blues: How a Big Hedge Fund Marketed Its Expertise and Shrouded Its Risks," *The Wall Street Journal,* September 25, 1998.

23. Author interview with Rob Adrian.

24. Author interviews with Steven Black and Thomas Maheras.

25. Carol Loomis, "A House Built on Sand," *Fortune,* October 26, 1998.

26. Author interview with John Whitehead.

27. Federal Reserve Bank of New York, "Chronology of Material Events in the Efforts Regarding Long-Term Capital Portfolio, L.P."; Alan Greenspan, letter to Senator Alfonse M. D'Amato, October 20, 1998 (enclosure).

28. Author interview with Jon Corzine.

29. Author interview with Warren Buffett.

10 • At the Fed

Epigraph: William J. McDonough, statement to Committee on Banking and Financial Services, U.S. House of Representatives, October 1, 1998.

1. Author interview with Peter Fisher; Jacob M. Schlesinger, "Long-Term Capital Bailout Spotlights a Fed 'Radical,'" *The Wall Street Journal,* November 2, 1998.

2. Author interview with Jon Corzine.

3. Author interview with Steven Black.

4. Author interview with Eric Rosenfeld.

5. Author interview with Richard Dunn.

6. Author interview with Andrew Siciliano.

7. Author interviews with Jon Corzine and Herbert Allison.

8. Alan Greenspan, testimony before Committee on Banking and Financial Services, U.S. House of Representatives, October 1, 1998.

9. William J. McDonough, statement to Committee on Banking and Financial Services, U.S. House of Representatives, October 1, 1998.

10. J. R. Wu, "Treasurys Gains Are Trimmed After Yield Hits Low of 5.05%, as Stocks Rally on Tape Release," *The Wall Street Journal,* September 22, 1998.

11. Robert Rubin, remarks at Woodrow Wilson International Center for Scholars, Washington, D.C., October 20, 1998.

12. Author interview with David Komansky.

13. Author interview with James Cayne.

14. Author interview with Herbert Allison.

15. Ibid.

16. The accounts of the meetings at the Federal Reserve were mostly drawn from interviews by the author, including ones with Herbert Allison, Jon Corzine, Peter Fisher, David Pflug, David Komansky, and Thomas Russo.

17. The letter was printed in *The Wall Street Journal;* see Mitchell Pacelle, Leslie Scism, and Steven Lipin, "How Buffett, AIG and Goldman Sought Long-Term Capital, but Were Rejected," September 30, 1998.

18. Author interview with Herbert Allison.

19. Author interview with David Pflug.

20. Gretchen Morgenson, "Seeing a Fund as Too Big to Fail, New York Fed Assists Its Bailout," *The New York Times,* September 24, 1998.

21. Michael Schroeder and Jacob M. Schlesinger, "Fed May Face Recriminations over Handling of Fund Bailout," *The Wall Street Journal,* September 25, 1998.

22. "Review & Outlook: Decade of Moral Hazard," *The Wall Street Journal,* September 25, 1998.

23. Gretchen Morgenson, "Fallen Star: The Overview; Hedge Fund Bailout Rattles Investors and Markets," *The New York Times,* September 25, 1998; Schroeder and Schlesinger, "Fed May Face Recriminations over Handling of Fund Bailout."

24. "Mullins Magic," *Financial Times,* September 25, 1998.

25. Author interviews with David Pflug and Herbert Allison.

26. Author interview with Steven Black.

27. Author interview with Herbert Allison.

Epilogue

1. John Greenwald, *Time,* October 5, 1998; *San Francisco Chronicle,* October 1, 1998; *The Boston Globe,* September 27, 1998; *The Philadelphia Inquirer,* September 27, 1998; *The Miami Herald,* September 27, 1998.

2. Michael Lewis, "How the Eggheads Cracked," *The New York Times Magazine,* January 24, 1999.

3. Author interview with Eugene F. Fama.

4. Lewis, "How the Eggheads Cracked."

5. Matt Murray, "Bankers Trust Is Hit by $488 Million Loss," *The Wall Street Journal,* October 23, 1998; Paul Beckett, "Former Chairman of Bankers Trust Is Expected to Quit Deutsche Bank Post," *The Wall Street Journal,* June 25, 1999.

6. Peter Truell, "Bailed-Out Hedge Fund Cutting 18% of Its Staff," *The New York Times,* October 28, 1998.

7. Lewis, "How the Eggheads Cracked."

8. See Lewis, "How the Eggheads Cracked," and Mitchell Pacelle, Randall Smith, and Anita Raghavan, "Investors May See 'LTCM, the Sequel,'" *The Wall Street Journal,* May 20, 1999.

9. Myron S. Scholes, "Risk-Reduction Methodology: Balancing Risk and Rate of Return Targets," talk at the *Economist* investment conference, New York, September 22–23, 1999.

10. Author interview with Eric Rosenfeld.

11. Alan Greenspan, letter to Senator Alfonse M. D'Amato, October 20, 1998.

12. Lynne Marek and Katherine Burton, "Long-Term Capital Near to Being Out of Business, McDonough Says," Bloomberg, October 1, 1999.

13. Remarks by Alan Greenspan before the Futures Industry Association, Boca Raton, Florida, March 19, 1999.

14. *Capitalism: The Unknown Ideal,* quoted in "Ayn Rand: Still Spouting," *The Economist,* November 27, 1999.

15. "Hedge Funds, Leverage, and the Lessons of Long-Term Capital Management," Report of the President's Working Group on Financial Markets, April 1999, 24, 29.

16. John Cassidy, "Annals of Finance: Time Bomb," *The New Yorker,* July 5, 1999.

17. Patrick M. Parkinson, "Progress report by the President's Working Group on Financial Markets," testimony before Committee on Agriculture, Nutrition, and Forestry, U.S. Senate, December 16, 1998.

18. Derivatives and Risk Management Symposium on Stability in

World Financial Markets, Fordham University School of Law, January 28, 1999, as reprinted in *Fordham: Finance, Securities & Tax Law Forum,* IV, no. 1 (1999), 21.

19. Figures are from a presentation made by LTCM in February 1999 to an investor.

20. Merrill Lynch, *1998 Annual Report,* 50.

Index

Long-Term Capital Management (*cont'd*):
  waivers on, 214–18
  warrant for, 85, 88–89, 91, 93–94,
    107–9, 111, 118, 134, 170, 223
  see also specific fund partners
Long-Term Capital Portfolio (LTCP),
  see Long-Term Capital
  Management, portfolio of
Lotus Development Corporation, 70

McCain, John, 223
McDonough, Robert, 129–30, 166
McDonough, William J.:
  Greenspan and, 184, 186
  Long-Term intervention
    orchestrated by, xvii–xxi, 153,
    166, 169, 183–84, 186–90, 192,
    194, 195, 198, 201–9, 218, 219,
    220, 230–31
  Meriwether and, 166, 169, 181,
    183, 204
McEntee, James J., 36, 113, 129,
    134–35, 145, 155, 157, 176, 227
McIntosh, William, 10, 19, 20, 220
McKinsey & Company, 38
Maheras, Thomas, 180
Malaysia, 111–12, 117
Malkiel, Burton, 98
margin calls, 86, 102–6, 201–2
markets:
  bond, xix, xx, 7–10, 12–13, 26,
    40–44, 52, 54, 72, 76–77,
    110–11, 130, 133, 151–52, 154,
    158–59, 171–72, 173
  correlation of, 7, 41–42, 98,
    117–18, 120, 134, 144–45, 160,
    162, 173, 188
  currency, xix, 7, 15, 24, 41, 54–55,
    128
  derivatives, xix, 12, 29–30, 37, 42,
    46, 92, 103–5, 118, 140
  distortion of, 234–35
  efficiency of, 13, 33, 34–35, 37,
    64–65, 68, 74, 75, 76–77, 97,
    123, 234
  emerging, 127–30, 133, 144–45,
    163, 168, 224, 234
  free, 175–76
  global, 144–45, 153, 161
  historical trends in, 63–64, 70–77,
    235
  liquidity of, 30, 42–43, 60, 76, 106,
    112, 116, 151, 161–62, 222, 228
  momentum of, 72–74
  mortgages, 16, 42, 52–53, 64,
    97–98
  random properties of, 34–35,
    65–66, 69, 72, 98, 173, 233
  "seizing up" of, 194–95
  stabilization of, 175–76, 230

  volatility of, 40–44, 72–77, 117–18,
    123–26, 136, 144–45, 153,
    163–64, 168–69, 173, 188–89
  see also stock market
Marron, Donald, 38
Massachusetts Institute of Technology
  (MIT), 11, 13, 29, 37, 58, 59, 69,
    70, 126
Mattone, Vincent, 85, 87, 156–57,
    164, 191
Maughan, Deryck, 21, 49, 114–15,
    198, 204, 207
MCI Communications, 102, 112
MCI/WorldCom, 148
Mead, John, 203, 204, 210–11, 212,
    213
Mendoza, Roberto, 93, 97, 150,
    166–67, 192, 195, 196, 198, 200
mergers, corporate, 100–102, 111,
    146, 147, 148–49, 168, 234
Meriwether, John W.:
  background of, 5–7, 10, 11
  Buffett and, 32, 153, 182, 184, 202,
    203, 204
  in China, 142, 147, 152
  competitiveness of, 10, 45–46,
    83–84
  Corzine and, 6–7, 32, 46, 47, 169,
    171, 172, 206, 223
  gambling by, 6, 10, 14
  golf played by, 6, 14, 15, 35, 36, 45,
    83–84, 90, 138, 150, 179
  Hilibrand and, 18–19, 21, 50, 218
  horse racing as interest of, 14, 45, 90
  investment strategies of, 3–5, 10–11,
    95
  investor letters of, 41, 57–58,
    61–62, 63, 72, 76, 77–78, 95,
    138, 159–62, 194
  as Irish Catholic, 5, 36, 50
  Long-Term managed by, xix, 26–28,
    31–33, 41, 45–63, 77–96, 101,
    113, 115, 120, 129–30, 133,
    137–38, 143, 155, 159–62, 167,
    177, 180, 184, 193, 221
  Long-Term's collapse and, 147–51,
    153, 155–58, 161–84, 190, 193,
    197, 199, 200, 202–6, 209, 211,
    214, 217–18, 221, 226
  loyalty to, 15, 16, 17–19, 21, 50, 128
  McDonough and, 166, 169, 181,
    183, 204
  mathematical ability of, 5, 6, 11
  media coverage of, 10, 16, 20, 55,
    209, 221
  in Mozer affair, 19–22, 23, 27, 28,
    37, 88, 114, 147, 148, 155
  offices of, 15, 16, 20, 50–51, 120
  reputation of, 19–22, 23, 27, 28, 37,
    209, 221

ABOUT THE TYPE

This book was set in Sabon, a typeface designed by the well-known German typographer Jan Tschichold (1902–74). Sabon's design is based on the original letterforms of Claude Garamond and was created specifically to be used for three sources: foundry type for hand composition, Linotype, and Monotype. Tschichold named his typeface for the famous Frankfurt typefounder Jacques Sabon, who died in 1580.